THE
STREETS
WE HAVE
COME DOWN
literature of the city

HAYDEN SERIES IN LITERATURE

Robert W. Boynton, Consulting Editor

*Former Principal, Senior High School
and Chairman, English Department
Germantown Friends School*

THE
STREETS
WE HAVE
COME DOWN

literature of the city

IVAN DOIG

HAYDEN BOOK COMPANY, INC.
Rochelle Park, New Jersey

Library of Congress Cataloging in Publication Data

Doig, Ivan, comp.
The streets we have come down.

(Hayden series in literature)
Includes bibliographical references.
1. City and town life—Literary collections.
2. American literature—20th century.   I. Title.
PS509.C57D6   810′.9′32   74-17213
ISBN 0-8104-5823-3

Printed in the United States of America

1   2   3   4   5   6   7   8   9   PRINTING

75 76 77 78 79 80 81 82   YEAR

TO THE READER

*...I cannot tell you how beautiful the city appeared,
and a little terrible.*

Robinson Jeffers, "The Purse-Seine"

As a city dweller come from the country and a small town, I look quizzically at the everyday hours I spend now amid more than a million other persons in a tiny precinct of the earth. *The Streets We Have Come Down* expresses for me something of the vivid mix of city life. Beyond that, it is intended to show how readily the twin emotions of Robinson Jeffers's poetic line take over my gaze across the American cityscape. For me, those emotions are read most clearly in the beauty of education and opportunity which the city can offer, the terror of crowding and concretizing which the city can impose. The emotions may read differently in other minds, but whatever appearance they take, I hope *The Streets We Have Come Down* will bring out their hues a bit.

The book begins as close to today as I could make it — Part One is about special insights into urban life as seen in several American cities; Part Two illuminates our metropolitan colossus, New York City. Part Three explores our past with the eternal hard question, "How Came We Here?" Part Four is some guessing ahead.

Seattle, Washington

Ivan Doig

ACKNOWLEDGMENTS

As always, the first and biggest thanks for all her help, editorial and otherwise, must go to my wife, Carol. Portions of the work were read by some good friends and true: once again I'm grateful to Ann and Marshall Nelson and to Linda and Clinton Miller. In his serendipitous fashion, John Roden led me to the "Letter from the North" in Part Three, and Jean Roden as usual contributed her research skills. My thanks to Lisa Roden for helping with the material from the files of the Seattle Rumor Center. The staffs of the University of Washington library and the Shoreline Community College library were unfailingly helpful and diligent; time and again, specific problems of research were made easier by the prompt efficiency of Melvylei Stone, Peggy O'Coyne, and Judy Murphy. And this book is much the better for having been proofread by Ainsley Roseen, one more unfailing friend.

I.D.

CONTENTS

THE
STREETS
WE HAVE
COME DOWN
literature of the city

PART 1

WHAT IS THIS PLACE?

INTRODUCTION

The woes of city life sometimes seem like a science fiction movie come off the bleary screen of midnight television. Little mutant monsters grow and grow as the citizenry bumps around in loud panic, and first thing we know, here's Godzilla crunching up our own block. Our current monster roster in the cities is whopping: crime, pollution, the blight of poverty and the tension of racial prejudice, snarled traffic, noise, more and more garbage, a soaring cost of living, faltering utilities, the tedium of commuting, unending strain on natural resources. The list becomes a catalogue. Brushing against only one or two of these daily calamities, let alone some exasperating combination, is enough to set today's city-dweller to wondering about how livable his surroundings really are.

And make no mistake, the city's headaches belong to all of us whether our mailing address is rural, small-town, suburban or metropolitan. The 1970 U.S. census counted 26 cities with populations of more than half a million: Baltimore, Boston, Chicago, Cleveland, Columbus, Dallas, Denver, Detroit, Houston, Indianapolis, Jacksonville, Kansas City, Los Angeles, Memphis, Milwaukee, New Orleans, New York, Philadelphia, Phoenix, Pittsburgh, St. Louis, San Antonio, San Diego, San Francisco, Seattle and Washington. Thirty others showed a population of 250,000 or more: Akron, Atlanta, Austin, Birmingham, Buffalo, Cincinnati, El Paso, Fort Worth, Honolulu, Jersey City, Long Beach, Louisville, Miami, Minneapolis, Nashville, Newark, Norfolk, Oakland, Oklahoma City, Omaha, Portland, Rochester, Sacramento, St. Paul, San Jose, Tampa, Toledo, Tucson, Tulsa, and Wichita. Dozens more among today's Anchorages and Raleighs and Waterburys and Salt Lake Citys have gone far on their way to many of the problems of their bigger neighbors. As all roads once led from Rome, so does a network of modern problems radiate from the American city. Seeping along river systems or down prevailing winds, pollution respects no boundaries. The cities ingest the rural poor and at vast financial and spiritual expense make them the urban poor. Downtown skylines gasp for our tax money, set our food and clothing prices, fashion our national culture. The murdered hills of West Virginia and Kentucky coalfields have yielded up their tonnages of power, and now the Arizona desert and the Montana prairie will have their turn to feed fuel to the lamps and neon signs of metropolitan America.

To look at all aspects of what urbanization is, has been, and might be would amount to a task which would far outweigh a book this size.

The selection of readings across almost 150 years and from thirty different viewpoints is not an attempt to provide master plans for urban living. Any respectable library can disgorge more of those than you can walk away with. Nor is it an effort to catalogue the daily woes which go with city life. A typical urban citizen's routine drums home such points every weekday. Rather the book is an effort to bring together some insights about humankind in the American city, how we come to be here, what it's like for us and our neighbors, and, in a few instances, where we might go from here. One way or another, journalists, social scientists, politicians, poets, historians and novelists have all worked with these topics. Some of each are in this collection, but the book does not belong to the camp of any of them. Instead, it tries to be a city dweller's book. The only theme is that cities are made of, by, and for people.

So to Part One—"What Is This Place?"—to try for some insights into urban life and what it does to us. Taking a moment for a long view, we may notice that the city probably does some of the same things to us that rural life did. The human flow past an old woman on a park bench can be as unspeaking as the prairie which pressed in on her grandmother's homestead cabin with lonely infinities. In larger terms, today's marginal neighborhoods perhaps are kin to certain hardscrabble farmlands earlier in our history. Those were the areas where the dreams and the national impetus lured settlers beyond fertile soil where a decent living could be earned. The same homestead laws applied there, and towns and roads and social patterns appeared there much the same as elsewhere. The people simply had overreached themselves, and instead of prosperity, there were hard acres and rural slums. Perhaps something similar has happened in our cities, for here too we frequently find ourselves in scantly understood territory beyond the frontiers of our competence.

New afflictions crowd in upon old. Pollution spewed up by the modern city must be charted to keep track of how unhealthy it is to breathe the air. Here and elsewhere a new vastness comes to our urban problems. Some of our most dismal ghettoes are more populous than entire nations were a few centuries ago. The commuter who averages 25 miles each workday for 45 years travels farther, through all that nerve-twitching nightmare, than Christopher Columbus did in all his explorations—and farther than it is to go from the earth to the moon.

A society can't come through daily trauma unscathed. This section presents intimations, from professional watchers of city man, of where we are now and what condition we are in:

One way or another, the city dwellers of Joan Didion's "Los Angeles Notebook" are fraying seriously. The quiet despair of her scenes suggests, in her view, what urban man pays for being who he is, where he is.

Loren Eiseley in "The Judgment of the Birds" is looking beyond man's walls into wildness. What he sees there, in the flight of pigeons among the skyscrapers, puts urban man in a perspective we seldom will confess to.

"Are We Invaded by Red China?" This and many thousand other flashes of fear were telephoned to the Seattle Rumor Center by fretful callers from 1968 to 1973. Perhaps one test of a civilization is to ask what its people are afraid of; these selections are from the day-by-day logbook of one small telephone nerve center in a single American city.

archy the cockroach wrote lower case poetry because he had no way to work the capital letters on his boss's typewriter in the new york sun newsroom. his saga of broadway the lightning bug is a tale lived out by many seekers of fame and fortune in our great cities.

The tremendous sounds of a city have been written about in countless ways. In "Flight," poet James Tate attunes us to the private sounds which would impel us to leave it all, if we had someone to go with us. If.

Mike Royko, columnist for the Chicago *Daily News*, is a reasonable man. Surely this is why the unreason which permeates our urban existence looks so shabby when he writes about it as he does in "No People Need Apply."

"On Saturday night, there is something happening for everybody in Harlem, regardless of what his groove might be," Claude Brown observes. He vividly describes the grooves to be found in our most famous city-within-a-city on the very last night of the week.

At the frayed corners of city life, "Children Are Not To Run, Shout or Play" or otherwise remind us that yet another generation of poverty is growing up. Ben Bagdikian investigates the lives of these country folk come to the city, our latest immigrants.

Los Angeles Notebook

JOAN DIDION

Our view of the colossal enigma that is California will long be shaded by the intense prose of native daughter Joan Didion, first in her columns for Saturday Evening Post *and* Life *and later in her novel* Play It As It Lays. *She has told an interviewer:* "*If I had to live and write away from the West, I would be working and projecting as an alien.*"

There is something uneasy in the Los Angeles air this afternoon, some unnatural stillness, some tension. What it means is that tonight a Santa Ana will begin to blow, a hot wind from the northeast whining down through the Cajon and San Gorgonio Passes, blowing up sandstorms out along Route 66, drying the hills and the nerves to the flash point. For a few days now we will see smoke back in the canyons, and hear sirens in the night. I have neither heard nor read that a Santa Ana is due, but I know it, and almost everyone I have seen today knows it too. We know it because we feel it. The baby frets. The maid sulks. I rekindle a waning argument with the telephone company, then cut my losses and lie down, given over to whatever it is in the air. To live with the Santa Ana is to accept, consciously or unconsciously, a deeply mechanistic view of human behavior.

I recall being told, when I first moved to Los Angeles and was living on an isolated beach, that the Indians would throw themselves into the sea when the bad wind blew. I could see why. The Pacific turned ominously glossy during a Santa Ana period, and one woke in the night troubled not only by the peacocks screaming in the olive trees but by the eerie absence of surf. The heat was surreal. The sky had a yellow cast, the kind of light sometimes called "earthquake weather." My only neighbor would not come out of her house for days, and there were no lights at night, and her husband roamed the place with a machete. One day he would tell me that he had heard a trespasser, the next a rattlesnake.

"On nights like that," Raymond Chandler once wrote about the Santa Ana, "every booze party ends in a fight. Meek little wives feel the edge of the carving knife and study their husbands' necks. Any-

---

thing can happen." That was the kind of wind it was. I did not know then that there was any basis for the effect it had on all of us, but it turns out to be another of those cases in which science bears out folk wisdom. The Santa Ana, which is named for one of the canyons it rushes through, is a *foehn* wind, like the *foehn* of Austria and Switzerland and the *hamsin* of Israel. There are a number of persistent malevolent winds, perhaps the best known of which are the mistral of France and the Mediterranean sirocco, but a *foehn* wind has distinct characteristics: it occurs on the leeward slope of a mountain range and, although the air begins as a cold mass, it is warmed as it comes down the mountain and appears finally as a hot dry wind. Whenever and wherever a *foehn* blows, doctors hear about headaches and nausea and allergies, about "nervousness," about "depression." In Los Angeles some teachers do not attempt to conduct formal classes during a Santa Ana, because the children become unmanageable. In Switzerland the suicide rate goes up during the *foehn*, and in the courts of some Swiss cantons the wind is considered a mitigating circumstance for crime. Surgeons are said to watch the wind, because blood does not clot normally during a *foehn*. A few years ago an Israeli physicist discovered that not only during such winds, but for the ten or twelve hours which precede them, the air carries an unusually high ratio of positive to negative ions. No one seems to know exactly why that should be; some talk about friction and others suggest solar disturbances. In any case the positive ions are there, and what an excess of positive ions does, in the simplest terms, is make people unhappy. One cannot get much more mechanistic than that.

Easterners commonly complain that there is no "weather" at all in Southern California, that the days and the seasons slip by relentlessly, numbingly bland. That is quite misleading. In fact the climate is characterized by infrequent but violent extremes: two periods of torrential subtropical rains which continue for weeks and wash out the hills and send subdivisions sliding toward the sea; about twenty scattered days a year of the Santa Ana, which, with its incendiary dryness, invariably means fire. At the first prediction of a Santa Ana, the Forest Service flies men and equipment from northern California into the southern forests, and the Los Angeles Fire Department cancels its ordinary non-firefighting routines. The Santa Ana caused Malibu to burn the way it did in 1956, and Bel Air in 1961, and Santa Barbara in 1964. In the winter of 1966-67 eleven men were killed fighting a Santa Ana fire that spread through the San Gabriel Mountains.

Just to watch the front-page news out of Los Angeles during a Santa Ana is to get very close to what it is about the place. The longest single Santa Ana period in recent years was in 1957, and it lasted not the usual three or four days but fourteen days, from November 21 until December 4. On the first day 25,000 acres of the San Gabriel Mountains were burning, with gusts reaching 100 miles an hour. In town, the wind reached Force 12, or hurricane force, on the Beaufort Scale; oil derricks were toppled and people ordered off the downtown streets to avoid injury from flying objects. On November 22 the fire in the San Gabriels was out of control. On November 24 six people were killed in automobile accidents, and by the end of the week the Los Angeles *Times* was keeping a box score of traffic deaths. On November 26 a prominent Pasadena attorney, depressed about money, shot and killed his wife, their two sons, and himself. On November 27 a South Gate divorcée, twenty-two, was murdered and thrown from a moving car. On November 30 the San Gabriel fire was still out of control, and the wind in town was blowing eighty miles an hour. On the first day of December four people died violently, and on the third the wind began to break.

It is hard for people who have not lived in Los Angeles to realize how radically the Santa Ana figures in the local imagination. The city burning is Los Angeles's deepest image of itself: Nathanael West perceived that, in *The Day of the Locust*; and at the time of the 1965 Watts riots what struck the imagination most indelibly were the fires. For days one could drive the Harbor Freeway and see the city on fire, just as we had always known it would be in the end. Los Angeles weather is the weather of catastrophe, of apocalypse, and, just as the reliably long and bitter winters of New England determine the way life is lived there, so the violence and the unpredictability of the Santa Ana affect the entire quality of life in Los Angeles, accentuate its impermanence, its unreliability. The wind shows us how close to the edge we are.

2

"Here's why I'm on the beeper, Ron," said the telephone voice on the all-night radio show. "I just want to say that this *Sex for the Secretary* creature—whatever her name is—certainly isn't contributing anything to the morals in this country. It's pathetic. Statistics *show*."

"It's *Sex and the Office*, honey," the disc jockey said. "That's the title. By Helen Gurley Brown. Statistics show what?"

"I haven't got them right here at my fingertips, naturally. But they *show*."

"I'd be interested in hearing them. Be constructive, you Night Owls."

"All right, let's take *one* statistic," the voice said, truculent now. "Maybe I haven't read the book, but what's this business she recommends about *going out with married men for lunch?*"

So it went, from midnight until 5 a.m., interrupted by records and by occasional calls debating whether or not a rattlesnake can swim. Misinformation about rattlesnakes is a leitmotiv of the insomniac imagination in Los Angeles. Toward 2 a.m. a man from "out Tarzana way" called to protest. "The Night Owls who called earlier must have been thinking about, uh, *The Man in the Gray Flannel Suit* or some other book," he said, "because Helen's one of the few authors trying to tell us what's really going *on.* Hefner's another, and he's also controversial, working in, uh, another area."

An old man, after testifying that he "personally" had seen a swimming rattlesnake, in the Delta-Mendota Canal, urged "moderation" on the Helen Gurley Brown question. "We shouldn't get on the beeper to call things pornographic before we've read them," he complained, pronouncing it porn-ee-oh-graphic. "I say, get the book. Give it a chance." The original *provocateur* called back to agree that she would get the book. "And then I'll burn it," she added.

"Book burner, eh?" laughed the disc jockey good-naturedly.

"I wish they still burned witches," she hissed.

3

It is three o'clock on a Sunday afternoon and 105° and the air so thick with smog that the dusty palm trees loom up with a sudden and rather attractive mystery. I have been playing in the sprinklers with the baby and I get in the car and go to Ralph's Market on the corner of Sunset and Fuller wearing an old bikini bathing suit. That is not a very good thing to wear to the market but neither is it, at Ralph's on the corner of Sunset and Fuller, an unusual costume. Nonetheless a large woman in a cotton muumuu jams her cart into mine at the butcher counter. *"What a thing to wear to the market,"* she says in a loud but strangled voice. Everyone looks the other way and I study a plastic package of rib lamb chops and she repeats it. She follows me all over the store, to the Junior Foods, to the Dairy Products, to the Mexican Delicacies, jamming my cart whenever she can. Her husband plucks at her sleeve. As I leave the check-out counter she raises her voice one last time: *"What a thing to wear to Ralph's,"* she says.

4

A party at someone's house in Beverly Hills: a pink tent, two orchestras, a couple of French Communist directors in Cardin evening jackets, chili and hamburgers from Chasen's. The wife of an English actor sits at a table alone; she visits California rarely although her husband works here a good deal. An American who knows her slightly comes over to the table.

"Marvelous to see you here," he says.

"Is it," she says.

"How long have you been here?"

"Too long."

She takes a fresh drink from a passing waiter and smiles at her husband, who is dancing.

The American tries again. He mentions her husband.

"I hear he's marvelous in this picture."

She looks at the American for the first time. When she finally speaks she enunciates every word very clearly. "He . . . is . . . also . . . a . . . fag," she says pleasantly.

5

The oral history of Los Angeles is written in piano bars. "Moon River," the piano player always plays, and "Mountain Greenery." "There's a Small Hotel" and "This Is Not the First Time." People talk to each other, tell each other about their first wives and last husbands. "Stay funny," they tell each other, and "This is to die over." A construction man talks to an unemployed screenwriter who is celebrating, alone, his tenth wedding anniversary. The construction man is on a job in Montecito: "Up in Montecito," he says, "they got one square mile with 135 millionaires."

"Putrescence," the writer says.

"That's all you got to say about it?"

"Don't read me wrong, I think Santa Barbara's one of the most— Christ, *the* most—beautiful places in the world, but it's a beautiful place that contains a . . . *putrescence.* They just live on their putrescent millions."

"So give me putrescent."

"No, no," the writer says. "I just happen to think millionaires have some sort of lacking in their . . . in their elasticity."

A drunk requests "The Sweetheart of Sigma Chi." The piano player says he doesn't know it. "Where'd you learn to play the piano?" the drunk asks. "I got two degrees," the piano player says. "One in musical education." I go to a coin telephone and call a friend in New York. "Where are you?" he says. "In a piano bar in Encino," I say. "Why?" he says. "Why not," I say.

The Judgment of the Birds

LOREN EISELEY

Loren Eiseley is an anthropologist who doubles as one of the most sensitive writers of twentieth century America. Such books of his as The Immense Journey *and* The Invisible Pyramid *have been acclaimed as eloquent excursions into the frontier between man and universe.*

It is a commonplace of all religious thought, even the most primitive, that the man seeking visions and insight must go apart from his fellows and live for a time in the wilderness. If he is of the proper sort, he will return with a message. It may not be a message from the god he set out to seek, but even if he has failed in that particular, he will have had a vision or seen a marvel, and these are always worth listening to and thinking about.

The world, I have come to believe, is a very queer place, but we have been part of this queerness for so long that we tend to take it for granted. We rush to and fro like Mad Hatters upon our peculiar errands, all the time imagining our surroundings to be dull and ourselves quite ordinary creatures. Actually, there is nothing in the world to encourage this idea, but such is the mind of man, and this is why he finds it necessary from time to time to send emissaries into the wilderness in the hope of learning of great events, or plans in store for him, that will resuscitate his waning taste for life. His great news services, his worldwide radio network, he knows with a last remnant of healthy distrust will be of no use to him in this matter. No miracle can withstand a radio broadcast, and it is certain that it would be no miracle if it could. One must seek, then, what only the solitary approach can give—a natural revelation.

Let it be understood that I am not the sort of man to whom is entrusted direct knowledge of great events or prophecies. A naturalist, however, spends much of his life alone, and my life is no exception. Even in New York City there are patches of wilderness, and a man by himself is bound to undergo certain experiences falling into the class of

---

which I speak. I set mine down, therefore: a matter of pigeons, a flight of chemicals, and a judgment of birds, in the hope that they will come to the eye of those who have retained a true taste for the marvelous, and who are capable of discerning in the flow of ordinary events the point at which the mundane world gives way to quite another dimension.

New York is not, on the whole, the best place to enjoy the downright miraculous nature of the planet. There are, I do not doubt, many remarkable stories to be heard there and many strange sights to be seen, but to grasp a marvel fully it must be savored from all aspects. This cannot be done while one is being jostled and hustled along a crowded street. Nevertheless, in any city there are true wildernesses where a man can be alone. It can happen in a hotel room, or on the high roofs at dawn.

One night on the twentieth floor of a midtown hotel I awoke in the dark and grew restless. On an impulse I climbed upon the broad old-fashioned window sill, opened the curtains and peered out. It was the hour just before dawn, the hour when men sigh in their sleep, or, if awake, strive to focus their wavering eyesight upon a world emerging from the shadows. I leaned out sleepily through the open window. I had expected depths, but not the sight I saw.

I found I was looking down from that great height into a series of curious cupolas or lofts that I could just barely make out in the darkness. As I looked, the outlines of these lofts became more distinct because the light was being reflected from the wings of pigeons who, in utter silence, were beginning to float outward upon the city. In and out through the open slits in the cupolas passed the white-winged birds on their mysterious errands. At this hour the city was theirs, and quietly, without the brush of a single wing tip against stone in that high, eerie place, they were taking over the spires of Manhattan. They were pouring upward in a light that was not yet perceptible to human eyes, while far down in the black darkness of the alleys it was still midnight.

As I crouched half asleep across the sill, I had a moment's illusion that the world had changed in the night, as in some immense snowfall, and that if I were to leave, it would have to be as these other inhabitants were doing, by the window. I should have to launch out into that great bottomless void with the simple confidence of young birds reared high up there among the familiar chimney pots and interposed horrors of the abyss.

I leaned farther out. To and fro went the white wings, to and fro. There were no sounds from any of them. They knew man was asleep and this light for a little while was theirs. Or perhaps I had only dreamed about man in this city of wings—which he could surely never have built. Perhaps I, myself, was one of these birds dreaming unpleasantly a moment of old dangers far below as I teetered on a window ledge.

Around and around went the wings. It needed only a little courage, only a little shove from the window ledge to enter that city of light. The muscles of my hands were already making little premonitory lunges. I wanted to enter that city and go away over the roofs in the first dawn. I wanted to enter it so badly that I drew back carefully into the room and opened the hall door. I found my coat on the chair, and it slowly became clear to me that there was a way down through the floors, that I was, after all, only a man.

I dressed then and went back to my own kind, and I have been rather more than usually careful ever since not to look into the city of light. I had seen, just once, man's greatest creation from a strange inverted angle, and it was not really his at all. I will never forget how those wings went round and round, and how, by the merest pressure of the fingers and a feeling for air, one might go away over the roofs. It is a knowledge, however, that is better kept to oneself. I think of it sometimes in such a way that the wings, beginning far down in the black depths of the mind, begin to rise and whirl till all the mind is lit by their spinning, and there is a sense of things passing away, but lightly, as a wing might veer over an obstacle.

"Are We Invaded by Red China?"

FROM THE SEATTLE RUMOR CENTER LOGBOOKS

> As rumors fed fear in the cities during the racially tense
> summer of 1968, the Seattle Rumor Center was started. The
> Center's volunteer staff checked on stories phoned in by
> anxious citizens and responded with facts. In the five years
> it operated, the Center handled tens of thousands of such
> calls.

Aug. 20, 1968—Man called looking for "anything exciting" going on he could go watch.

Oct. 9, 1968—What are the Black Panthers?

Oct. 17, 1968—Jackie Kennedy to marry shipping magnate?

Oct. 22, 1968—Is the small sign over "WE" on the Kennedy half dollar a hammer and sickle?

Oct. 24, 1968—Woman called to say Jackie Kennedy poisoned—by her husband!

Nov. 1, 1968—Who do I contact about my son-in-law who threatens my daughter?

June 30, 1969—If demands aren't met by August, are the Black Panthers going to bomb the Bon Marche?[1]

July 3, 1969—Are prisoner of war camps being renovated for concentration camps for Negroes in New Prague, Minnesota?

July 7, 1969—Did the Chinese invade Canada, and are on the Canadian border?

July 15, 1969—Are the Black Panthers going to see the Supremes?

July 17, 1969—Is it true there was an epidemic of boys in Vietnam bleeding to death through their pores?

July 20, 1969—Is a Russian ship firing on our astronauts?

July 31, 1969—Are hiccups caused by a misbeat of the heart?

Sept. 10, 1969—Is Paul McCartney dead?

Sept. 24, 1969—Where can you take a mentally disturbed old lady?

Oct. 14, 1969—If you are against the war, should you keep your children home from school tomorrow?

Oct. 25, 1969—Have you heard anything about a baby food that causes brain damage?

Oct. 26, 1969—Do cats carry leukemia and give it to people?

---

[1]Department store in downtown Seattle.

Oct. 27, 1969—Are a group of people at Meadowdale Elementary planning to put LSD and razor blades in Halloween candy?

Nov. 14, 1969—Have there been castrations at Tacoma Mall and Southcenter?[2]

Nov. 18, 1969—Is an unidentified flying object following the Apollo 12?

May 1, 1970—Is speed addictive?

May 1, 1970—Is there going to be a riot?

May 1, 1970—Is John Lennon dead?

May 5, 1970—Are we invaded by Red China?

May 8, 1970—Were there 4 or 5 Kent State students killed?

Aug. 13, 1970—A kidnapping in northeast Seattle reported?

Aug. 14, 1970—What's happening with the nerve gas?

Aug. 19, 1970—The FBI keep a list of gay people?

Aug. 26, 1970—How can I find out if a cosmetics company has Commie affiliations?

Aug. 27, 1970—Will there be a riot at Sealth the first day of school?[3]

Aug. 31, 1970—Did McCartney quit the Beatles?

March 23, 1971—Is it true that large dogs are taken from their homes in the Seattle area and sold to researchers?

April 8, 1971—Was a lady bit by a deadly snake in Southcenter and is in a coma now?

June 27, 1971—Can you get the chicken pox twice?

July 14, 1971—What's the latest rumor?

July 17, 1971—Will a baby die if stung by a bee?

July 21, 1971—Is there a submarine anchored off Sand Point?

July 21, 1971—Did a plane blow up at Boeing Field?

July 27, 1971—Is it true that blacks will have an armed revolution in 1972?

Aug. 3, 1971—Did a Chinese restaurant get closed for serving cat food?

Aug. 15, 1971—Does Lee Trevino play golf with a Coke bottle to give his friends a chance?

Sept. 5, 1971—Was a Sasquatch sighted at Bellingham?[4]

Sept. 12, 1971—How much blood do you need to exist?

Sept. 30, 1971—Any possibility of danger to the female organs of mother's little girl who sits too close to color TV?

---

[2] Shopping centers in Tacoma and Seattle.

[3] Sealth High School in Seattle.

[4] Sasquatch: Pacific Northwest version of the legendary abominable snowman. Bellingham: city in northwest corner of Washington state.

Oct. 26, 1971—Have Children of God been putting LSD in cookies?[5]

Jan. 3, 1972—Is there some kind of an epidemic in the Hawaiian Islands?

March 11, 1972—Is there an incurable strain of VD going around in our area?

May 21, 1972—What kind of nettles are edible?

May 23, 1972—Did someone just jump off the Medical-Dental Building?

May 24, 1972—Was Elvis Presley involved in a car accident?

May 25, 1972—Are Hell's Angels coming to town?

May 26, 1972—Where are the Hell's Angels?

June 7, 1972—Does the Fire Department charge to put out a fire?

June 9, 1972—Did Howard Hughes die?

June 26, 1972—Was a police officer shot in Buffalo, N.Y., by a group of blacks?

July 11, 1972—My husband is keeping another woman. How can I get her for prostitution?

July 18, 1972—Is fluoridation a Communist plot?

July 18, 1972—Is sugar a cure for hiccups?

July 20, 1972—Did a man jump off the Aurora Bridge?

July 26, 1972—Did Tiny's fruit stand burn down?

July 27, 1972—Was there an earthquake today?

July 29, 1972—Is McGovern going to drop his running mate?

Aug. 17, 1972—Was there a flying saucer in Vancouver, Canada?

Aug. 24, 1972—A UFO spotted in Kansas City?

Sept. 22, 1972—Does smoking aspirins in cigarettes produce a "high"?

Sept. 28, 1972—Are they planning to kill off fish in Green Lake the first of the month?

Oct. 4, 1972—Why is the noon whistle blowing so long?

Oct. 5, 1972—Is it true Mr. Onassis owns all the marijuana fields in Mexico?

Oct. 16, 1972—Does a chemical used in freezing TV dinners cause cancer?

Nov. 1, 1972—Has Frank Sinatra died?

Nov. 3, 1972—Is Henry Kissinger in the centerfold of *Cosmopolitan*?

---

[5] Children of God: religious sect.

the flattered lightning bug

DON MARQUIS

In his column for the New York Sun, *Don Marquis (1878-1938) invented a pair of our most memorable city dwellers, archy, the bardic cockroach, and mehitabel, the free-spirited alley cat. Through them he twitted a civilization taking itself too seriously; as he once had archy say, "that stern and rockbound coast felt like an amateur when it saw how grim the puritans that landed on it were."*

a lightning bug got
in here the other night a
regular hick from
the real country he was
awful proud of himself you
city insects may think
you are some punkins
but i don t see any
of you flashing in the dark
like we do in
the country all right go
to it says i mehitabel the
cat and that green
spider who lives in your locker
and two or three cockroach
friends of mine and a
friendly rat all gathered
around him and urged him on
and he lightened and
lightened and lightened you
don t see anything like this
in town often he says go to it
we told him it s a
real treat to us and
we nicknamed him broadway
which pleased him

this is the life
he said all i
need is a harbor
under me to be a
statue of liberty and
he got so vain of
himself i had to take
him down a peg you ve
made lightning for two hours
little bug i told him
but i don t hear
any claps of thunder
yet there are some men
like that when he wore
himself out mehitabel
the cat ate him

            archy

Flight

JAMES TATE

The smooth ironies of James Tate's poems mark him as one of the most notable of America's younger generation of poets. An assistant professor of English at Columbia University, he has set a number of his poems in odd crannies of urban life where, as in this work, there are even "conspiracies of dust."

Like a glum cricket
the refrigerator is singing
and just as I am convinced

that it is the only noise
in the building, a pot falls
in 2B. The neighbors on

both sides of me suddenly
realize that they have not
made love to their wives

since 1947. The racket
multiplies. The man down hall
is teaching his dog to fly.

The fish are disgusted
and beat their heads blue
against a cold aquarium. I too

lose control and consider
the dust huddled in the corner
a threat to my endurance.

Were you here, we would not
tolerate mongrels in the air,
nor the conspiracies of dust.

We would drive all night,
your head tilted on my shoulder.
At dawn, I would nudge you

with my anxious fingers and say,
Already we are in Idaho.

No People Need Apply

MIKE ROYKO

Mike Royko went a classic journalistic route to fame as an observer of Chicago life: from neighborhood reporting on the North Side to the day-in, day-out legwork of the City News Bureau to the Chicago Daily News *as a reporter and columnist. He has become best known to a national audience for his scathing columns about the political organization of Mayor Richard J. Daley; a selection from* Boss, *his biography of Daley, is included in Part Three.*

The manager of a high-rise building on Lake Shore Drive recently sent this letter to his tenants:

"Dear Tenant:

"We have been receiving numerous complaints on the misuse of the lobbies by adults as well as children.

"We must ask, therefore, that 'Lobby Sitting' be discontinued.

"Please note under Rules and Regulations:

"Children shall not be permitted to loiter or play on the stairways, halls, porches or court areas or in public places generally used by the public or other tenants.

"The sidewalks, entryways, passages, vestibules, halls and stairways outside of the several apartments shall not be used for any other purpose than ingress and egress to and from the respective rooms or apartments.

"We have been asked by many, why we have sofas and chairs in the lobby if we do not permit their use.

"It is the intention of the owners that seating be available for the FEW MINUTES that a guest may be waiting for a tenant, or that a tenant and guest be waiting for a taxi or driver to pick them up, and to enhance our lobby.

"We are sure you will agree that we are constantly extending efforts to maintain our lobbies and public areas in a manner that will be pleasing to you and reflect the prestige of our building. It is our sincere hope that you will co-operate with us."

From I MAY BE WRONG, BUT I DOUBT IT by Mike Royko. Reprinted by permission of Henry Regnery Company.

The letter angered a lady who lives in the building. She said it was directed at the elderly people, who, during the great blizzard, had no place to go. So they sat in the lobby just to get out of their apartments for a few hours.

The lady sent it to me because she felt I would share her anger.

I can't get angry about the letter because I think I understand the feelings of the building manager and the people who complained to him about all those old people hanging around the lobby.

Life just happens to be different in a high-rise than, say, in a bungalow or three-flat neighborhood.

And High-Rise Man sees things—himself included—in a different way.

High-Rise Man is like his building—soaring, lean, modern, gracious, cool, handsome, push-button, filter-tipped, a symbol of today and today's young, calorie-free living.

In the morning, he can leap out of bed and stand there in his shorts, looking out of his sweeping glass window at the sun rising over Lake Michigan.

At night, with the lights dimmed, he might stand there sipping something-on-the-rocks, listening to something tasteful on his stereo, gazing down at the twinkling lights on Lake Shore Drive. With a slight smile, he thinks:

"This is It. And I have made It."

Contrast him to Bungalow Man and Three-Flat Man. We think of ourselves as kind of squat, pot-bellied, ordinary, brick, mortar, sidewalks-by-WPA—just like the real estate.

The sight of old people is not offensive to Three-Flat Man and Bungalow Man because even when he is young he thinks he is getting old.

Besides, old people are part of Three-Flat Man's world. They're always there, sitting on the front steps, watering a lawn, watering a dog, taking a walk for the paper, complaining about somebody's punk kids.

But when High-Rise Man and his High-Rise Mate step out of the cab, nod to the doorman's respectful greeting and stride through their lobby, it can be jarring—shocking—to see a bunch of old people sitting around, dozing, knitting, cackling, or even, heaven forbid, coughing.

Not in their lean, young, soaring world.

Children are just as distasteful. When you see a child, you think of runny noses, scabby knees, diapers, boisterous behavior—none of which belongs in the world of muted tones, indirect lighting, thick-rugged hallways and gleaming lobbies.

This is a problem, of course, because old people do live in those buildings. And a few children, too.

And it seems somewhat harsh to bar them from the lobbies entirely.

Possibly the building managers could work out some sort of schedule, as second lieutenants used to do with the day rooms in the service.

They might tell them something like this:

"Dear Tenant:

"It has come to our attention that due to the cold weather some of our elderly tenants would like to leave their apartments and sit in the lobby.

"Therefore, we have amended our rules to permit 'Limited Lobby Sitting.'

"No more than six (6) elderly people will be permitted to sit in the lobby at one time.

"They will space themselves and will use those chairs that are arranged to face AWAY from the main entrance.

"Lobby Sitting will not be permitted during morning hours when tenants are leaving for their offices or during evening hours when dinner guests might be arriving.

"It is NOT allowed on Friday and Saturday nights.

"Lobby Sitting privileges will be revoked, of course, for violations of the above or for repeated complaints of cackling, knitting, dozing, coughing or cracking sounds from joints.

"Regarding children: We suggest that tenants who possess them consider giving them away."

Manchild on a Harlem Saturday Night

CLAUDE BROWN

Claude Brown's parents were sharecroppers who moved from rural poverty in the South to city poverty in New York. His youth in Harlem was a gauntlet of street fighting, drugs and correction schools, a bootstrap adolescence from which he was one of the few to emerge to a college education. Of the other street boys, he wrote: "Almost everybody was dead or in jail."

Saturday night. I suppose there's a Saturday night in every Negro community throughout the nation just like Saturday night in Harlem. The bars will jump. The precinct station will have a busy night. The hospital's emergency ward will jump.

Cats who have been working all their lives, who've never been in any trouble before, good-doing righteous cats, self-respecting, law-abiding citizens—they'll all come out. Perhaps it'll be their night in the bar, their night in the police station, maybe their night in the emergency ward.

They tell me that young doctors really try hard for a chance to do their internship in Harlem Hospital—it offers such a wide variety of experiences. They say it's the best place in the city where a surgeon can train. They say you get all kinds of experience just working there on Saturday nights.

It's usually the older folks who practice this Saturday night thing, or some of the younger cats who haven't come out of the woods yet, young cats who drink a lot of liquor, who didn't quite finish junior high school, who still have most of the Southern ways . . . the young cats who carry knives, the young cats who want to be bad niggers. It's usually the guys around eighteen to twenty-five, guys who haven't separated themselves yet from the older generation or who just haven't become critical of the older generation. They follow the pattern that has been set by the older generation, the Saturday night pattern of get-

---

ting drunk, getting a new piece of cunt, and getting real bad—carrying a knife in your pocket and ready to use it, ready to curse, ready to become a Harlem Saturday night statistic, in the hospital, the police station, or the morgue.

The intern who comes to Harlem and starts his internship around April will be ready to go into surgery by June. He's probably already tried to close up windpipes for people who've had their throat slit. Or tried to put intestines back in a stomach. Or somebody has hit somebody in the head with a hatchet. Or somebody has come into his house at the wrong time and caught somebody else going out the window. That's quite a job too, putting a person back together after a four- or five-story fall.

I suppose any policeman who's been in Harlem for a month of Saturday nights has had all the experience he'll ever need, as far as handling violence goes. Some of them will have more experience than they'll ever be able to use.

To me, it always seemed as though Saturday night was the down-home night. In the tales I'd heard about down home—how so-and-so got bad and killed Cousin Joe or knocked out Cousin Willie's eye—everything violent happened on Saturday night. It was the only time for anything to really happen, because people were too tired working all week from sunup to sundown to raise but so much hell on the week nights. Then, comes Saturday, and they take it kind of easy during the day, resting up for another Saturday night.

Down home, when they went to town, all the niggers would just break bad, so it seemed. Everybody just seemed to let out all their hostility on everybody else. Maybe they were hoping that they could get their throat cut. Perhaps if a person was lucky enough to get his throat cut, he'd be free from the fields. On the other hand, if someone was lucky enough to cut somebody else's throat, he'd done the guy a favor, because he'd freed him.

In the tales about down home that I'd heard, everybody was trying to either cash out on Saturday night or cash somebody else out. There was always the good corn liquor that Cy Walker used to make, and there was always that new gun that somebody had bought. The first time they shot the gun at so-and-so, he jumped out of the window and didn't stop running until he got home—and got his gun. You'd sit there and say, "Well, I'll be damned. I never knew they had all those bad niggers in the South. I always thought the baddest cat down there was Charlie." But it seemed as though on Saturday night, the niggers got bad. Of course, they didn't get bad enough to mess with Charlie, but they got bad. They were bad enough to cut each other's throats, shoot each other, hit each other in the head with axes, and all that sort of action. Women were bad enough to throw lye on one another.

Saturday night down home was really something, but, then, Saturday night in Harlem was really something too. There is something happening for everybody on Saturday night: for the cat who works all day long on the railroad, in the garment center, driving a bus, or as a subway conductor. On Saturday night, there is something happening for everybody in Harlem, regardless of what his groove might be. Even the real soul sisters, who go to church and live for Sunday, who live to jump up and clap and call on the Lord, Saturday night means something to them too. Saturday night is the night they start getting ready for Sunday. They have to braid all the kids' hair and get them ready. They have to iron their white usher uniforms and get pretty for Sunday and say a prayer. For the devoted churchgoers, Saturday night means that Sunday will soon be here.

Saturday night is a time to try new things. Maybe that's why so many people in the older generation had to lose their lives on Saturday night. It must be something about a Saturday night with Negroes. . . . Maybe they wanted to die on Saturday night. They'd always associated Sunday with going to heaven, because that was when they went to church and sang all those songs, clapped and shouted and stomped their feet and praised the Lord. Maybe they figured that if they died on Sunday morning, the Lord's day, they'd be well on their way.

Everybody has this thing about Saturday night. I imagine that before pot or horse or any other drugs hit Harlem good and strong, the people just had to try something else, like knifing or shooting somebody, because Saturday night was the night for daring deeds. Since there was no pot out on a large scale then, I suppose one of the most daring deeds anyone could perform was to shoot or stab somebody.

Many of the chicks in the neighborhood took some of their first really big steps on Saturday night. Some cats—or as a girl I knew might say, "no-good niggers"—talked many girls into turning their first tricks on a Saturday night just because the cats needed some money. That's how that thing goes on Saturday night. I recall talking a girl into a trick on a Saturday night. She said it was her first, but I like to tell myself it wasn't. If it was, that was okay. She was a part of Harlem, and Saturday night was a time for first things, even for girls turning their first tricks, pulling their first real John.

Saturday night has also been a traditional night for money to be floating around in places like Harlem. It's a night of temptation, the kind of temptation one might see on Catfish Row at the end of the cotton season on the weekend. Most of the people got paid on Friday night, and Saturday they had some money. If they didn't get paid on Friday, there was a good chance that they'd be around playing the single action on Saturday in the afternoon. By the time the last figure came out, everybody might have some change, even if it was only eight dollars—one dollar on the 0 that afternoon. It was still some money.

Then there were all the crap games floating around. The stickup artists would be out hunting. The Murphy boys would be out strong. In the bars, the tricks would be out strong. All the whores would be out there, and any decent, self-respecting whore could pull at least two hundred dollars on Saturday night in some of the bad-doing bars on 125th Street.

As a matter of fact, Reno used to say, "The cat who can't make no money on Saturday night is in trouble." There was a lot of truth to it, because there was so much money floating around in Harlem on Saturday night, if anyone couldn't get any money then, he just didn't have any business there.

It seemed as though Harlem's history is made on Saturday nights. You hear about all the times people have gotten shot—like when two white cops were killed on 146th Street a couple of years ago—on a Saturday night. Just about every time a cop is killed in Harlem, it's on a Saturday night.

People know you shouldn't bother with Negroes on Saturday night, because for some reason or another, Negroes just don't mind dying on Saturday night. They seem ready to die, so they're not going to take but so much stuff. There were some people who were always trying to get themselves killed. Every Saturday night, they'd try it all over again.

One was Big Bill. When I was just a kid on Eighth Avenue in knee pants, this guy was trying to get himself killed. He was always in some fight with a knife. He was always cutting or trying to cut somebody's throat. He was always getting cut or getting stabbed, getting hit in the head, getting shot. Every Saturday night that he was out there, something happened. If you heard on Sunday morning that somebody had gotten shot or stabbed, you didn't usually ask who did it. You'd ask if Big Bill did it. If he did it, no one paid too much attention to it, because he was always doing something like that. They'd say, "Yeah, man. That cat is crazy."

If somebody else had done it, you'd wonder why, and this was something to talk about and discuss. Somebody else might not have been as crazy. In the case of Big Bill, everybody expected that sooner or later somebody would kill him and put him out of his misery and that this was what he was trying for. One time Spanish Joe stabbed him. He just missed his lung, and everybody thought he was going to cool it behind that. But as soon as the cat got back on the street, he was right out there doing it again.

Even now, he's always getting in fights out on the streets on Saturday nights. He's always hurting somebody, or somebody's hurting him. He just seems to be hanging on. I think he's just unlucky. Here's a cat who's been trying to get himself killed every Saturday night as far back as I can remember, and he still hasn't made it. I suppose you've got to sympathize with a guy like that, because he's really been trying.

"Children Are Not to Run, Shout, or Play"

BEN BAGDIKIAN

Ben Bagdikian's diligent reporting has appeared in many of the major magazines and newspapers. In recent years he has become an eminent critic of American journalism. His study of poverty in America began as an assignment for Saturday Evening Post *and grew into the book* In the Midst of Plenty.

Into the cities they pour, refugees from a silent revolution.

In Chicago the white folk from the countryside come mostly by Trailway bus, carrying all they own: a suitcase tied with rope, an old trunk, three shopping bags, a folded baby buggy, a bag of grits, clutching a letter from a relative come earlier with an address and a warning, "Don't take the cabs, they'll cheat you."

If they are colored they come mostly by that great iron artery in Southern Negro life, the Illinois Central Railroad, getting off in awe under the largest building they ever saw, carrying their old suitcases and trunks, cardboard boxes with clothes and pans, and they, too, have a carefully written address, an address that may no longer exist because newcomers go to the slums and massive redevelopment is turning many slums into vacant lots or luxury apartments.

If they are American Indians they may come in rickety old cars from the Dakotas and Utah and Arizona, fleeing the hunger of the reservations, making Chicago the fourth largest concentration of aborigines in the United States.

They all gravitate toward the city, entering Chicago at the rate of fifty a day.

In a city as big as Chicago the newcomers face a strange new world. Old courage is not enough, previous skills meaningless, and what may have been minor disadvantages in education or family cohesion suddenly become catastrophic. It is possible, walking among the newcomers in their tenements, to hear these stories and these voices, and to see these signs:

"Why, this contract you signed says you have to pay carrying charges for the furniture that are more than the furniture itself! Didn't you read this before you signed it?"

"Well, Sister, the man said it would be a small charge and I couldn't find my glasses that day."

"You mean you can't read, don't you?"

"Well, not very well, Sister."

The twenty-four-year-old white girl, infant in arms, herding two other small children before her, has hitchhiked continuously for two days and two nights from West Virginia and found her husband in the middle of Chicago during a blizzard, but when a social worker gives her applications to fill out and bus tokens to get to the agency for help, the girl who has braved four hundred miles of the unknown, telephones five times in panic because the buses, the city, and the forms in triplicate are frightening.

"Mr. Donovan, my husband's back from jail so the welfare cut out my ADC because I got a unreported male in the house. Does that mean my kids can't eat because their Daddy's home?"

At Stewart Elementary School in Chicago about one thousand students enter in the fall and about one thousand students leave before June because their parents have been evicted, have departed the district for another house, or have gone back South. A teacher said, "It's hard to teach a child much of anything in a school with a 100 per cent turnover every year."

"Joe, you got to stay and help me. I need help."

"Ma, I'm going. I'm leaving for good. I don't know what I'll do but I can't stand it no more. I'm seventeen and I'll get along somehow. It's not my fault Pa's a drunk and you got eleven kids. Now you'll only have ten."

The heavy black pencilled letters, written large and painfully, are on grey cardboard tacked to the plaster in the damp corridor of 4860 North Winthrop: "Absolutely Do Not Throw Trash Out Bathroom Windows. Children Are Not to Run, Shout, or Play in Halls."

But it is not just Chicago. It is the same in New York, Los Angeles, Philadelphia, Detroit, Cleveland, Washington, St. Louis—all the great cities. In the last four decades a vast migration of 27,000,000 men, women, and children have flocked to metropolis. It is greater than the international migration which at its fullest flow from 1880 to 1920 brought 24,000,000 foreigners to America's cities. This time it is native Americans.

Almost all of them are poor. An alarming number of them remain poor for a long time.

The poverty of the newcomers is familiar and at the same time different. Prolonged lack of money can arise from a number of causes but whatever its cause it can have serious side effects that deepen the disease.

There are enormous differences in each person's response to adversity and because some people have been celebrated for personal triumph over poverty this has led to the assumption—usually by the well-fed—that to be poor makes one more noble. This was never true for most of the poor and it is not true now. Yet the belief persists that the poor compared with the affluent ought to be more honest, more resourceful, more puritanical, more disciplined, more resilient against despair, more emotionally stable, and simultaneously more aggressive and more submissive. They are not. Poverty is the pressure of living at the bottom of the social sea and this pressure finds the weakness in every personality. Poverty is dirty, vermin-infested, cold in winter, broiling in summer, and worst of all it is lonely and self-reproaching.

Ironically, the native American poor of the 1960's are worse off in some ways than the foreign immigrants of two generations ago. Both came practically penniless, went into the worst housing, got the worst jobs, and suffered the isolation and discrimination that comes to the impoverished stranger.

But the foreigners had their own culture and countrymen and history to give them assurance while they were being shunned by the new culture. In the old days if a man was disdained as a "wop" or a "mick" or a "kike" he or his parents knew that there were a time and a place in which the Italians ruled the world and created a great culture, or the Irish wrenched freedom from the world's greatest power and defended their Roman Catholic faith, or the Jews shared the making of modern civilization and survived the suffering millennia with learning and art. The lash of prejudice made its scars, as it always does, but there was some psychological solace in one's own history and bitter satisfaction that the tormentor was so ignorant he didn't even know this history. But the Negro called "nigger" or turned away with a crocodilian "Sir," and the Alabama white sneeringly called "hillbilly" hear this from their own countrymen. From the viper within the nest there is little room for retreat.

The foreign immigrant had his small solace but he also had a spur to drive him on. His was a total commitment to the new land: he had no way to leave. He could not hitchhike back to the farm, or take a bus to the home village, or go back again to the stream of migrant agricultural workers. Most had barely managed the ocean voyage here. There was no turning back.

They came from abroad at an opportune time. The New World was abuilding—railroads, canals, factories—and this was still done mainly by human hands. Pick and shovel required no diploma; there was work for the unskilled and the illiterate. It was a simple time of no application forms or Social Security cards or suitability tests or pension plans, the lack of which the workingman would feel bitterly one day, but which made the entry to casual work quicker. It was also a time for the small entrepreneur, the pushcart operator, the door-to-door peddler, the sidewalk salesman.

The foreign immigrants, too, were crowded into the worst housing. But cities were still growing in a more or less haphazard way, still mixtures of rich and poor, old and new, all living within sight and sound of each other. In the tightest immigrant slum it was possible to see or hear the ways of older settlements with all the clues these offered to successful living in a metropolis. The foreigner was highly conscious that he was in a new land and needed to learn new ways. He may have come from a city abroad. But his greatest advantage over his native contemporary was the presence of older inhabitants from whom he could learn. The friendly neighbor—or even an unfriendly one—was a powerful figure in the making of new Americans. In the city of fifty years ago, the established Americans could hardly avoid knowing the immigrants were there. People walked. The center of business and industry was downtown. All parts of the city were close at hand and brushing against each other.

The young foreigners went to schools populated by the native-born. From the American children and their teachers the immigrants not only learned the habits and idioms of city living, but they also absorbed the ambitions and standards of normal hope. This was not always a pleasant process and integration often came with bitterness and cruelty. But the country recognized that it had masses of newcomers. In the great cities of the East and Midwest no one doubted that the new element in the American population required some reaction from native society. Hundreds of organizations, some from within the immigrant groups and some from outside, turned to the job of integrating the newcomers with public schools, adult education, community houses, and systematic visitations by religious groups, private charities, and the local political chieftains.

The modern American immigrant comes to the city at a bad time. The Negro and, to a lesser extent, the white rural migrant encounter discrimination harsher for coming from their own countrymen. From this the white man and the American Indian can usually retreat. There is a constant shuttling between farm and city, or reservation and city, in one direction when conditions at home get too grim, in the other when jobs in the city are too scarce. But the periodic retreats increase family instability, disrupt education, and prevent serious commitment to making a decent, permanent home. For the Negro there is no such easy return, since he escapes not only hunger but repression. But other conditions delay his setting down roots: an even lower level of education than the rural white, more discrimination against him with jobs and the almost impermeable barrier that keeps the Negro out of the housing market.

The chief disadvantage for the native migrant is the erosion of the traditional foothold for the novice in the metropolis: the unskilled job. The ditchdigger, the factory hand, the street peddler—these were typical roles for the newcomer starting upward from 1880 to 1920. But these are the jobs that are now shrinking, to the peculiar disadvantage of the newcomer to the city who comes with poor education from an agrarian culture unconcerned with industrial and white collar skills. In factories, about 1,500,000 jobs a year are abolished by automation. In construction work between 1956 and 1962 work accomplished went up 30 per cent while the number of workers was cut 25 per cent. The open jobs are mostly for skilled technicians or white collar and managerial positions. The only place with a consistent increase in available jobs has been in government and that has been relatively small—less than 300,000 new positions a year—and most of those teaching jobs in the public schools. As production-per-man goes up in industry, the working population continues to go up. . . . For the pushcart and door-to-door peddler, the times are bad, too. In 1900 there were 77,000 licensed hucksters and peddlers, but even though licensing and nose-counting are far more complete today, by 1950 there were only 24,000. In a rich economy, success in merchandising comes from volume of sales at low prices. This requires large investment and access to credit. The supermarket and discount house are creatures of this generation and they can undersell the lone proprietor.

The city itself has changed, almost entirely to the disadvantage of the impoverished newcomer. The transition from rural poverty to urban poverty is bewildering under any circumstances. The newcomer probably came from dilapidated farmhouses or shacks in the field without running water or electricity. In 1960 there were still 7,000,000 dwellings, 12 per cent of the total, that lacked running water or a toilet. In the city a gas stove, plaster on the walls, electric wiring, plumbing, rigid rules of trash and garbage disposal may be unfamiliar and seem unimportant. Life in the city is almost always overwhelming. The lifetime face-to-face personal relations of the village are replaced by fast-moving, fast-talking, impatient people in business suits sitting in remote high offices requesting forms in triplicate. Mass transit—subways, multiple bus lines, transfers, endless blocks of huge buildings—can be dizzying. The punctuality and impersonality of city jobs can be depressing. The new legal and social demands for proper clothing and medical care for school children and the competition on the basis of writing on school applications and job forms and welfare reports, all may seem mysteries comparable to the language barrier of the earlier foreigners and, in one way, worse. Most bureaucrats assume that any native-born American can write the mother tongue, can fill out forms, understand rapidly-uttered directions in business protocol, and can get around un-aided in his own city. It is not a valid assumption. But few native migrants are willing to admit it. There is a glossary for the semi-literate—"I don't have my glasses with me," or "My hands are dirty, would you please fill it out?" or, "Oh, was I supposed to bring that paper with me?"—phrases used not only to avoid admission of difficulty with writing or reading, but also to avoid the painful moment when a parent has to admit to his own child that he is illiterate.

The new city deepens all the traditional problems. Since World War II the experienced city-dwellers have moved to the suburbs or to new housing developments away from downtown. With them have gone the big stores, the supermarkets, many of the factories and office buildings. The private car squeezed mass transit offstage and prosperous American life accommodated itself to the victor. Homes, stores, working places, even entertainment (Philadelphia has five downtown theaters but thirty summer suburban ones) all built themselves for the convenience of the automobile rather than for the railroad or bus or subway or pedestrian. This left the central cores of cities decayed and abandoned and this is where the newcomers settle. Instead of living interspersed among older residents, they crowd into whole blocks and entire neighborhoods that have emptied out their original residents en masse, sometimes in a matter of a few months. This process has broken an important chain of inheritance by which the accumulated experience of civilized urban living was normally passed on to the newcomer. Conformity, a curse to those who have learned the crucial mechanics of living, serves its purpose in the struggle to master a new environment. A vital part of this learning process is the urge of the newcomer to adjust to the prevailing standards and to the expectations of his neighbors. But now there was no prevailing standard, no expectation by anyone, no model to follow, nothing to adjust to.

Many of the rural migrants had never before lived under the same roof with another family. Certainly they had never conducted their total family ritual within chambers that were only a few feet away from a dozen other chambers where other families were living out their lives, all without the cleansing action of open land and sun and wind. The almost automatic conditions of city-life cooperation—embodied in the commonplace concept of "the people downstairs" or, also alien to the rural family, "the people next door" —are slow to come to families

who for generations had space and open fields for neighbors. The mechanics of tenement living can be awesome, its integration into the unconscious skills of day-to-day living can take a long time. For many,
modern plumbing—the toilet bowl and water closet, the kitchen sink
drain—seems governed by principles as arcane as those for a nuclear
reactor. Plaster walls seem made for graffiti or for drilling and explora-
tion, especially by children not yet initiated to winter winds in the
North. No hogs or chickens care for the garbage, and it is often unclear
who does.

For people raised in a forgiving climate in dwellings that have
been immemorially ramshackle, there is little skill in carpentering. It
is the old-time urbanite who is the irrepressible handyman. Newcomers to the city will sometimes shiver in cruel cold for lack of a dozen
nails and a hammer and an eye for defense against the weather. For
those brought up in the ageless shacks of the South, the family shelter
is taken for granted as a part of nature, like a tree or a creek, and as
unalterable to the unaided hand. The niceties of the city—swept sidewalks and a patch of lawn out front—are alien to those who never had
sidewalks and for whom grass was self-tending, like leaves on a tree. In
the untypical neighborhoods where old-timers have remained, the newcomers are noticeably quicker to adopt these habits of care for home
and neighborhood.

Confusing though his own dwelling may be, the newcomer is even
more appalled by the machinery of the city itself. Officialdom, "the
law," is a different animal entirely. In the rural preserves there is little
recourse to officialdom. "The law" is something to be avoided. But if
authority needs to be approached or comes unasked, it is in the form of
a flesh-and-blood individual known by name, face, and reputation. In
the city, "the law" is far more demanding than in the countryside. It
governs the attendance of children at school, their vaccinations, the
collection of garbage and trash, condition of the house, operation of
electrical wiring and plumbing, behavior of family members, the place
and nature of one's work, or more likely, the receipt and expenditure of
welfare money. But this more pervasive "law" is not a single authority,
nor is it a familiar person, consistent and knowable, but a remote and
abstract concoction of formal offices, sheets of paper, and a shifting
cast of strangers. It is part of the wave of nervous signals that keep
pouring into the newcomer, signals he has never heard before, whose
meaning he has trouble comprehending, that he may not even recognize as messages, and that even when recognized as something directed
at him he associates with trouble. The older neighbor would have been
helpful; but mastery comes only with time and experience. For a surprisingly long time, the unpredictable outside world frightens the rural
newcomer. In the disruption of the new life, he clings to the tiny part of

this world, his own neighborhood, that he at least knows by sight. This is why there are people more terrified of moving ten blocks than they are of hitchhiking 400 miles. The translation of these weird signals is one service that the experienced neighbor can provide, either by advice or by example. But for vast stretches of today's slums there are no second-generation neighbors, no old hands, friendly or unfriendly. Their absence accelerates the breakdown of order to produce wild and primitive neighborhood conditions, confusion and chaos in the family, wretchedness of lonely individuals. When the latest arrival from the countryside enters the neighborhood, this is all he sees; to the newcomer, as with children, whatever happens is normal. If the novice adjusts to this, he finds himself at war with the outer world. But often he is at war without knowing it. He finds out only when he is shunned in the fashionable shopping districts or when he goes to school or when he is arrested.

The schools reflect their neighborhoods. With the home-owning taxpayers gone, and the articulate city-wise resident moved away, the district loses its influence in municipal politics. Street pavements deteriorate, trash collections are missed and rats multiply until they invade the distant respectable neighborhoods, increasing the dread of the newcomer. Friendly intercessions with the police by neighborhood patriarch or priest disappear because the patriarch has probably moved away and the priest and minister have followed their parishioners. In the dreary decline, the most damaging single loss is the neighborhood school. The building becomes decrepit and the weariest teachers are assigned to maintain order in them: newcomers have no powerful PTA or organized voting bloc to threaten aldermen. Primary purpose of the classroom becomes discipline, which is often genuinely difficult to impose, partly because the children are untouched by any spirit of learning, partly because teaching staffs are generally inadequate, and partly because a segment of the student body already is in fierce revolt. Classroom education is filled with white collar symbols and values and these usually mean nothing to the slum students, either in their own experience or in the example of anyone they know.

The public school has been the social seedbed of modern American democracy but with a few brilliant exceptions it is failing in America's central cities. Traditionally the community school has established personal links among children from different classes and cultures. Even under unsympathetic circumstances, a few irrepressible talents have sprung, obvious and unmistakable, from all cultures represented in a school, a phenomenon that has in its own quiet way contributed to the basic national ethic of respect for the potential of the individual rather than for his class. For the children of the affluent, this has been a deep, if largely unconscious, social lesson. Furthermore, it has forced the middle and upper classes to compete in excellence rather than drift in the complacence of imagined superiority of inherited position. The continuing vigor of American society owes much to this demonstration before the young in their schools. For the children of the poor and deprived, the association in the classroom has meant respect, sometimes grudging, for the possibility of talent and decency among the affluent, and, more important, it has provided the most helpful clues to academic and social achievement. It has been the greatest single bridge for escape from destitution and despair. But the homogeneous school, with all the children from the slums or all from college-degree households, loses that function. The school in the slum has a greater role to play than in any other single kind of neighborhood, for it is the most likely place that the child can find new directions after the culture break with his parents' past, rise above deficiencies at home, and allay the confusion of the unsettled migrant. Yet, these are the most neglected schools in America. James Conant estimates that they spend less than half the money per student and have fewer than half the ratio of teachers to students, compared with schools in affluent districts. The slum school, often the dumping ground for unsatisfactory teachers, is populated by bewildered, unprepared, and unhappy children who can only re-infect each other with apathy and confusion.

When the newcomer looks for a job he seldom carries convincing credentials of experience and training, but worse, he usually carries the ineffable stigma of his neighborhood. The millions of the poor who are Negroes carry the extra burden of discrimination against their skin. This takes from them the technique of quiet success by which other ethnic groups in the past have overcome prejudice. The Negro has no chance quietly to become a success selling vacuum cleaners door-to-door in the better neighborhoods, or to fake his way into a white collar job, or to slip unnoticed into a skilled occupation. The Horatio Alger tradition applied to the European immigrant called for the ambitious chap to insinuate himself into a job and become such a smashing success that he won the admiration of the boss and his fellow-employees before they remembered that all Germans are stupid, all Irish are drunks, and all Italians are gangsters. For the man with a dark skin there is no such bypass of the stereotype.

It has been a long time, in the memory of contemporaries, since the mass migrations from Europe. In the 1920's the immigration gates were closed except for the precisely selected people whose education and skills were pre-scheduled. In the meantime, the country convinced itself that poverty has disappeared. Societies to help newcomers are long gone or evolved into something else. The settlement houses are either torn down or are splendid edifices in established neighborhoods, though some have lately been responding to the old sounds of need. In the place of the immigrant societies and the patronizing politicians have come the welfare agencies, which in terms of cash do more than any settlement house or ward heeler ever did and have prevented mass starvation and political chaos. But they are not humanity expressed so much as humanity administered. They are indispensable but they are not enough. Fewer children in the slums starve or freeze than in the 1890's, but fewer are recognized by name and face by someone from the outside world.

There is a final irony for the newly arrived poor in the cities. It costs them more to be poor than it used to. Living standards are higher, not only in the expectation of the community, but of the law. The number of persons per room, the temperature of the house in winter, the stability of stairways, the dental and medical condition of school children—often honored in the breach—are nevertheless regulated by law and one way or another the poor pay for it. These are good things for the law to demand, but for the benefits provided they complicate the economy of poverty in the city (rural areas are usually devoid of such law and of welfare). The greatest complication of all is the domination of the American economy by the automobile. Public transportation between the centers of human activity has shrivelled. The poor no longer live in the shadow of the majority of jobs. There are fewer garment shops whose owners can be charmed, or foundry foremen to nag, or shoe factories to hang around. These are dispersed over the landscape where there is free parking, along with the supermarkets with the cheapest prices. But few of the poor can get to them. The poor today are stranded in an island of slums surrounded by indifference.

The indifference is no unique callousness among Americans. Americans, in fact, are less inured to the suffering of others than most established peoples. They still long, happily, to do something about tragedy. But poverty has never been pleasant to look at and the average citizen, even of a humane society, does not actively seek it out. When cities were mixtures of differing economic groups, living cheek by jowl, and a man going to work walked by the poor, or perhaps saw them at the downtown employment office, or had his children sit next to their children in school, there was no choice. The middle-class citizen knew there was poverty because it was in the next block, or he saw it from the trolley, or he saw men selling buttons or repairing umbrellas in the street. The middle-class man may have protected himself with a smug explanation of why this happened, but he knew it existed. Today the middle-class American lives in the suburbs or in an entirely different part of the city. He does not usually have to go daily through the central city, or at least not through the littered streets behind the big hotels. He is much more apt to move outward to the fringes for working and shopping. He and his children may go for years without ever seeing a slum. (Indeed, the socially conscious parent in the city has been known to take his children on a deliberate tour of the slums to open young eyes to what exists in his own community.) His highways loop around or leap over these distant anonymous blocks at sixty miles an hour.

Forty years ago two-thirds of the population of the United States was in serious economic trouble. Today a smaller proportion of Americans is poor, not so small as the affluent seem to think, but small enough to drop below the threshold of national consciousness. Because they are miserable out in the distant farmlands and mountains or in their cramped slums in the abandoned cores of cities, the poor are poor all by themselves.

Besides, the poor used to look poor and very often they don't any more. For centuries the literature of poverty was filled with words like "rags" and "faded" and "torn." This was the state of clothing among the poor until American poverty became the best-dressed in the world. In recent years clothes have become casual and dyes have become perfect.

It was possible recently to watch a girl at a dance in a Chicago community house, in a pink cotton dress with a bright blue bow at the collar; she could have been picked up by a parent in a big car and gone home to an apartment with a doorman. A boy in chinos and sports shirt walked down a San Francisco street with books under his arm; he might have entered a hillside villa without raising eyebrows. It would be an imprudent man who bet on the income level of the children's families. The Chicago girl went to a dark and uriniferous stairway beside a gin mill and walked into her tenement where drunken adults yelled at her and babies in cribs cried to be changed. The boy in San Francisco went up a back fire escape to a dingy pair of rooms where his husbandless mother fed her children from cold cans. The dyes in American clothing do not fade and in their fidelity they have removed from the streets one of the historic clues to poverty.

Paradoxically, the poor in America now are materially better off than the impoverished of the past, but they are poor nonetheless and they may be poorer in spirit. . . . They are unnourished by their native countryside, so they have become refugees in the cities where they are hidden from their own countrymen, sustained by welfare payments that keep them fed and clothed, but for the most part without hope of deliverance. The American city which once demonstrated for the world how to receive masses of penniless newcomers and from them produce a generation of productive citizens seems to have forgotten how it did it.

QUESTIONS

1a. Tension is a theme in Joan Didion's "Los Angeles Notebook." What specific details does she use to convey this?

 b. Do any of her episodes suggest similar experiences that you have had? If so, try writing a page of your own to add to her notebook. If not, try to explain why similar moments of tension are not part of your experience.

2a. What exactly is "the miraculous" in Loren Eiseley's article?

 b. Both Eiseley and Didion are writing about the far edges of human experience; what is the difference in their views of what lies beyond those edges?

3a. Of the questions phoned to the Seattle Rumor Center, are there any which you find reasonable? Which ones and why? Compare your "reasonable" rumors with those of others in the class. Are they the same? If not, what do the differences show about you?

 b. What features of city life seem to foster the rumors listed in the article?

4a. What does the poem by Don Marquis say about broadway's attitude as a newcomer to the city? What details are used by the poet to bring out this attitude?

 b. What makes the poem amusing and at the same time a serious comment on the pitfalls of city life?

5a. James Tate's poem mentions several examples of loss of control. From his descriptions of the building and its tenants, what has driven the characters beyond control?

 b. Why is the title of the poem appropriate? How is the humor here essentially the same as, or different from, that in Marquis's poem?

 c. Compare the Tate poem with the last episode of Didion's "Los Angeles Notebook." What is the difference between the responses of the narrators, and why?

6a. Mike Royko has set scenes to contrast his apartment dwellers. How does he use specific adjectives and verbs to do this?

 b. His article begins and ends with a letter. What changes does he make in the second version to satirize the first?

 c. Author Royko says he "understands the feelings" of the building manager and the high rise types who complained. Does "understanding" include "sympathizing with"? What is Royko saying about city living patterns?

7a. Claude Brown writes about the excitement of a Harlem Saturday night. Why are the persons in his story following the "pattern" of behavior?

b. What is the difference between how Brown's Harlem characters behave and how Didion's Los Angeles characters behave? Is the difference simply a matter of "adjusting" better to a situation? Why or why not?

8a. Dialogue is used in several places in the article by Ben Bagdikian. What is the author illustrating in each case?

b. What comparisons show up between earlier immigrants to the city and the modern newcomers Bagdikian is reporting on? How convinced are you that his comparisons are accurate and fair? Explain.

9a. The title of Part One is "What Is This Place?" Are the considerations here peculiar to city life, or do they apply to other "places" as well, such as suburbs or small towns? If so, why?

b. The selections in Part One comprise several types of writing: notebook entries, essay, logbook, poetry, satire, memoir, investigative article. If you live or have lived in a city, choose one of these forms of writing and give your own account of some aspect of life in the city you know. If you've never lived in a city, take as your topic one of the problems raised in Part One that you hadn't thought of before and write about it as if you were a newcomer to a city.

FURTHER SOURCES

Much more material is available about both the topics and the authors found in this book. These end-of-chapter lists include further sources to go with each article, plus some suggestions for use with each major part of the book.

As a start, a pair of books for general reading on the American city and how it came to be: *The Urban Wilderness*, by Sam Bass Warner, Jr. (Harper & Row, 1972) and *The Americans: The Democratic Experience*, by Daniel J. Boorstin (Random House, 1973).

Many films deal with the contemporary city, and some of the best are: *Time Piece* and *Cosmopolis* (both from Contemporary/McGraw-Hill Films, 1221 Avenue of the Americas, New York, N.Y. 10020); *1985* and *Nothing But a Man* (both from Macmillan Films, Inc., 34 Mac-Questen Pky. S., Mt. Vernon, N.Y. 10550); *The Marshes of "Two" Street* (NET Film Service, Audio Visual Center, Indiana University, Bloomington, Ind. 47401); *The Cool World* and *Law and Order* (both from Zipporah Films, 54 Lewis Wharf, Boston, Mass. 02110). A current source of material about cities is *Update, the Urban News File*, a monthly microfiche series (Bell & Howell, Micro Photo Division, Old Mansfield Road, Wooster, Ohio 44691). The *Update* collection indexes articles from newspapers in 95 American cities, covering ten major categories: education, employment, environment, government and politics, health, housing and urban development, human and economic relations, law and order, transportation, welfare and poverty.

For comparison's sake with current writings about the cities, an interesting set of articles is the *Saturday Evening Post* series, profiling 121 cities in intermittent issues between Aug. 25, 1945, and July 5, 1952.

Los Angeles Notebook *Joan Didion* Collected articles can be found in the author's *Slouching Toward Bethlehem* (Farrar, Straus & Giroux, 1968). Her novel *Play It As It Lays* (Farrar, Straus & Giroux, 1970) was made into a movie in 1973. A profile of Joan Didion and her work is "Joan Didion: portrait of a professional," by Alfred Kazin, *Harper's*, Dec., 1971, pp. 112-22.

The Judgment of the Birds *Loren Eiseley* The most notable books by this author are *The Immense Journey* (Random House, 1957) and *The Invisible Pyramid* (Charles Scribner's Sons, 1970). An excellent article about Loren Eiseley is "The Immense Journey of Loren Eiseley," by John Medelman, *Esquire*, March, 1967, pp. 92-94.

Are We Invaded by Red China? *Seattle Rumor Center log-books* For an article about the Center, see "The Rumor Fighters," by Ivan Doig, *Kiwanis*, June, 1972, pp. 31-33. Material about the study of rumors is sparse; the standard work is *The Psychology of Rumor*, by Gordon Allport and Leo Postman (Holt and Co., 1947).

the flattered lightning bug *Don Marquis* See *the lives and times of archy and mehitabel* (Doubleday and Co., 1950); for a detailed biography of the poet, see *O Rare Don Marquis*, by Edward Anthony (Doubleday, 1962).

Flight *James Tate* This poet's best-known collections are *The Lost Pilot* (Yale University Press, 1967) and *Absences* (Little, Brown, 1972). An illustrated anthology of urban poetry is *On City Streets*, edited by Nancy Larrick (Bantam, 1969). Perhaps the most notable American poem on a single city is *Paterson*, by William Carlos Williams (New Directions, 1963).

No People Need Apply *Mike Royko* Royko's columns are syndicated by the Chicago *Daily News* and appear in many U.S. newspapers. A collection of his columns is titled *I May Be Wrong, But I Doubt It* (Henry Regnery Co., 1968).

Manchild on a Harlem Saturday Night *Claude Brown* For a profile of the author, see "A Cry from Harlem," by Chandler Brossard, *Look*, Dec. 14, 1965, pp. 125-28. Historical material on Harlem can be found in *The Negro in New York*, edited by Roi Ottley and William J. Weatherby (New York Public Library, 1967). For comparing Claude Brown's life with the Black experience in another generation in a different city, see *Long Old Road*, by Horace R. Cayton (University of Washington Press, 1963).

"Children Are Not To Run, Shout, or Play" *Ben Bagdikian* A similarly perceptive book is *The Other America: Poverty in the United States*, by Michael Harrington (The Macmillan Co., 1963).

PART 2

MEGATOWN REPORTS

INTRODUCTION

New York City comes to mind thoroughly swathed in strings of clichés. To the more than 200 million Americans who do *not* live there, New York exists mostly as a stupendous gauzy silhouette seen limping dimly through some news report of crime or disaster, some latest drama of the asphalt jungle. We can scarcely see the place for the platitudes, and we can't explore it because of its immensity, yet we know we must try because this biggest city serves as an early warning gauge for metropolitan problems coursing toward the rest of us. Reveal the colossus with facts and figures? We can try:

When the 1970 census was taken, the number of persons living in New York City was 7,894,862. Forty-three of our states have populations smaller than this total. It is more people, living within a space of 300 square miles, than could be counted by going from north to south down the entire nation through the states of Montana, Idaho, Utah, Wyoming, Colorado, Arizona and New Mexico. New York's Black population alone would constitute the sixth largest city in America; its Jewish population is far and away the largest of any city in the world. The famed skyline thrusts up more buildings of 50 stories or higher than all the rest of the U.S. cities combined. Thirty-six newspapers, including the country's two biggest in circulation, are published in the city; the editorial offices of most of the nation's influential magazines are there; so are the headquarters of the two national news services, and of the three major broadcasting networks. Our national folklore credits New York with the first automobile accident (1896) and the first bank robbery (1831). The city currently employs more than 30,000 police, the equivalent of about two Army divisions. Nearly six million telephones are in use by New Yorkers. The city's annual budget runs to more than eight *billion* dollars. . . .

The huge numbers run on and on, bunching up next to the clichés. With even its most casual statistics making us think in the millions or more, New York truly is our megatown. Part Two attempts to reach through the clichés and statistics toward some human dimensions of our biggest city:

Survival skills for fending in the urban wilderness should include a sturdy sense of humor. *Village Voice* reporter Clark Whelton watches the inspired mischief of "Papo and the Hydrant."

A giant city lives by giant systems. Looking at the man who runs the electrical empire of Consolidated Edison, William W. Prochnau wonders: "Can He Keep New York Bright?"

Meyer Berger of the New York *Times* knew his city from steel root to concrete pinnacle. He takes us under the pavement with the warning that "New York Is a Brittle City."

In the spires of the metropolis glimmer dreams of fame and glory. "The Golden City" is novelist Thomas Wolfe's personal hymnal of such dreams.

James Baldwin's letters to White America have been thoughtful, compelling messages across our racial chasms. In "Fifth Avenue, Uptown" he talks of how Black people live in a city shared with neglect and inequity.

Many ways the city knows to twang our nerve ends. Tom Wolfe watches anthropologist Edward T. Hall watching New Yorkers twitch: "Oh Rotten Gotham—Sliding Down Into the Behavioral Sink."

Papo and the Hydrant:
Lower East Side Summer

CLARK WHELTON

As a staff writer for The Village Voice, *Clark Whelton has searched out many memorable stories from the New York streets. "Papo and the Hydrant" typically shows his fine blend of reporter's detail and narrator's style.*

Papo opened the hydrant for the first time on an airless Saturday afternoon. The sun was straight up in the hot, hazy sky and when the kids saw Papo with the wrench in his hand some of them ran inside for their bathing suits while the rest just emptied their pockets, stashed their possessions on the brownstone stoops, and waited for the water. East of Avenue B other hydrants were already open and flailing away at the heat like lawn sprinklers at a five-alarm fire. Papo removed his shirt and shoes and unscrewed the nozzle cover from the smaller of the two hydrant openings. Then he fitted the wrench to the valve nut on top of the hydrant and pushed.

The water gushed up out of its iron well and spilled into the sunlight, brown with rust and sediment. Papo slowly turned the wrench with one hand and strained the water with the fingers of the other, feeling for stones and jewels of shattered glass that the kids had dropped into the hydrant during the winter. The water began to clear and Papo, satisfied that the hydrant had passed its stones, twisted the wrench in a complete circle. A horizontal shaft of water jetted out into the middle of the street. The kids came off the sidewalk, dancing with anticipation. A man jumped into a car opposite the hydrant and moved it down the block. Papo glanced at the new space and gave the wrench another twist. The water skidded along the asphalt into the other curb.

The kids darted in and out of the water, backing toward the hydrant as far as they could until the force of the stream shoved them aside. Papo straddled the hydrant, hitching up his pants, bareback in the afternoon sun. Bracing his heels on the curb, he lowered himself slowly until his buttocks were just above the nozzle and the silvery column of water was spurting out between his legs. He reached down and

---

rubbed his hands along the fluid flanks of the rushing torrent. Then he picked up a beer can and examined it carefully. Both ends had been cleanly removed. Papo was ready.

A truck came down the block, slowed briefly while the driver rolled up the window on the hydrant side, then picked up speed. The children scattered. Papo jammed the beer can into the nozzle and as the truck came even with the hydrant a plume of water smacked the cab window and boomed along the aluminum van as the truck roared by.

The kids came back into the street. Papo tilted the beer can back and sent a geyser into the air. The kids opened their mouths, trying to catch the water as it fell, and while they were looking up Papo leveled the can and hit them with the channeled stream. They screamed and yelled, twisting away, trying to maintain their balance. Then they came back, approaching the shaft at the point where it splintered into fluid fragments, trying to catch the water in their mouths without getting knocked down. Papo held the can between his thighs and followed them with the stream as they tried to get away. A car sped by and Papo hit it on the fly with a flip of his wrist. Then someone shouted in Spanish and Papo closed his legs. Some of the water bubbled up between his legs and the rest was deflected downward into the gutter. The kids jumped back on the sidewalk and looked up the block. A wide, maroon convertible, top down, was approaching cautiously.

Papo tightened his legs. The convertible edged up to the water-streaked street and stopped, just out of range. Behind the wheel sat a girl in a blue kerchief with her hair wrapped around pink plastic curlers. Next to her a pretty man in sunglasses, his carefully groomed hair just brushing the top of his green silk collar, sat looking straight ahead. The girl looked at Papo on the hydrant, then turned and looked behind her. A delivery truck and two cars were waiting for her to move. The convertible from New Jersey, its cream-colored license plates proclaiming its innocence, had been caught in the hydrant trap.

"Put the top up!" the truck driver yelled, leaning out of his cab.

"It's broken," the girl answered. "I have to put it up by hand and it takes 20 minutes." A horn sounded. The girl looked at Papo, who was watching the water run down his legs.

"Can we please go through?" she asked.

Papo looked up as if he were surprised to see the convertible. He waved an arm in a casual gesture and said: "Go ahead."

The girl didn't move. "I *told* you," her companion said, his eyes still fixed on a spot above the glove compartment.

"Shut up, Ronnie," the girl said. Then to Papo: "Really? You won't squirt us?"

More horns began to blare. A man on a motorcycle coasted up to the hydrant and stopped. He lowered his helmet toward Papo.

'Go ahead, sock it to me!'' he shouted.

Papo shook his head solemnly. "Can't do it, man. Might get water on the lady's car." The biker gunned his engine and peeled away. Three or four kids began to circle the convertible, rubbing their wet hands over the polished maroon metal. They stopped next to Ronnie. Ronnie looked straight ahead. Other kids began to touch the car. One of them pulled on the radio antenna and left it quivering. The horns continued their discordant chorus. The girl reached over and rolled up the windows on Ronnie's side. The kids knocked on the glass next to Ronnie's head. Ronnie stared at the dashboard, his mouth set. The girl looked at Papo again.

"You really promise?" she pleaded.

"Sure," Papo said. "Sure I do."

The truck driver jumped down to the street and walked over by the hydrant. "Go ahead, lady," he said. "I won't let him do anything. You're holding up traffic."

The girl settled down behind the wheel and let the car crawl forward several yards. Papo looked down at the water which was once again bubbling up between his thighs. The girl gripped the wheel with both hands and stamped on the accelerator. The convertible leaped ahead and Papo in one smooth motion opened his legs, rammed the beer can into the nozzle, and arched a rooster-tail of water into the air. His timing was perfect and the arc of water dropped in over the rolled-up windows and broke in a shining explosion on the dashboard, grazed the back of Ronnie's neck and swiped the girl across the shoulders, and the convertible was out of range.

The truck driver climbed back into his cab. "Some protector," a voice called. The truck driver shrugged. "They was from Jersey," he explained.

The convertible hit the green light at Avenue B and turned left, its tires squealing, but Papo was already looking up the block at the other cars, watching their windows, waiting for an opening.

Can He Keep New York Bright?

WILLIAM W. PROCHNAU

Based in Washington, D.C., for several years as a corre-
spondent for the Seattle Times, *William W. Prochnau*
ranged the eastern seaboard from the launch towers of Cape
Canaveral to the executive towers of Manhattan. He moved
from reporting to the staff of U.S. Senator Warren G. Mag-
nuson.

It was early on a June morning and the view from the executive suite
looked out over the classic profile of Lower Manhattan. The slate-gray
sky-piercers of corporate America melded with the crumbling-brown
buildings of another America, flags flying from the one, laundry flying
from the other. Down below, the city was awakening. It is a late
awakener, and the tumult of its curse, the automobile, penetrated the
whirr of the air-conditioning, even on the 16th floor. It was the begin-
ning of a good New York day. Not a cloud in the sky—just the custom-
ary smoke, hanging brown and thick, and the unseen hydrocarbons and
sulfur dioxide. Nearby, on a tenement roof, a single sunbather sought
the filtered rays and breathed in the spring morning. Breathed in the
crud.

The Consolidated Edison Co. of New York is, by most measures,
the largest private utility in the world. It supplies electricity and natural gas to most of the metropolitan area of the country's largest—and
the world's most significant—city.

Con Ed's huge blue generators pump the lifeblood of Wall Street,
feed the ozones of the great television networks, turn the presses of The
New York Times. They give Broadway its garishness and the Village
its psychedelia. They light the slums of a million blacks and Puerto
Ricans, illuminate the varying affluence of millions of other New
Yorkers. If Con Ed bobbles, civilization rocks in the mass metropolis.
In New York, Con Ed is The Source.

Over the years, the Consolidated Edison Co. has developed a reputation as black as the city was itself during the great power failure of
1965. It has been seen as the archetype of everything that is wrong with
laissez faire capitalism.

Reprinted with permission of the author.

It has been socially unresponsive. It has been civically uncaring. It has charged high rates for poor service. It has been an incredibly poor planner, leading to critical power shortages. It has been a polluter. It has scarred the landscape.

It has hired few blacks, few Puerto Ricans, even few Jews in this most Jewish of cities. The titles of three recent magazine articles about this giant corporation describe the mood as well as anything: "Con Ed —The Arrogance of Power" (New York Magazine); "All Power (Sometimes) to the People" (The New York Times Magazine). "Con Ed— The Company You Love To Hate" (Fortune).

It was shortly after the Fortune article that Con Ed's overseers decided that it was time to join the modern world. In a move that caused fluttering throughout the electric-power industry the archaic, mossback, superconservative Consolidated Edison Co. set out to change its image and, hopefully, its performance.

The board of directors sacked the company's aging chief executive officer, Charles Able, a man who had started his Con Ed career 50 years earlier as a $6-a-week messenger boy. To replace Able the directors did a most unusual thing. They went to Washington, D.C., and hired a man who seemed antithetical to everything Con Ed had stood for. He was a liberal, a Democrat, a public-power advocate, a man totally uninitiated in corporate life and uninitiated in Wall Street, a man who had spent his entire life west of the Hudson River, much of it tucked away in the remoteness of Walla Walla, Wash.

Charles Franklin Luce, however, was not exactly without credits. At the time of his move in 1967 Luce was under-secretary of the interior and one of the most respected members of Lyndon Johnson's "little" Cabinet. Earlier he had guided the giant Bonneville Power Administration through one of its most tumultuous periods—laying the groundwork for a huge Western power grid and implementing a treaty with Canada that led to joint development of power in the Columbia Basin.

Still, Luce was an odd choice. He was such a public man, a man whose life goal was to become a federal judge. In Walla Walla, during the late '40s and '50s, he had made his legal reputation representing the Indian tribes of Southeast Washington. Before the Supreme Court, he added luster to that reputation by defending indigent convicts.

It is not surprising that in some public-power circles, and in some not-so-shrouded Washington conversations, there were murmurs of a sellout. Much of the animosity has gone out of the legendary dispute between public and private power. But not all. One of Luce's Interior Department aides, invited to join the New York adventure but reluctant to go along, put it to him squarely.

The aide's challenge exasperated Luce more than it angered him. "Public service?" Luce asked him. "What greater public service do you expect to perform than to go up there and serve 9 million people?"

The remark was clearly atypical of the traditional Con Ed executive. But it was typical of Luce. Like most successful executives, he sees life as a series of challenges. No challenge would be greater than this one.

In part the challenge of Con Ed was primarily a local one with problems peculiar only to the almost unmanageable metropolis of New York. But in other, probably more important ways, Con Ed's problems were those of the nation. The United States, like Con Ed, is in a power crisis. Probing questions are being asked and the answers could change the very way of American life.

Power is a polluter—of the air, of the water, of the landscape. But power is basic. In the Great Blackout of 1965, some 600,000 persons were trapped in the black holes of the New York subways. So how do you match the absolute necessity of conserving the environment with the almost desperate need for new power? Or is the risk to the environment that great? Or is the need for power that desperate? Are we properly using electricity?

Is it logical to pollute the rivers to produce power to produce aluminum to produce aluminum cans to pollute the rivers? Is it sensible to produce electricity to power the huge neon signs that uglify our cities? Is it plausible to hold that the environment should never be changed to serve man?

In the executive suite it was 8:15 in the morning and the beginning of a Dawn Patrol meeting. The ruling clique of Con Ed is sitting in a circle facing the chairman, assessing the problems of the empire . . . "two generators down, Chuck, temperatures due in the 90s by midweek" . . . and an ad campaign for electric lawn lamps. Lawn lamps? The chairman frowns. "They're great profit-makers," Luce concedes, "but, good God, when you're short of electricity and they are burning all day in the front yard. It's symbolic of another era." Scratch one ad campaign.

It is the beginning of the annual summer crisis, when Con Ed is called upon to power the billions of BTU's required to cool the simmering metropolis. Lawn lamps are frivolities, because The Source, as usual, is dangerously low on power reserves. Given a cool June, all might be well. By the end of summer's first month Indian Point, Con Ed's showplace atomic plant, would be back on line with enough power for a quarter-million people . . . On the last weekend in June, a ther-

mal shield will rupture at Indian Point, scattering metal throughout the plant and closing it until September. In the executive suite, the summer will look hotter.

The Chairman's chauffeur is a burly, cheerful Italian named Angie, whose father used to have a farm out near Flushing and raised goats. Angie got his start at Con Ed driving trucks, moved up to the Cadillacs and Imperials and now has the top job, driving a Chevy. "He don't like limousines," Angie said of the chairman. "The public looks at you and says you're spending their money."

Angie is good at reminiscing and he remembers how Con Ed used to be. The big, black limousines were an institution then, with city license plates "so nobody'd get in trouble." The wives would take them out shopping and you'd see them parked in lines in front of the cabarets. A favorite was the Engineers Club and the line of Con Ed cars sometimes stretched half a block. Angie remembers that shortly after Luce arrived the new chairman saw a Con Ed booze bill from the Engineers Club. He also remembers what Luce said: "Jesus Christ, what do they do, bathe in the stuff?" Out went the Engineers Club and the limousines.

Those were not the only changes. Luce's arrival at Con Ed was something like Castro's march into Havana. He switched ad agencies and law firms, ending decades-long associations. In short order most of the old-line management officials were gone, many of them by simply lowering the retirement age.

He accelerated the programs for hiring blacks and Puerto Ricans. He sought out Jews, although that wasn't always so easy. "What can we say to people? 'Hey, come on over, we're not anti-Semitic anymore?' " lamented one of the new vice presidents.

Luce also began writing public "letters from the chairman," frankly outlining Con Ed's shortcomings. He started holding press conferences—something that the old management, uncomfortable outside the executive suite, rarely did. He even began appearing on the New York talk shows which have used Con Ed as a comedy prop as regularly as Bob Hope uses Phyllis Diller.

Dick Cavett is fond of introducing voluptuous female guests as producing more electricity than Con Ed. "But that's not difficult," he usually adds. "So can two Size D flashlight batteries."

And the changes at Con Ed often got down to the almost picayune: Cloth towels were eliminated from the executive wash room.

Many of the changes were more in form than substance. After three years of Luce, rates still were high (with an additional increase pending) and power still desperately short. But New Yorkers looked on the new regime with at least tolerant suspicion. It was grand theater to watch someone try to humanize Con Ed.

Luce, as a personality, is as straight as a Seneca arrow—serious, unflashy, stolid. But, for a Con Ed chairman, he is thoroughly unconventional, almost eccentric at times.

At lunch he and Angie stop the executive Chevy at busy Manhattan street corners and eat hotdogs at an umbrella stand. On Sundays he often hops on a bicycle at his Bronxville home and pedals off for surprise visits to isolated Con Ed installations.

Even if the substance of his changes is yet to be seen, Luce's maneuverings, his economies, his almost messianic effort to restructure Con Ed have won him at least begrudging admiration from some of the utility's longtime critics.

Ben Nerzberg is a tough Manhattan lawyer who represents Con Ed's largest customer, the City Housing Authority which runs up a $10-million-a-year light bill. No large customer (perhaps no small one, either) can be too happy with Con Ed. The utility's electric rates run 17 per cent higher than the national average. . . . Nerzberg's voice is like grinding gravel, the first hint that he is a rough adversary, and he is an avowed opponent of new rate increases. But he likes Luce.

"You just can't believe how bad the last management was," Nerzberg says. "It was God-awful. There is no question that Luce is setting about to do a good job. Maybe in five years he can turn it around."

But Nerzberg, like many New Yorkers, retains that tolerant suspicion of anything Con Ed. Luce's changes will have to amount to more than "promising statements to the unfortunate consumers of Con Ed," he says. And he warns that the upheavals at corporate headquarters could cause morale problems. "He may be too much of a martinet."

Other critics are far less yielding than Nerzberg. Rod Vandivert is the executive director of the Scenic Hudson Preservation Conference, a group of highly successful environmentalists who have been the gremlins in Con Ed's power-development plans. Vandivert offers an almost interminable, staccato recital of what he considers the evils of New York's "primitive" electric utility.

"Luce very possibly is trying," Vandivert says. "But the only real achievements are that Con Ed trucks are now painted blue, which is cleaner than the old orange, and the company's fossil-fuel generating plants are now using lower-sulfur fuel. But even that is in anticipation of stronger regulations. On brownie points, Con Ed has a long way to go."

Vandivert, both because of his successes and his unbending antagonism, causes spasms at Con Ed. "Rod has a conspiracy complex," one executive wearily moaned. But with Con Ed's past history and present problems a conspiracy complex, wrong as it might be, is not the worst that someone might conjure up about New York's beleaguered superutility.

It is not too surprising that The New York Times concluded recently that what Luce really needs from the public is a "willing suspension of disbelief."

In the executive suite, cerebrum of The Source, the lights flickered and then went out just before 5:30 in the afternoon of November 9, 1965. Simultaneously, New York went black—the ink enveloping the tenements below the 16th floor, shrouding the Bowery and Chinatown and the Village, hobbling Wall Street and making a jungle of Central Park. Uptown, on West 65th Street, a Con Ed operator had made a grievous error. The Great Blackout of '65 was not Con Ed's fault. It had started, ten minutes earlier, somewhere along upstate New York's Niagara frontier. Then it had moved, like a disastrous black tidal wave, through Canada, New England and finally into the city. As system after system failed, the losers desperately sucked power away from The Source—until The Source had none. At the West 65th Street control center the instruments could follow the wave rolling relentlessly toward the city. Power ties with the outside, interstate exchanges, should have been cut. The Source should have isolated itself. Instead, the city went black. For 14 hours The Source was dead.

If New York were not New York, perhaps the problems of Con Ed would have only marginal interest beyond the Hudson River. Even as the world's largest private utility, the company serves an area of less than 600 square miles. During a Con Ed brownout light bulbs dim in less than 1 per cent of America. But New York, bleak and frustrating as it is in the 1970s, still is the commercial, financial and even social hub of the country.

"As a result of its close relationship to the economy of New York City, Consolidated Edison Co. is, from some standpoints, an important factor in the socioeconomic scheme of the entire United States and other parts of the world," a Federal Power Commission study said recently. "The impacts of any serious power shortages in New York are felt in the economic and trade channels far beyond the confines of the city."

A serious power shortage has, of course, arrived. While nothing as horrendous as the Great Blackout has occurred since 1965, brownouts (voltage reductions ordered by Con Ed when electricity demand threatens to outstrip supply) are on the verge of becoming commonplace.

The future, if all goes well, should be brighter. But Luce must unsnarl some staggering problems to make the future work for Con Ed—and for New York.

Some of these problems, peculiar to the city, probably are beyond solution. The company shoulders a huge tax burden. Con Ed paid more in local taxes last year than it paid out in payroll.

Luce is bleakly fond of recalling that he used to sell a kilowatt-hour of electricity at Bonneville for less than the taxes on a kilowatt-hour in New York. The population density of New York has made underground wiring, an esthetic nicety elsewhere, an absolute necessity in the city. Con Ed has 50,000 miles of expensive underground cable, much of it buried decades ago.

New Yorkers also are unusual electricity consumers. Because many of them are apartment dwellers, Con Ed's average residential customer uses only half as much electricity as his national-average counterpart. Because there are few large industrial electricity-users in the city, Con Ed's load factor is highly fluctuating—soaring in the daytime and evening, dropping to almost nothing late at night.

Other problems have rather obvious, if not always simple, solutions. Because of its historically bad planning, many of Con Ed's generating plants are badly outmoded. One plant is 69 years old. Others were built 50 or more years ago.

But the classic problem, hardly unique to New York, pits Con Ed against the environment. Electric-power producers have polluted since Thomas Alva Edison's tinkerings a century ago and the company which took his name has been no exception. Con Ed may not be the worst polluter of the air over New York (the automobile and its vile hydrocarbons long have held that distinction) or the water around the city (the very municipal governments that often harangue Con Ed have fouled the Hudson and killed New York harbor).

But Con Ed has done its share. In the past, its old coal-fired plants spewed tons of crud into the air. Even now, with most of its plants burning low-sulfur fuel, the company is a consistent violator of the city's antismoke regulations. With Con Ed struggling to move into the nuclear age, some environmentalists are concerned that the company might treat the city's water resources even worse.

In the mid-1960s, as Con Ed engineers began to foresee the potentially disastrous power shortages of the 1970s, nuclear generation seemed the logical solution. It was fairly economical and it resolved the old environmental bugaboo of fossil-fuel plants—air pollution. There seemed to be, at that time, no major environmental problems with nuclear power. So Con Ed began planning a number of nuclear plants.

But as preservation of the environment became a national cause in the late 1960s, it grew apparent that nuclear power had problems, too. There were atomic scare stories about potential explosions and some scientists warned about the effects of low-level radiation in populated areas.

But thermal pollution was the real concern and it was a problem discovered very late by the public. Nuclear-power production heats vast quantities of water which, in Con Ed's case, will be pumped into the Hudson River. This hot water could affect the ecology of the river, possibly endangering the survival of fish species and other aqua life. Con Ed's researchers believe the effect on the Hudson will be minimal, but the company's credibility is not always high in New York.

In any case, the uneasiness over Con Ed's nuclear plan helps illuminate why the Federal Power Commission concluded that the company is "severely handicapped" in trying to handle New York's future power needs. New York's tolerant suspicion of even the new regime at Con Ed can quickly give away to simple suspicion. Much of the company's planning has been exasperatingly poor. Environmental considerations probably will grow. "No one was talking about thermal pollution when we started planning the nuclear installation," one engineer said, "and now no one will stop talking about it."

Despite the problems, Luce sees nuclear power as the long-range salvation of Con Ed. He sees the new nuclear plants on the Hudson, plus some new fossil-fuel plants, getting the company and New York through the crisis of the 1970s. By the 1980s, he hopes the company will begin building nuclear installations on the ocean where the vastness of the Atlantic should minimize whatever problems there are with thermal pollution.

"I don't want to be remembered as the guy who destroyed the aquatic life of the Hudson," Luce said. But he doesn't want to be remembered as the guy who failed to light New York City, either. The way Charles Franklin Luce, 53, a liberal and socially motivated man, solves that dilemma, if he solves it at all, could affect the way Americans live far beyond the fouled rivers that confine New York City.

On July 21, 1970, across the feculent East River from the executive suite, Big Allis groaned and stopped. Big Allis is the bulging-blue bulwark of The Consolidated Edison Co.—Big Allis, a million-kilowatt generator, biggest in the retinue of The Source. But Big Allis was dead, dead until September. With Allis gone, The Source was without reserve power as New York braced itself for the heat storms of late July and August. In the executive suite, the chairman switched off his air-conditioner. The summer looked long and hot, long and hot indeed.

New York Is A Brittle City

MEYER BERGER

Meyer Berger was cherished by fellow newsmen for the sureness of his reporting and the quick grace of his writing. The human interest stories he tracked down daily for his column in the New York Times *remain a remarkable chronicle of the myriad details which add up to big-city life. Berger died in 1959 at the age of 60.*

New York is a brittle city, but the weakness doesn't show up until a big parade is scheduled. The Army's atomic cannon was ruled off Fifth Avenue because its eighty tons would have snapped sub-pavement ganglia—the eight water mains that run abreast only four feet under street surface, and the sewer mains that lie another nine feet down. Fifth Avenue is weakest in dead center. The water mains are of cast iron eighty to ninety years old, and couldn't take the big cannon's weight. Consolidated Edison's gas mains, though set in close to the curbs, would probably have cracked, too.

The Police Department's chief engineer calls all Army, municipal and utility experts into a huddle before a big parade is staged in the city. These men get out their maps and figure the route to be taken by the heavy equipment. They know how much each street can bear. They make sure, for example, that no vehicle's load distribution will put more than 400 pounds to the inch on Fifth Avenue's pavement. Park Avenue could never have an Army parade because its asphalt crust over the New York Central tracks at Fifty-ninth Street is only four inches thick, thinnest in all Gotham.

Getting big pieces of Army equipment into the city is another worry. Army's radar Skysweeper, originally routed through one of the vehicular tunnels, had to rumble over George Washington Bridge instead. The tunnels have only 13 feet 2 inches clearance; the bridge has 13 feet 2½ inches. At that, the radar machine had to let some air out of its tires to make it.

Parades are a menace to manholes on any city route. When the Eighty-second Airborne moved up Fifth Avenue at war's end, its equipment cracked Fifth Avenue's manhole covers as if they were so many plastic tiddlywinks buttons. Now Army orders detour tanks and cannon around the covers.

Engineers always see to it that a few cross streets are kept traffic-clear for fire apparatus. They work out a careful parade dispersal plan, too—fix things so that marching units drain off at different blocks without jamming post-parade traffic.

The Golden City

THOMAS WOLFE

*The novels of North Carolina-born Thomas Wolfe are rich
with autobiography, and clearly the New York he adopted in
his mid-twenties appeared to him with the intensity of light
and atmosphere he describes here. Famous in the Depression years for his huge lyrical works,* Look Homeward, Angel
and Of Time and the River, *Wolfe died in 1938, a few weeks
before his 38th birthday. This selection is from the novel*
The Web and the Rock.

Always and forever when the boy thought of his father, and of the
proud, the cold, the secret North, he thought, too, of the city. His father had not come from there, yet strangely, through some subtle
chemistry of his imagination, some magic of his boy's mind and heart,
he connected his father's life and figure with the bright and shining
city of the North.

In his child's picture of the world, there were no waste or barren
places: there was only the rich tapestry of an immense and limitlessly
fertile domain forever lyrical as April, and forever ready for the harvest, touched with the sorcery of a magic green, bathed forever in a
full-hued golden light. And at the end, forever at the end of all the
fabled earth, there hung the golden vision of the city, itself more fertile, richer, more full of joy and bounty than the earth it rested on. Far-
off and shining, it rose upward in his vision from an opalescent mist,
upborne and sustained as lightly as a cloud, yet firm and soaring with
full golden light. It was a vision simple, unperplexed, carved from deep
substances of light and shade, and exultant with its prophecy of glory,
love, and triumph.

He heard, far off, the deep and beelike murmur of its million-foot-
ed life, and all the mystery of the earth and time was in that sound. He
saw its thousand streets peopled with a flashing, beautiful, infinitely
varied life. The city flashed before him like a glorious jewel, blazing
with countless rich and brilliant facets of a life so good, so bountiful, so
strangely and constantly beautiful and interesting, that it seemed in-

tolerable that he should miss a moment of it. He saw the streets
swarming with the figures of great men and glorious women, and he
walked among them like a conqueror, winning fiercely and exultantly
by his talent, courage, and merit the greatest tributes that the city had
to offer, the highest prize of power, wealth, and fame, and the great
emolument of love. There would be villainy and knavery as black and
sinister as hell, but he would smash it with a blow, and drive it cring-
ing to its hole. There would be heroic men and lovely women, and he
would win and take a place among the highest and most fortunate people on the earth.

Thus, in a vision hued with all the strange and magic colors of his
adolescence, the boy walked the streets of his great legendary city.
Sometimes he sat among the masters of the earth in rooms of manlike
opulence: dark wood, heavy leathers of solid, lavish brown, were all
around him. Again he walked in great chambers of the night, rich with
the warmth of marble and the majesty of great stairs, sustained on
swelling columns of a rich-toned onyx, soft and deep with crimson carpets in which the foot sank down with noiseless tread. And through
this room, filled with a warm and undulant music, the deep and mellow thrum of violins, there walked a hundred beautiful women, and all
were his, if he would have them. And the loveliest of them all was his.
Long of limb and slender, yet lavish and deep of figure, they walked
with proud, straight looks on their fragile and empty faces, holding
their gleaming shoulders superbly, and their clear, depthless eyes alive
with love and tenderness. A firm and golden light fell over them, and
over all his love.

He also walked in steep and canyoned streets, blue and cool with a
frontal steepness of money and great business, brown and rich somehow with the sultry and exultant smell of coffee, the good green smell
of money, and the fresh, half-rotten odor of the harbor with its tide of
ships.

Such was his vision of the city—adolescent, fleshly, and erotic, but
drunk with innocence and joy, and made strange and wonderful by the
magic lights of gold and green and lavish brown in which he saw it.
For, more than anything, it was the light. The light was golden with
the flesh of women, lavish as their limbs, true, depthless, tender as
their glorious eyes, fine-spun and maddening as their hair, as unuttera-
ble with desire as their fragrant nests of spicery, their deep melon-
heavy breasts. The light was golden like a morning light that shines
through ancient glass into a room of old dark brown. The light was rich
brown shot with gold, lavish brown like old stone houses gulched in
morning on a city street. The light was also blue, like morning underneath the frontal cliff of buildings, vertical, cool blue, hazed with thin

morning mist, cold-flowing harbor blue of clean, cool waters, rimed brightly with a dancing morning gold.

The light was amber-brown in vast, dark chambers shuttered from young light, where, in great walnut beds, the glorious women stirred in sensual warmth their lavish limbs. The light was brown-gold like ground coffee, merchants, and the walnut houses where they lived; brown-gold like old brick buildings grimed with money and the smell of trade; brown-gold like morning in great gleaming bars of swart mahogany, the fresh wet beer-wash, lemon rind, and the smell of Angostura bitters. Then it was full-golden in the evening in the theatres, shining with full-golden warmth and body on full-golden figures of the women, on fat red plush, and on the rich, faded, slightly stale smell, and on the gilt sheaves and cupids and the cornucopias, on the fleshly, potent, softly-golden smell of all the people. And in great restaurants the light was brighter gold, but full and round like warm onyx columns, smooth, warmly-tinted marble, old wine in dark, rounded, age-encrusted bottles, and the great blonde figures of naked women on rose-clouded ceilings. Then the light was full and rich, brown-golden like great fields in Autumn; it was full-swelling golden light like mown fields, bronzered picked out with fat, rusty-golden sheaves of corn, and governed by huge barns of red and the mellow, winy fragrance of the apples.

That vision of the city was gathered from a thousand isolated sources, from the pages of books, the words of a traveler, a picture of Brooklyn Bridge with its great, winglike sweep, the song and music of its cables, even the little figures of the men with derby hats as they advanced across it. These and a thousand other things all built the picture of the city in his mind, until now it possessed him and had got somehow, powerfully, exultantly, ineradicably, into everything he did or thought or felt.

That vision of the city blazed outward not only from those images and objects which would evoke it literally, as the picture of the Bridge had done: it was now mixed obscurely and powerfully into his whole vision of the earth, into the chemistry and rhythm of his blood, into a million things with which it had no visible relation. It came in a woman's laughter in the street at night, in sounds of music and the faint thrumming of a waltz, in the guttural rise and fall of the bass violin; and it was in the odor of new grass in April, in cries half-heard and broken by the wind, and in the hot daze and torpid drone of Sunday afternoon.

It came in all the sounds and noises of a carnival, in the smell of confetti, gasoline, the high, excited clamors of the people, the wheeling music of the carousel, the sharp cries and strident voices of the barkers. And it was in the circus smells and sounds as well—in the ramp and reek of lions, tigers, elephants, and in the tawny camel smell. It came somehow in frosty Autumn nights, in clear, sharp, frosty sounds of Hallowe'en. And it came to him intolerably at night in the receding whistle-wail of a distant and departing train, the faint and mournful tolling of its bell, and the pounding of great wheels upon the rail. It came also in the sight of great strings of rusty freight cars on the tracks, and in the sight of a rail, shining with the music of space and flight as it swept away into the distance and was lost from sight.

In things like these, and countless others, the vision of the city would come alive and stab him like a knife.

Fifth Avenue, Uptown:
A Letter from Harlem

JAMES BALDWIN

The civil rights struggle of the 1960s was the dramatic back-drop for James Baldwin's famous set of essays which were published in book form as The Fire Next Time. *Acclaimed for their passion and eloquence, his articles and novels have focused on the disparity between shares of American life for Black and White citizens. The following essay is from the collection* Nobody Knows My Name.

There is a housing project standing now where the house in which we grew up once stood, and one of those stunted city trees is snarling where our doorway used to be. This is on the rehabilitated side of the avenue. The other side of the avenue—for progress takes time—has not been rehabilitated yet and it looks exactly as it looked in the days when we sat with our noses pressed against the windowpane, longing to be allowed to go "across the street." The grocery store which gave us credit is still there, and there can be no doubt that it is still giving credit. The people in the project certainly need it—far more, indeed, than they ever needed the project. The last time I passed by, the Jewish proprietor was still standing among his shelves, looking sadder and heavier but scarcely any older. Further down the block stands the shoe-repair store in which our shoes were repaired until reparation became impossible and in which, then, we bought all our "new" ones. The Negro proprietor is still in the window, head down, working at the leather.

These two, I imagine, could tell a long tale if they would (perhaps they would be glad to if they could), having watched so many, for so long, struggling in the fishhooks, the barbed wire, of this avenue.

The avenue is elsewhere the renowned and elegant Fifth. The area I am describing, which, in today's gang parlance, would be called "the turf," is bounded by Lenox Avenue on the west, the Harlem River on the east, 135th Street on the north, and 130th Street on the south. We

---

never lived beyond these boundaries; this is where we grew up. Walking along 145th Street—for example—familiar as it is, and similar, does not have the same impact because I do not know any of the people on the block. But when I turn east on 131st Street and Lenox Avenue, there is first a soda-pop joint, then a shoeshine "parlor," then a grocery store, then a dry cleaners', then the houses. All along the street there are people who watched me grow up, people who grew up with me, people I watched grow up along with my brothers and sisters; and, sometimes in my arms, sometimes underfoot, sometimes at my shoulder—or on it—their children, a riot, a forest of children, who include my nieces and nephews.

When we reach the end of this long block, we find ourselves on wide, filthy, hostile Fifth Avenue, facing that project which hangs over the avenue like a monument to the folly, and the cowardice, of good intentions. All along the block, for anyone who knows it, are immense human gaps, like craters. These gaps are not created merely by those who have moved away, inevitably into some other ghetto; or by those who have risen, almost always into a greater capacity for self-loathing and self-delusion; or yet by those who, by whatever means—War II, the Korean war, a policeman's gun or billy, a gang war, a brawl, madness, an overdose of heroin, or, simply, unnatural exhaustion—are dead. I am talking about those who are left, and I am talking principally about the young. What are they doing? Well, some, a minority, are fanatical churchgoers, members of the more extreme of the Holy Roller sects. Many, many more are "moslems," by affiliation or sympathy, that is to say that they are united by nothing more—and nothing less—than a hatred of the white world and all its works. They are present, for example, at every Buy Black street corner meeting—meetings in which the speaker urges his hearers to cease trading with white men and establish a separate economy. Neither the speaker nor his hearers can possibly do this, of course, since Negroes do not own General Motors or RCA or the A&P, nor, indeed, do they own more than a wholly insufficient fraction of anything else in Harlem (those who *do* own anything are more interested in their profits than in their fellows). But these meetings nevertheless keep alive in the participators a certain pride of bitterness without which, however futile this bitterness may be, they could scarcely remain alive at all. Many have given up. They stay home and watch the TV screen, living on the earnings of their parents, cousins, brothers, or uncles, and only leave the house to go to the movies or to the nearest bar. "How're you making it?" one may ask, running into them along the block, or in the bar. "Oh, I'm TV-ing it"; with the saddest, sweetest, most shamefaced of smiles, and from a great distance. This distance one is compelled to respect; anyone who has traveled so far will not easily be dragged again into the world. There are further retreats, of course, than the TV screen or the bar. There are those who are simply sitting on their stoops, "stoned," animated for a moment only, and hideously, by the approach of someone who may lend them the money for a "fix." Or by the approach of someone from whom they can purchase it, one of the shrewd ones, on the way to prison or just coming out.

And the others, who have avoided all of these deaths, get up in the morning and go downtown to meet "the man." They work in the white man's world all day and come home in the evening to this fetid block. They struggle to instill in their children some private sense of honor or dignity which will help the child to survive. This means, of course, that they must struggle, stolidly, incessantly, to keep this sense alive in themselves, in spite of the insults, the indifference, and the cruelty they are certain to encounter in their working day. They patiently browbeat the landlord into fixing the heat, the plaster, the plumbing; this demands prodigious patience; nor is patience usually enough. In trying to make their hovels habitable, they are perpetually throwing good money after bad. Such frustration, so long endured, is driving many strong, admirable men and women whose only crime is color to the very gates of paranoia.

One remembers them from another time—playing handball in the playground, going to church, wondering if they were going to be promoted at school. One remembers them going off to war—gladly, to escape this block. One remembers their return. Perhaps one remembers their wedding day. And one sees where the girl is now—vainly looking for salvation from some other embittered, trussed, and struggling boy —and sees the all-but-abandoned children in the streets.

Now I am perfectly aware that there are other slums in which white men are fighting for their lives, and mainly losing. I know that blood is also flowing through those streets and that the human damage there is incalculable. People are continually pointing out to me the wretchedness of white people in order to console me for the wretchedness of blacks. But an itemized account of the American failure does not console me and it should not console anyone else. That hundreds and thousands of white people are living, in effect, no better than the "niggers" is not a fact to be regarded with complacency. The social and moral bankruptcy suggested by this fact is of the bitterest, most terrifying kind.

The people, however, who believe that this democratic anguish has some consoling value are always pointing out that So-and-So, white, and So-and-So, black, rose from the slums into the big time. The existence—the public existence—of, say, Frank Sinatra and Sammy Davis, Jr. proves to them that America is still the land of opportunity and that inequalities vanish before the determined will. It proves nothing of the sort. The determined will is rare—at the moment, in this century, it is unspeakably rare—and the inequalities suffered by the many are in no way justified by the rise of a few. A few have always risen—in every country, every era, and in the teeth of regimes which can by no stretch of the imagination be thought of as free. Not all these people, it is worth remembering, left the world better than they found it. The determined will is rare, but it is not invariably benevolent. Furthermore, the American equation of success with the big time reveals an awful disrespect for human life and human achievement. This equation has placed our cities among the most dangerous in the world and has placed our youth among the most empty and most bewildered. The situation of our youth is not mysterious. Children have never been very good at listening to their elders, but they have never failed to imitate them. They must, they have no other methods. That is exactly what our children are doing. They are imitating our immorality, our disrespect for the pain of others.

All other slum dwellers, when the bank account permits it, can move out of the slum and vanish altogether from the eye of persecution. No Negro in this country has ever made that much money and it will be a long time before any Negro does. The Negroes in Harlem, who have no money, spend what they have on such gimcracks as they are sold. These include "wider" TV screens, more "faithful" hi-fi sets, more "powerful" cars, all of which, of course, are obsolete long before they are paid for. Anyone who has ever struggled with poverty knows how extremely expensive it is to be poor; and if one is a member of a captive population, economically speaking, one's feet have simply been placed on the treadmill forever. One is victimized, economically, in a thousand ways—rent, for example, or car insurance. Go shopping one day in Harlem—for anything—and compare Harlem prices and quality with those downtown.

The people who have managed to get off this block have only got as far as a more respectable ghetto. This respectable ghetto does not even have the advantages of the disreputable one, friends, neighbors, a familiar church, and friendly tradesmen; and it is not, moreover, in the nature of any ghetto to remain respectable long. Every Sunday, people who have left the block take the lonely ride back, dragging their increasingly discontented children with them. They spend the day talking, not always with words, about the trouble they've seen and the trouble—one must watch their eyes as they watch their children—they are only too likely to see. For children do not like ghettos. It takes them nearly no time to discover exactly why they are there.

The projects in Harlem are hated. They are hated almost as much as policemen, and this is saying a great deal. And they are hated for the same reason: both reveal, unbearably, the real attitude of the white world, no matter how many liberal speeches are made, no matter how many lofty editorials are written, no matter how many civil-rights commissions are set up.

The projects are hideous, of course, there being a law, apparently respected throughout the world, that popular housing shall be as cheerless as a prison. They are lumped all over Harlem, colorless, bleak, high, and revolting. The wide windows look out on Harlem's invincible and indescribable squalor: the Park Avenue railroad tracks, around which, about forty years ago, the present dark community began; the unrehabilitated houses, bowed down, it would seem, under the great weight of frustration and bitterness they contain; the dark, the ominous schoolhouses from which the child may emerge maimed, blinded, hooked, or enraged for life; and the churches, churches, block upon block of churches, niched in the walls like cannon in the walls of a fortress. Even if the administration of the projects were not so insanely humiliating (for example: one must report raises in salary to the management, which will then eat up the profit by raising one's rent; the management has the right to know who is staying in your apartment; the management can ask you to leave, at their discretion), the projects would still be hated because they are an insult to the meanest intelligence.

Harlem got its first private project, Riverton—which is now, naturally, a slum—about twelve years ago because at that time Negroes were not allowed to live in Stuyvesant Town.[1] Harlem watched Riverton go up, therefore, in the most violent bitterness of spirit, and hated it long before the builders arrived. They began hating it at about the time people began moving out of their condemned houses to make room for this additional proof of how thoroughly the white world despised them. And they had scarcely moved in, naturally, before they began smashing windows, defacing walls, urinating in the elevators, and fornicating in the playgrounds. Liberals, both white and black, were appalled at the spectacle. I was appalled by the liberal innocence —or cynicism, which comes out in practice as much the same thing. Other people were delighted to be able to point to proof positive that nothing could be done to better the lot of the colored people. They were, and are, right in one respect: that nothing can be done as long as

---

[1] Stuyvesant Town: privately owned complex of residential high-rises on lower Manhattan Island.

they are treated like colored people. The people in Harlem know they are living there because white people do not think they are good enough to live anywhere else. No amount of "improvement" can sweeten this fact. Whatever money is now being ear-marked to improve this, or any other ghetto, might as well be burnt. A ghetto can be improved in one way only: out of existence.

Similarly the only way to police a ghetto is to be oppressive. None of Commissioner Kennedy's[2] policemen, even with the best will in the world, have any way of understanding the lives led by the people they swagger about in two's and three's controlling. Their very presence is an insult, and it would be, even if they spent their entire day feeding gumdrops to children. They represent the force of the white world; and that world's real intentions are, simply, for that world's criminal profit and ease, to keep the black man corraled up here, in his place. The badge, the gun in the holster, and the swinging club make vivid what will happen should his rebellion become overt. Rare, indeed, is the Harlem citizen, from the most circumspect church member to the most shiftless adolescent, who does not have a long tale to tell of police incompetence, injustice, or brutality. I myself have witnessed and endured it more than once. The businessmen and racketeers also have a story. And so do the prostitutes. (And this is not, perhaps, the place to discuss Harlem's very complex attitude towards black policemen, nor the reasons, according to Harlem, that they are nearly all downtown.)

It is hard, on the other hand, to blame the policeman, blank, good-natured, thoughtless, and insuperably innocent, for being such a perfect representative of the people he serves. He, too, believes in good intentions and is astounded and offended when they are not taken for the deed. He has never, himself, done anything for which to be hated—which of us has?—and yet he is facing, daily and nightly, people who would gladly see him dead, and he knows it. There is no way for him not to know it: there are few things under heaven more unnerving than the silent, accumulating contempt and hatred of a people. He moves through Harlem, therefore, like an occupying soldier in a bitterly hostile country; which is precisely what, and where, he is, and is the reason he walks in two's and three's. And he is not the only one who knows why he is always in company: the people who are watching him know why, too. Any street meeting, sacred or secular, which he and his colleagues uneasily cover has as its explicit or implicit burden the cruelty and injustice of the white domination. And these days, of course, in terms increasingly vivid and jubilant, it speaks of the end of that domination. The white policeman, standing on a Harlem street corner,

[2] Commissioner Kennedy: Stephen P. Kennedy, New York City police commissioner, 1955-61.

finds himself at the very center of the revolution now occurring in the world. He is not prepared for it—naturally, nobody is—and, what is possibly much more to the point, he is exposed, as few white people are, to the anguish of the black people around him. Even if he is gifted with the merest mustard grain of imagination, something must seep in. He cannot avoid observing that some of the children, in spite of their color, remind him of children he has known and loved, perhaps even of his own childen. He knows that he certainly does not want *his* children living this way. He can retreat from his uneasiness in only one direction: into a callousness which very shortly becomes second nature. He becomes more callous, the population becomes more hostile, the situation grows more tense, and the police force is increased. One day, to everyone's astonishment, someone drops a match in the powder keg and everything blows up. Before the dust has settled or the blood congealed, editorials, speeches, and civil-rights commissions are loud in the land, demanding to know what happened. What happened is that Negroes want to be treated like men.

Negroes want to be treated like men: a perfectly straightforward statement, containing only seven words. People who have mastered Kant, Hegel, Shakespeare, Marx, Freud, and the Bible find this statement utterly impenetrable. The idea seems to threaten profound, barely conscious assumptions. A kind of panic paralyzes their features, as though they found themselves trapped on the edge of a steep place. I once tried to describe to a very-well-known American intellectual the conditions among Negroes in the South. My recital disturbed him and made him indignant; and he asked me in perfect innocence, "Why don't all the Negroes in the South move North?" I tried to explain what *has* happened, unfailingly, whenever a significant body of Negroes move North. They do not escape jim-crow: they merely encounter another, not-less-deadly variety. They do not move to Chicago, they move to the South Side; they do not move to New York, they move to Harlem. The pressure within the ghetto causes the ghetto walls to expand, and this expansion is always violent. White people hold the line as long as they can, and in as many ways as they can, from verbal intimidation to physical violence. But inevitably the border which has divided the ghetto from the rest of the world falls into the hands of the ghetto. The white people fall back bitterly before the black horde; the landlords make a tidy profit by raising the rent, chopping up the rooms, and all but dispensing with the upkeep; and what has once been a neighborhood turns into a "turf." This is precisely what happened when the Puerto Ricans arrived in their thousands—and the bitterness thus caused is, as I write, being fought out all up and down those streets.

Northerners indulge in an extremely dangerous luxury. They seem to feel that because they fought on the right side during the Civil War, and won, that they have earned the right merely to deplore what is going on in the South, without taking any responsibility for it; and that they can ignore what is happening in Northern cities because what is happening in Little Rock or Birmingham is worse. Well, in the first place, it is not possible for anyone who has not endured both to know which is "worse." I know Negroes who prefer the South and white Southerners, because "At least there, you haven't got to play any guessing games!" The guessing games referred to have driven more than one Negro into the narcotics ward, the madhouse, or the river. I know another Negro, a man very dear to me, who says, with conviction and with truth, "The spirit of the South is the spirit of America." He was born in the North and did his military training in the South. He did not, as far as I can gather, find the South "worse"; he found it, if anything, all too familiar. In the second place, though, even if Birmingham *is* worse, no doubt Johannesburg, South Africa, beats it by several miles, and Buchenwald was one of the worst things that ever happened in the entire history of the world. The world has never lacked for horrifying examples; but I do not believe that these examples are meant to be used as justification for our own crimes. This perpetual justification empties the heart of all human feeling. The emptier our hearts become, the greater will be our crimes. Thirdly, the South is not merely an embarrassingly backward region, but a part of this country, and what happens there concerns every one of us.

As far as the color problem is concerned, there is but one great difference between the Southern white and the Northerner: the Southerner remembers, historically, and in his own psyche, a kind of Eden in which he loved black people and they loved him. Historically, the flaming sword laid across this Eden is the Civil War. Personally, it is the Southerner's sexual coming of age, when, without any warning, unbreakable taboos are set up between himself and his past. Everything, thereafter, is permitted him except the love he remembers and has never ceased to need. The resulting, indescribable torment affects every Southern mind and is the basis of the Southern hysteria.

None of this is true for the Northerner. Negroes represent nothing to him personally, except, perhaps, the dangers of carnality. He never sees Negroes. Southerners see them all the time. Northerners never think about them whereas Southerners are never really thinking of anything else. Negroes are, therefore, ignored in the North and are under surveillance in the South, and suffer hideously in both places. Neither the Southerner nor the Northerner is able to look on the Negro simply as a man. It seems to be indispensable to the national self-esteem that the Negro be considered either as a kind of ward (in which case we are told how many Negroes, comparatively, bought Cadillacs last year and how few, comparatively, were lynched), or as a victim (in which case we are promised that he will never vote in our assemblies or go to school with our kids). They are two sides of the same coin and the South will not change—*cannot* change—until the North changes. The country will not change until it re-examines itself and discovers what it really means by freedom. In the meantime, generations keep being born, bitterness is increased by incompetence, pride, and folly, and the world shrinks around us.

It is a terrible, an inexorable, law that one cannot deny the humanity of another without diminishing one's own: in the face of one's victim, one sees oneself. Walk through the streets of Harlem and see what we, this nation, have become.

Oh Rotten Gotham—Sliding Down Into the Behavioral Sink

TOM WOLFE

Early in the 1960s, Tom Wolfe's imaginative reportage helped set the style of what became known as the New Journalism. Many of his vividly impressionistic magazine articles have been collected in a trio of books: The Kandy-Kolored Tangerine-Flake Streamline Baby *(1965);* The Pump House Gang *(1968); and* Radical Chic and Mau-Mauing the Flak Catchers *(1970).*

I just spent two days with Edward T. Hall, an anthropologist, watching thousands of my fellow New Yorkers short-circuiting themselves into hot little twitching death balls with jolts of their own adrenalin. Dr. Hall says it is overcrowding that does it. Overcrowding gets the adrenalin going, and the adrenalin gets them hyped up. And here they are, hyped up, turning bilious, nephritic, queer, autistic, sadistic, barren, batty, sloppy, hot-in-the-pants, chancred-on-the-flankers, leering, puling, numb—the usual in New York, in other words, and God knows what else. Dr. Hall has the theory that overcrowding has already thrown New York into a state of behavioral sink. Behavioral sink is a term from ethology, which is the study of how animals relate to their environment. Among animals, the sink winds up with a "population collapse" or "massive die-off." Oh rotten Gotham.

It got to be easy to look at New Yorkers as animals, especially looking down from some place like a balcony at Grand Central at the rush hour Friday afternoon. The floor was filled with the poor white humans, running around, dodging, blinking their eyes, making a sound like a pen full of starlings or rats or something.

"Listen to them skid," says Dr. Hall.

He was right. The poor old etiolate animals were out there skidding on their rubber soles. You could hear it once he pointed it out. They stop short to keep from hitting somebody or because they are disoriented and they suddenly stop and look around, and they skid on their rubber-sole shoes, and a screech goes up. They pour out onto the floor down the escalators from the Pan-Am Building, from 42nd Street, from Lexington Avenue, up out of subways, down into subways, railroad trains, up into helicopters—

"You can also hear the helicopters all the way down here," says Dr. Hall. The sound of the helicopters using the roof of the Pan-Am Building nearly 50 stories up beats right through. "If it weren't for this ceiling"—he is referring to the very high ceiling in Grand Central— "this place would be unbearable with this kind of crowding. And yet they'll probably never 'waste' space like this again."

They screech! And the adrenal glands in all those poor white animals enlarge, micrometer by micrometer, to the size of cantaloupes. Dr. Hall pulls a Minox camera out of a holster he has on his belt and starts shooting away at the human scurry. The Sink!

Dr. Hall has the Minox up to his eye—he is a slender man, calm, 52 years old, young-looking, an anthropologist who has worked with Navajos, Hopis, Spanish-Americans, Negroes, Trukese. He was the most important anthropologist in the government during the crucial years of the foreign aid program, the 1950's. He directed both the Point Four[1] training program and the Human Relations Area Files. He wrote *The Silent Language* and *The Hidden Dimension*, two books that are picking up the kind of "underground" following his friend Marshall McLuhan started picking up about five years ago. He teaches at the Illinois Institute of Technology, lives with his wife, Mildred, in a high-ceilinged townhouse on one of the last great residential streets in downtown Chicago, Astor Street; has a grown son and daughter, loves good food, good wine, the relaxed, civilized life—but comes to New York with a Minox at his eye to record—perfect!—The Sink.

We really got down in there by walking down into the Lexington Avenue line subway stop under Grand Central. We inhaled those nice big fluffy fumes of human sweat, urine, effluvia, and sebaceous secretions. One old female human was already stroked out on the upper level, on a stretcher, with two policemen standing by. The other humans barely looked at her. They rushed into line. They bellied each other, haunch to paunch, down the stairs. Human heads shone through the gratings. The species North European tried to create bubbles of space around themselves, about a foot and a half in diameter—

"See, he's reacting against the line," says Dr. Hall.

—but the species Mediterranean presses on in. The hell with bubbles of space. The species North European resents that, this male

---

[1] Point Four: U.S. program of technical assistance to foreign countries, beginning in the early 1950s.

human behind him presses forward toward the booth . . . *breathing* on him, he's disgusted, he pulls out of the line entirely, the species Mediterranean resents him for resenting it, and neither of them realizes what the hell they are getting irritable about exactly. And in all of them, the old adrenals grow another micrometer.

Dr. Hall whips out the Minox. Too perfect! The bottom of The Sink.

It is the sheer overcrowding, such as occurs in the business sections of Manhattan five days a week and in Harlem, Bedford-Stuyvesant, Southeast Bronx every day—sheer overcrowding is converting New Yorkers into animals in a sink pen. Dr. Hall's argument runs as follows: All animals, including birds, seem to have a built-in, inherited requirement to have a certain amount of territory, space, to lead their lives in. Even if they have all the food they need, and there are no predatory animals threatening them, they cannot tolerate crowding beyond a certain point. No more than 200 wild Norway rats can survive on a quarter acre of ground, for example, even when they are given all the food they can eat. They just die off.

But why? To find out, ethologists have run experiments on all sorts of animals, from stickleback crabs to Sika deer. In one major experiment, an ethologist named John Calhoun put some domesticated white Norway rats in a pen with four sections to it, connected by ramps. Calhoun knew from previous experiments that the rats tend to split up into groups of 10 to 12 and that the pen, therefore, would hold 40 to 48 rats comfortably, assuming they formed four equal groups. He allowed them to reproduce until there were 80 rats, balanced between male and female, but did not let it get any more crowded. He kept them supplied with plenty of food, water and nesting materials. In other words, all of their more obvious needs were taken care of. A less obvious need—space—was not. To the human eye, the pen did not even look especially crowded. But to the rats, it was crowded beyond endurance.

The entire colony was soon plunged into a profound behavioral sink. "The sink," said Calhoun, "is the outcome of any behavioral process that collects animals together in unusually great numbers. The unhealthy connotations of the term are not accidental: a behavioral sink does act to aggravate all forms of pathology that can be found within a group."

For a start, long before the rat population reached 80, a status hierarchy had developed in the pen. Two dominant male rats took over the two end sections, acquired harems of 8 to 10 females each, and forced the rest of the rats into the two middle pens. All the overcrowding took place in the middle pens. That was where the "sink" hit. The aristocrat rats at the ends grew bigger, sleeker, healthier, and more secure the whole time.

In The Sink, meanwhile, nest building, courting, sex behavior, reproduction, social organization, health—all of it went to pieces. Normally, Norway rats have a mating ritual in which the male chases the female, the female ducks down into a burrow and sticks her head up to watch the male. He performs a little dance outside the burrow, then she comes out, and he mounts her, usually for a few seconds. When The Sink set in, however, no more than three males—the dominant males in the middle sections—kept up the old customs. The rest tried everything from satyrism to homosexuality or else gave up on sex altogether. Some of the subordinate males spent all their time chasing females. Three or four might chase one female at the same time, and instead of stopping at the burrow entrance for the ritual, they would charge right in. Once mounted, they would hold on for minutes instead of the usual seconds.

Homosexuality rose sharply. So did bisexuality. Some males would mount anything—males, females, babies, senescent rats, anything. Still other males dropped sexual activity altogether, wouldn't fight and, in fact, would hardly move except when the other rats slept. Occasionally a female from the aristocrat rats' harems would come over the ramps and into the middle sections to sample life in The Sink. When she had had enough, she would run back up the ramp. Sink males would give chase up to the top of the ramp, which is to say, to the very edge of the aristocratic preserve. But one glance from one of the king rats would stop them cold and they would return to The Sink.

The slumming females from the harems had their adventures and then returned to a placid, healthy life. Females in The Sink, however, were ravaged, physically and psychologically. Pregnant rats had trouble continuing pregnancy. The rate of miscarriages increased significantly, and females started dying from tumors and other disorders of the mammary glands, sex organs, uterus, ovaries, and fallopian tubes. Typically, their kidneys, livers, and adrenals were also enlarged or diseased or showed other signs associated with stress.

Child-rearing became totally disorganized. The females lost the interest or the stamina to build nests and did not keep them up if they did build them. In the general filth and confusion, they would not put themselves out to save offspring they were momentarily separated from. Frantic, even sadistic competition among the males was going on all around them and rendering their lives chaotic. The males began unprovoked and senseless assaults upon one another, often in the form of tail-biting. Ordinarily, rats will suppress this kind of behavior when it crops up. In The Sink, male rats gave up all policing and just looked out for themselves. The "pecking order" among males in The Sink was never stable. Normally, male rats set up a three-class structure. Under the pressure of over-crowding, however, they broke up into all sorts of unstable subclasses, cliques, packs—and constantly pushed, probed, explored, tested one another's power. Anyone was fair game, except for the aristocrats in the end pens.

Calhoun kept the population down to 80, so that the next stage, "population collapse" or "massive die-off," did not occur. But the autopsies showed that the pattern—as in the diseases among the female rats—was already there.

The classic study of die-off was John J. Christian's study of Sika deer on James Island in the Chesapeake Bay, west of Cambridge, Maryland. Four or five of the deer had been released on the island, which was 280 acres and uninhabited, in 1916. By 1955 they had bred freely into a herd of 280 to 300. The population density was only about one deer per acre at this point, but Christian knew that this was already too high for the Sikas' inborn space requirements, and something would give before long. For two years the number of deer remained 280 to 300. But suddenly, in 1958, over half the deer died; 161 carcasses were recovered. In 1959 more deer died and the population steadied at about 80.

In two years, two-thirds of the herd had died. Why? It was not starvation. In fact, all of the deer collected were in excellent condition, with well-developed muscles, shining coats, and fat deposits between the muscles. In practically all the deer, however, the adrenal glands had enlarged by 50 percent. Christian concluded that the die-off was due to "shock following severe metabolic disturbance, probably as a result of prolonged adrenocortical hyperactivity. . . . There was no evidence of infection, starvation, or other obvious cause to explain the mass mortality." In other words, the constant stress of overpopulation, plus the normal stress of the cold of the winter, had kept the adrenalin flowing so constantly in the deer that their systems were depleted of blood sugar and they died of shock.

Well, the white humans are still skidding and darting across the floor of Grand Central. Dr. Hall listens a moment longer to the skidding and the darting noises, and then says, "You know, I've been on commuter trains here after everyone has been through one of these rushes, and I'll tell you, there is enough acid flowing in the stomachs in every car to dissolve the rails underneath."

Just a little invisible acid bath for the linings to round off the day. The ulcers the acids cause, of course, are the one disease people have already been taught to associate with the stress of city life. But overcrowding, as Dr. Hall sees it, raises a lot more hell with the body than just ulcers. In everyday life in New York—just the usual, getting to work, working in massively congested areas like 42nd Street between Fifth Avenue and Lexington, especially now that the Pan-Am Building is set in there, working in cubicles such as those in the editorial offices at Time-Life, Inc., which Dr. Hall cites as typical of New York's poor handling of space, working in cubicles with low ceilings and, often, no access to a window, while construction crews all over Manhattan drive everybody up the Masonite wall with air-pressure generators with noises up to the boil-a-brain decibel levels, then rushing to get home, piling into subways and trains, fighting for time and for space, the usual day in New York—the whole now-normal thing keeps shooting jolts of adrenalin into the body, breaking down the body's defenses and winding up with the work-a-daddy human animal stroked out at the breakfast table with his head apoplexed like a cauliflower out of his $6.95 semi-spread Pima-cotton shirt, and nosed over into a plate of No-Kloresto egg substitute, signing off with the black thrombosis, cancer, kidney, liver or stomach failure, and the adrenals ooze to a halt, the size of eggplants in July.

One of the people whose work Dr. Hall is interested in on this score is Rene Dubos at the Rockefeller Institute. Dubos's work indicates that specific organisms, such as the tuberculosis bacillus or a pneumonia virus, can seldom be considered "the cause" of a disease. The germ or virus, apparently, has to work in combination with other things that have already broken the body down in some way—such as the old adrenal hyperactivity. Dr. Hall would like to see some autopsy studies made to record the size of adrenal glands in New York, especially of people crowded into slums and people who go through the full rush-hour-work-rush-hour cycle every day. He is afraid that until there is some clinical, statistical data on how overcrowding actually ravages the human body, no one will be willing to do anything about it. Even in so obvious a thing as air pollution, the pattern is familiar. Until people can actually see the smoke or smell the sulphur or feel the sting in their eyes, politicians will not get excited about it, even though it is well known that many of the lethal substances polluting the air are invisible and odorless. For one thing, most politicians are like the aristocrat rats. They are insulated from The Sink by practically sultanic buffers—limousines, chauffeurs, secretaries, aides-de-camp, doormen, shuttered houses, high-floor apartments. They almost never ride subways, fight rush hours, much less live in the slums or work in the Pan-Am Building.

We took a cab from Grand Central to go up to Harlem, and by 48th Street we were already socked into one of those great, total traffic jams on First Avenue on Friday afternoon. Dr. Hall motions for me to survey the scene, and there they all are, humans, male and female, behind the glass of their automobile windows, soundlessly going through torture of their own adrenalin jolts. This male over here contracts his jaw muscles so hard that they bunch up into a great cheese Danish pattern. He twists his lips, he bleeds from the eyeballs, he shouts . . . soundlessly behind glass . . . the fat corrugates on the back of his neck, his whole body shakes as he pounds the heel of his hand into the steering wheel. The female human in the car ahead of him whips her head around, she bares her teeth, she screams . . . soundlessly behind glass . . . she throws her hands up in the air, Whaddya expect me—Yah, yuh stupid—and they all sit there, trapped in their own congestion, bleeding hate all over each other, shorting out the ganglia and—goddam it—

Dr. Hall sits back and watches it all. This is it! The Sink! And where is everybody's wandering boy?

Dr. Hall says, "We need a study in which drivers who go through these rush hours every day would wear GSR bands."

GSR?

"Galvanic skin response. It measures the electric potential of the skin, which is a function of sweating. If a person gets highly nervous, his palms begin to sweat. It is an index of tension. There are some other fairly simple devices that would record respiration and pulse. I think everybody who goes through this kind of experience all the time should take his own pulse—not literally—but just be aware of what's happening to him. You can usually tell when stress is beginning to get you physically."

In testing people crowded into New York's slums, Dr. Hall would like to take it one step further—gather information on the plasma hydrocortisone level in the blood or the cortico steroids in the urine. Both have been demonstrated to be reliable indicators of stress, and testing procedures are simple.

The slums—we finally made it up to East Harlem. We drove into 101st Street, and there was a new, avant-garde little church building, the Church of the Epiphany, which Dr. Hall liked—and, next to it, a pile of rubble where a row of buildings had been torn down, and from the back windows of the tenements beyond several people were busy "airmailing," throwing garbage out the window, into the rubble, beer cans, red shreds, the No-Money-Down Eames roller stand for a TV set, all flying through the air onto the scaggy sump. We drove around some more in Harlem, and a sequence was repeated, trash, buildings falling down, buildings torn down, rubble, scaggy sumps or, suddenly, a cluster of high-rise apartment projects, with fences around the grass.

"You know what this city looks like?" Dr. Hall said. "It looks bombed out. I used to live at Broadway and 124th Street back in 1946 when I was studying at Columbia. I can't tell you how much Harlem has changed in 20 years. It looks bombed out. It's broken down. People who live in New York get used to it and don't realize how filthy the city has become. The whole thing is typical of a behavioral sink. So is something like the Kitty Genovese case—a girl raped and murdered in the courtyard of an apartment complex and 40 or 50 people look on from their apartments and nobody even calls the police. That kind of apathy and anomie is typical of the general psychological deterioration of The Sink."

He looked at the high-rise housing projects and found them mainly testimony to how little planners know about humans' basic animal requirements for space.

"Even on the simplest terms," he said, "it is pointless to build one of these blocks much over five stories high. Suppose a family lives on the 15th floor. The mother will be completely cut off from her children if they are playing down below, because the elevators are constantly broken in these projects, and it often takes half an hour, literally half an hour, to get the elevator if it is running. That's very common. A mother in that situation is just as much a victim of overcrowding as if she were back in the tenement block. Some Negro leaders have a bitter joke about how the white man is solving the slum problem by stacking Negroes up vertically, and there is a lot to that."

For one thing, says Dr. Hall, planners have no idea of the different space requirements of people from different cultures, such as Negroes and Puerto Ricans. They are all treated as if they were minute, compact middle-class whites. As with the Sika deer, who are overcrowded at one per acre, overcrowding is a relative thing for the human animal, as well. Each species has its own feeling for space. The feeling may be "subjective," but it is quite real.

Dr. Hall's theories on space and territory are based on the same information, gathered by biologists, ethologists, and anthropologists, chiefly, as Robert Ardrey's. Ardrey has written two well-publicized books, *African Genesis* and one just published, *The Territorial Imperative. Life* magazine ran big excerpts from *The Territorial Imperative*, all about how the drive to acquire territory and property and add to it and achieve status is built into all animals, including man, over thousands of centuries of genetic history, etc., and is a more powerful drive than sex. *Life's* big display prompted Marshall McLuhan to crack, "They see this as a great historic justification for free enterprise and Republicanism. If the birds do it and the stickleback crabs do it, then it's right for man." To people like Hall and McLuhan, and Ardrey, for that matter, the right or wrong of it is irrelevant. The only thing they find inexcusable is the kind of thinking, by influential people, that isn't even aware of all this. Such as the thinking of most city planners.

"The planners always show you a bird's-eye view of what they are doing," he said. "You've seen those scale models. Everyone stands around the table and looks down and says that's great. It never occurs to anyone that they are taking a bird's-eye view. In the end, these projects do turn out fine, when viewed from an airplane."

As an anthropologist, Dr. Hall has to shake his head every time he hears planners talking about fully integrated housing projects for the year 1980 or 1990, as if by then all cultural groups will have the same feeling for space and will live placidly side by side, happy as the happy burghers who plan all the good clean bird's-eye views. According to his findings, the very fact that every cultural group does have its own peculiar, unspoken feeling for space is what is responsible for much of the uneasiness one group feels around the other.

It is like the North European and the Mediterranean in the subway line. The North European, without ever realizing it, tries to keep a bubble of space around himself, and the moment a stranger invades that sphere, he feels threatened. Mediterranean peoples tend to come from cultures where everyone is much more involved physically, publicly, with one another on a day-to-day basis and feels no uneasiness about mixing it up in public, but may have very different ideas about space inside the home. Even Negroes brought up in America have a different vocabulary of space and gesture from the North European Americans who, historically, have been their models, according to Dr. Hall. The failure of Negroes and whites to communicate well often boils down to things like this: some white will be interviewing a Negro for a job; the Negro's culture has taught him to show somebody you are interested by looking right at him and listening intently to what he has to say. But the species North European requires something more. He expects his listener to nod from time to time, as if to say, "Yes, keep going." If he doesn't get this nodding, he feels anxious, for fear the listener doesn't agree with him or has switched off. The Negro may learn that the white expects this sort of thing, but he isn't used to the precise kind of nodding that is customary, and so he may start overresponding, nodding like mad, and at this point the North European is liable to think he has some kind of a stupid Uncle Tom on his hands, and the guy still doesn't get the job.

The whole handling of space in New York is so chaotic, says Dr. Hall, that even middle-class housing now seems to be based on the bird's-eye models for slum projects. He took a look at the big Park West Village development, set up originally to provide housing in Manhattan for families in the middle-income range, and found its handling of space very much like a slum project with slightly larger balconies. He felt the time has come to start subsidizing the middle class in New York on its own terms—namely, the kind of truly "human" spaces that still remain in brownstones.

"I think New York City should seriously consider a program of encouraging the middle-class development of an area like Chelsea, which is already starting to come up. People are beginning to renovate houses there on their own, and I think if the city would subsidize that sort of thing with tax reliefs and so forth, you would be amazed at what would result. What New York needs is a string of minor successes in the housing field, just to show everyone that it can be done, and I think the middle class can still do that for you. The alternative is to keep on doing what you're doing now, trying to lift a very large lower class up by main force almost and finding it a very slow and discouraging process."

"But before deciding how to redesign space in New York," he said, "people must first simply realize how severe the problem already is. And the handwriting is already on the wall."

"A study published in 1962," he said, "surveyed a representative sample of people living in New York slums and found only 18 percent of them free from emotional symptoms. Thirty-eight percent were in need of psychiatric help, and 23 percent were seriously disturbed or incapacitated. Now, this study was published in 1962, which means the work probably went on from 1955 to 1960. That's six years ago. There is no telling how bad it is now. In a behavorial sink, crises can develop rapidly."

Dr. Hall would like to see a large-scale study similar to that undertaken by two sociopsychologists, Chombart de Lauwe and his wife, in a French working-class town. They found a direct relationship between crowding and general breakdown. In families where people were crowded into the apartment so that there was less than 86 to 108 square feet per person, social and physical disorders doubled. That would mean that for four people the smallest floor space they could tolerate would be an apartment, say, 12 by 30 feet.

What would one find in Harlem? "It is fairly obvious," Dr. Hall wrote in *The Hidden Dimension*, "that the American Negroes and people of Spanish culture who are flocking to our cities are being very seriously stressed. Not only are they in a setting that does not fit them, but they have passed the limits of their own tolerance of stress. The

United States is faced with the fact that two of its creative and sensitive peoples are in the process of being destroyed and like Samson could bring down the structure that houses us all."

Dr. Hall goes out to the airport, to go back to Chicago, and I am coming back in a cab, along the East River Drive. It is four in the afternoon, but already the damned drive is clogging up. There is a 1959 Oldsmobile just to the right of me. There are about eight people in there, a lot of pop-eyed silhouettes against a leopard-skin dashboard, leopard-skin seats—and the driver is classic. He has a moustache, sideburns down to his jaw socket, and a tattoo on his forearm like a Rossetti painting of Jane Burden Morris with her hair long. All right; it is even touching, like a postcard photo of the main drag in San Pedro, California. But suddenly Sideburns guns it and cuts in front of my cab so that my driver has to hit the brakes, and then hardly 100 feet ahead Sideburns hits a wall of traffic himself and has to hit his brakes, and then it happens. A stuffed white angora animal, a dog, no, it's a Pekingese cat, is mounted in his rear window—as soon as he hits the brakes its *eyes* light up, Nighttown pink. To keep from ramming him, my driver has to hit the brakes again, too, and so here I am, out in an insane, jammed-up expressway at four in the afternoon, shuddering to a stop while a stuffed Pekingese grows bigger and bigger and brighter in the eyeballs directly in front of me. Jolt! Nighttown pink! Hey—that's me the adrenalin is hitting, *I* am this white human sitting in a projectile heading amid a mass of clotted humans toward a white angora stuffed goddam leopard-dash Pekingese freaking cat—kill that damned angora—Jolt!—got me—another micrometer on the old adrenals—

QUESTIONS

1a. We are never given a full description of the main characters in "Papo and the Hydrant," yet the figures come alive as Clark Whelton tells the story. Describe them as Whelton makes you see them, pointing out how specific details reveal character.

b. How does the author keep the hydrant in the foreground of the story?

c. The story relies heavily on Papo's skill with the hydrant and the excitement he creates. Is Papo a heroic figure? Why or why not?

2a. In William Prochnau's article, what are the differences between what is happening in the italicized sections about The Source and in the main sections about Charles Luce and his staff?

b. Power resources have become a vital problem in our way of life. What uses of electricity are relatively new to us, and why have they come about? What changes in our living pattern might ease the power problem? What obstacles would you foresee in making such changes?

3a. What precise details are used by Meyer Berger to show how "brittle" the city's streets are?

b. Normally we don't think about such a subject as brittle streets, unless a skilled observer such as Berger brings it to our attention. Looking at a city as Berger might, find some other points of concern in our mode of urban life.

4a. Certain themes recur throughout Thomas Wolfe's "The Golden City." What are they?

b. How does the author use color to portray the city? Why does he?

c. The novel in which "The Golden City" appears was written in the 1930s. Do you think Wolfe would feel differently about New York today? Why or why not? How do you feel about the author's sentiments and the way they are expressed?

d. If you are fascinated by cities as author Wolfe was, try to explain in writing what it is you find fascinating. If you aren't, try to explain why not.

5a. How does James Baldwin detail the failure of the Harlem housing projects?

b. What are the day-to-day differences between the Harlem scene he describes and White suburbia? Between Baldwin's view of the city and Thomas Wolfe's vision?

6a. How has Tom Wolfe used his writing style to convey the aggravations of a crowded city?

 b. Wolfe's topic is the crowding to be found in a city. Are there also kinds of "crowding" in the suburbs or in the rural areas? Explain. As an individual, what are some situations of crowding you dislike, and what are some you don't mind or even enjoy? What are the differences you see between the situations?

FURTHER SOURCES

New York is portrayed exhaustively in print and other media. Some sources of high quality: E.B. White's small eloquent book, *Here Is New York* (Harper & Brothers, 1949); the picture-and-caption approach in *New York: A Serendipiter's Journey,* by Gay Talese (Harper, 1961); and two plays offering views of metropolitan life, Neil Simon's comedy *The Prisoner of Second Avenue* and Black playwright Charles Gordone's *No Place To Be Somebody.* A critically acclaimed television series set in New York was *East Side, West Side,* starring George C. Scott. A pair of the best episodes, each dealing with an aspect of racial relationships in the city, are "No Hiding Place" (Carousel Films, 1501 Broadway, New York, N.Y. 10036, or Mass Media Ministries, 2116 North Charles St., Baltimore, Md. 21218) and "Who Do You Kill?" (also from Carousel Films). An award-winning production on New York's street life is *Superfluous People* (Contemporary/McGraw Hill Films, 1221 Avenue of the Americas, New York, N.Y. 10020).

A perceptive newspaper series about day-to-day life on a block in New York City can be found in John Corry's articles in the *New York Times,* beginning on August 23, 1971, and continuing into 1972. The articles are indexed in the *New York Times Index* under "New York City—Description and Impressions," with the individual entries designated "NY Times series on variety of life on W. 85th St."

Papo and the Hydrant *Clark Whelton* This reporter's by-lined stories have appeared in *The Village Voice* for the past several years.

Can He Keep New York Bright? *William W. Prochnau* For articles about the Consolidated Edison Company, see: "Con Ed's Charles Luce: All Power (Sometimes) to the People," by Susan Brownmiller, *New York Times Magazine,* April 12, 1970, pp. 24-25; and "Con Ed: The Arrogance of Power," by Lucy Komisar, *New York* magazine, Sept. 8, 1969, pp. 24-30. For material about national power resources, see: *The Energy Crisis,* by Lawrence Rocks and Richard P. Runyon (Crown, 1972) and *Brown-out: the Power Crisis in America,* by William Rodgers (Stein and Day, 1972).

New York Is A Brittle City *Meyer Berger* This reporter's column, "About New York," can be found in issues of the New York *Times,* 1953-1959. A collection of the columns in book form is titled *Meyer Berger's New York* (Random House, 1960), and biographical material about Berger is in Gay Talese's history of the *Times,* entitled *The Kingdom and the Power* (Bantam, 1969).

The Golden City   *Thomas Wolfe*   Wolfe's novels that include material about New York City are *The Web and the Rock* (Grosset & Dunlap, 1939) and *You Can't Go Home Again* (Sun Dial Press, 1940). For biography, see *Thomas Wolfe*, by Andrew Turnbull (Charles Scribner's Sons, 1967). An interesting kinship in music to Wolfe's literary praise of the city is *Manhattan Tower* by Gordon Jenkins.

Fifth Avenue, Uptown   *James Baldwin*   Perhaps the best-known of this author's work are his set of essays, *The Fire Next Time* (Dial, 1963), and his novel, *Another Country* (Dell, 1962). A critical study of housing projects is *Urban Renewal and American Cities*, by Scott Greer (Bobbs-Merrill, 1966).

Oh Rotten Gotham—Sliding Down Into the Behavioral Sink   *Tom Wolfe*   A good example of Wolfe's work in book-length form is *Radical Chic & Mau-Mauing the Flak Catchers* (Bantam, 1971). Anthropologist E.T. Hall has written two important books: *The Silent Language* (Doubleday, 1959) and *The Hidden Dimension* (Doubleday, 1966).

PART 3

HOW CAME WE HERE?

INTRODUCTION

One thing America lost on the way to today: the settlers' sense of how empty this big continent seemed.

Through three centuries, about three-fourths of the white man's time here, that sense held true. The new Americans came here by fearful voyage, spent perhaps two or three months in frail ships across the colossal parabola of ocean. The first of them huddled then in whittled spots on the edge of forests which seemed to loom westward forever. Even as the restless among them pushed on toward the Pacific, it took months to cross the land by foot, horse and wagon; or several weeks to sail there by even the swiftest clipper ship; or with the coming of the train nearly a week to jounce cross-country even by that relentless vehicle. The farthest thing in their minds was using up an endless continent.

No surprise, then, that country America grew into city America without chronic worry about the consequences of crowding. That was mostly left to this past century. So, in looking at today's complex cities we take some account of yesterday's simpler workaday notions which were put into the building of these urban centers. With a little prying, insights about our own era may be offered up by history. For many of our modern city's features begin showing up far back: the building patterns which give us an orderly network of streets and utilities; the social patterns leaving us a faltering and often corrupt system of governing cities; the dreams of reward available in the vast enterprise of America; and the daunting reality of slum life for generation upon generation of newcomers to the American city.

We haven't come to where we are without going some special routes. Part Three is a sampler of our history, both from people who were there and from current practitioners of hindsight:

Building a city means someone has to put down the streets, put up a city hall, put in the lifelines a community needs. Ivan Doig shows how some lasting patterns were made for us in "Street of Dreams, Street of Life."

Of all the scrutiny undergone by young America, the looking over by Frances Trollope in the late 1820s was probably the sharpest and funniest. Here she chronicles her stay in the muddy metropolis of the frontier—"Cincinnati."

A later visitor, this time from the Southern rural elegance built on cotton and slavery, made a perceptive journey through Buffalo, Cleveland, Cincinnati and Louisville. In "Letter from the North," Charles

C. Jones, Jr., reports on the wonders and woes of the burgeoning cities in 1854.

Until immigration was sharply controlled by a 1924 act of Congress, the city limits of America were the docks where the newcomers stepped ashore. Novelist Henry Roth works with the emotions of one such arrival in 1907: "I Pray Thee Ask No Questions, This Is That Golden Land."

The province of the political boss is that neighborhood of civics where dead men vote amply when the ballot count is close and where a favor has a long promissory note. Look then to a quartet of metropolitan bosses—Plunkitt of New York, Ruef of San Francisco, Crump of Memphis, Daley of Chicago—for first-hand glimpses of men who ran the cities in the late 19th century and into the 20th.

Our cities have had to house newcomers by the millions, and the results usually have been squalid. Crusading journalist Jacob Riis in 1890 campaigned hard against the wretched tenement slums, the scandal of "How the Other Half Lives."

"The same winds blow spring on all men's dreams," writes historian Frank R. Kramer. In "Homestead, Incorporated" he looks at some of the myths of free enterprise, as transplanted from the soil of Midwestern farms to the productiveness of the automobile factory.

Street of Dreams, Street of Life

IVAN DOIG

Ivan Doig is a former newspaperman and magazine editor who now is a full-time writer. His articles reporting on urban topics have appeared in several national magazines, and he and his wife Carol have co-authored a book about the news media, News: A Consumer's Guide.

Suppose a street of dreams for the newcomer fresh to an American city a century ago:

Before the hard routines of job and ghetto life have worn into him, this stranger from across the ocean or out of the hinterland can see the city street as a pageant of progress and hope. The downtown buildings, many stories high and ornately made of brick, stone or iron, are marvelous to him in their size and texture. Here between their high noble profiles a day's traffic of wagons, carriages and horsecars adds up to perhaps more vehicles and people than he has seen in all his life before. Above, on tall ranks of poles, spans of wire are stretched against the sky, the telegraph ganglia carrying words in some mysterious manner. In this fabulous cityscape even the outdoors is lighted at night, gas lamps overhead shining like small bright moons. And at eye level, perhaps the grandest vision of all, beckon the proudly lettered windows of men who work in shops and businesses and trades of their own.

Swing your imagination, now, to a street where the urban immigrant actually begins his golden life:

Block upon looming block from the door of his steep stairwell he sees the tenements where families crowd into a few dismal and ill-ventilated rooms. In the backyards stand wooden privies, seeping disease out into a populace which has scant health care. The neighborhood by night is dimly suffused with yellow light from oil wicks. By day or night, close at hand are the saloons, the gambling dens, the brothels, enough concentrated deviltry to astound any unworldly soul.

Street of dreams, street of life. Even yet we walk routes as desperately far apart as those which held our wide-eyed newcomer of one hundred years ago. And like him, we make a start down at pedestrian level to understand something of city ways of life, because in these lines of fact and fancy which form the American meshwork of streets we say much about ourselves. Our modern surroundings show a number of imprints set for us long ago.

A glance around from most corner curbs will tell us one basic piece of information: our streets run straight and intersect each other at right angles, like the crosshatch design of some mammoth game of tic-tac-toe. Visit the European cities which are the ancestors of our own urban life and you find there streets curved like crescents, streets radiating from a plaza like the spokes of a wheel, streets which veer in ancient meanderings where village haphazardly grew onto neighbor village a millennium ago. For glories of architecture and heritage, and to skirt barriers of water and hill, the loveliest of European cities have allowed many of their streets to wander casually or to trace elegant designs. But rare is the map of an American city which doesn't show a plain grid design, block upon block out to where the fields are giving up to the latest suburb. The American pattern, for reasons deeply set in our history, is the straight line and the square corner.

When landholder William Penn worked out plans in the early 1680s for "a green country town, which will never be burnt, and always be wholesome," in all likelihood he had in mind the grid street systems tried in British colonies in Northern Ireland, as well as experiments by some urban planners in London. His idea was close, too, to the style of village greens in towns spreading across New England. So the first great American city grew from a checkerboard design carefully traced onto the wilderness.

The site, which the Quaker Penn dubbed Philadelphia from the Greek words for "brotherly love," was a flat tract stretching two miles long and a mile wide, crosshatched into straight-sided blocks, with main streets one hundred feet wide and with five open squares for parks. Penn's plan was embedded in the future growth of Philadelphia by a 1721 law providing for "surveyors and regulators" in charge of new streets. In turn, the Philadelphia example did much to embed this grid pattern at future town sites throughout the land. By 1776, Philadelphia stood foremost among the American settlements as an orderly, thriving community, and its population of approximately 25,000 marked it as London's New World rival for esteem and influence. When the American colonies broke free of Great Britain, the city became the first capital of the newly independent nation. All the while Philadelphia prospered and earned admiration, its street system was duplicated out in the growing frontier settlements and along the Atlantic seaboard as well.

Cities such as Tallahassee and Raleigh followed William Penn's pattern down to the exact number of public squares left open for parks. In the new clapboard Gothams of the frontier—Cincinnati, Lexington, Louisville, Pittsburgh—the ultimate in flattery was for a visitor to scan the boggy but arrow-straight streets and proclaim that the place looked like Philadelphia. Meanwhile the most influential southern city in early America, Charleston, South Carolina, had long since mapped its own grid pattern of streets. Then in 1811, New York's street commissioners disclosed that they had pondered "circles, ovals, and stars, which certainly embellish a plan," but because "strait sided and right angled houses are the most cheap to build, and the most convenient to live in," they were imposing a rigid grid system to shape their city's development.

By the end of the Civil War, the grid pattern truly had stamped its imprint all across the continent. On the Strait of Juan de Fuca in Washington Territory, almost as far west as a person could go without sloshing in the Pacific, a transplanted Ohioan laid out his townsite at Port Angeles in exact imitation of Cincinnati—which a half century before had imitated Philadelphia.

Straight lines and square intersections have come down to us not only from William Penn's blueprint, but from the laws which set up the American system for selling land. Installed in American government even before the Constitution, our system of township surveys has a mixed ancestry of features from English examples. But it is fervently American in its main point: it scrapped the feudal vestiges operating in several of the original colonies, under which big landlords parceled out sites to their settlers as they pleased, and relied instead on the New England custom of setting up carefully-measured townships with numbered plots for the individual claimants. After the cramped confines of European society, America stretched before its newcomers as a feast of acreage. The patterns put on the fresh continent were to make land sales easy and indisputable—and not just incidentally, to make those sales a source of funds both for a revenue-hungry federal government and for speculators who resold acreage gained from the public domain.

As a result, the system born in the Land Ordinance of 1785 was all straight lines and reference numbers, all ease of claim filing and official registry at the land office. By the work of surveyors driving marker stakes, America became the vast plaid pattern we see most clearly today by flying over the quilted terrain of the Midwest. Not surprisingly, the lesson that farm land was most simply sold and legal title most easily defined by this mesh of handy rectangles has helped to align building lots into the straight blocks of our town and city sites. Indeed, when the Ohio town of Circleville was imaginatively laid out in 1810 atop the circle designs of an early Indian civilization on the same site, residents complained about the irregular lots until the town was gradually reshaped. By 1856, a redevelopment corporation called the Circleville Squaring Company had the job done, in impeccably straight lines and square corners.

The alignment of our streets, then, owes to notions born early in the settlement of the land. What has filled in the details of today's street scene, the profiles of our buildings, the pipes and wires of utilities above and below ground—all has followed from a lineage of innovation and municipal needs.

Innovation perhaps has worked most relentlessly on our streets in the long revolution in transportation—or rather, the busy series of revolutions which add up to a century and a half of major consequences for city living. History seldom fits neat time spans, but with more ease than usual in making a mock piece of the past it can be shown what continual change has been at work in our means of transport. Take a look at American urban history about every thirty years since 1800, and at each glance you find some new transportation system—and just as importantly, you also find governmental policies underwriting costs of the latest innovation and insuring its spread throughout urban America:

1830—Canals are becoming the craze. The state of New York first hit it rich in building the 364-mile Erie Canal as a cargo route to the Great Lakes. After the Erie's completion in 1825, the other states from New Jersey to Illinois and up and down the Atlantic Coast dig their own waterways for the trade generated by the growing cities. Costs run high for construction, maintenance, and repair, but New York shows the way in financing, too: the sale of bonds to the public, a device which has provided the bankroll for countless public works ever since.

1860—Railroads have come. As the New Yorkers were finishing their Erie Canal, the first railroad went into business in England. The combination of steam power and rails was ready-made for the expanses of the United States. Thirty thousand miles of track have been laid in the three decades since 1830. And a system of land grants earlier used on a small scale to help finance wagon roads and some canals is expanded mightily for the newcomer: the state and federal governments give the railroad companies large tracts of land along the tracks they build.

1890—Next the streetcar becomes the transportation rage. Horse-drawn cars had long been in use, and San Francisco's cable cars began their hilly routes in 1873. Then in the late 1880s, Baltimore and Richmond introduced streetcars powered by electricity. By 1890, such systems are operating in 51 cities, and suburbs multiply mightily as the new lines make it easy to commute to and from jobs in the city. The streetcar lines are franchises granted to private companies, virtually without regulation. As open invitations to monopoly and corruption, they produce some of the fattest fortunes and biggest scandals in our municipal history.

1920—Now the automobile. The Model T which trundled off Henry Ford's assembly line in 1908 has set the pattern of low-priced mass-produced cars. The auto is the nation's new plaything which rapidly turns into a necessity. From the 4,000 cars built in 1900, the annual total is zooming toward the production of nearly five million cars in 1929, before the Depression temporarily slows the frenzy. And the tools necessary to pave the roadway for the new chariot have been quickly fashioned: the gas tax is invented to finance road-building out of motorists' purchases, and the 1916 Federal Aid Roads Act forms a lasting partnership of state highway departments and federal money.

1950—Finally the airplane. Outgrowing its early uses as an airborne machine-gun nest or a flying letter carrier, the airplane has come into its own as a passenger service. The first transcontinental passenger service began in 1929, a simple grasshoppering across the country by Ford Trimotor. Since then, the airlines have grown into a huge network providing the fastest transportation yet known to traveling man —and the jet airliner, five hours coast to coast, is soon to come. This air revolution is fed by military contracts for the companies which build the planes and, ever since the 1946 Federal Airport Act, by federal aid to the municipalities which build the airports.

Inevitably our streets have lagged behind in trying to cope with all this. An urban pattern originally laid out for foot and wagon was diverted by canal schemes which used up enormous public expenditure. It was expanded colossally by the marketing power of the railroad and the suburb-building of the streetcar. Most recently it has been jammed with the omnipresent automobile, and hit with both jet noise and the headache of funneling the terrific traffic to and from airports. No wonder the cities continually struggle to keep up with the latest varieties of traffic. Perhaps the surprise is that the streets haven't clogged for good long ago.

Clearly the powerful spawn of the Industrial Revolution has had great effect on the way we live in cities, especially through the transportation innovations just recited. But the American street has become what it is because of a number of smaller technical stunts, too, and a select few might be mentioned.

In the 1830s appeared a structure derisively called a "balloon frame" house, so named because it seemed frailly built of two-by-four inch studs and factory nails instead of the customary sturdy beams and mortises. The derision quickly faded, and the frame house with its ease and efficiency of construction has become a standard shelter across America.

Similarly, a pair of inventions now taken for granted lifted the national skyline: from the early 1880s, steel frame construction which sent skyscrapers towering above street level, and from 1872, the geared hydraulic elevator to provide a quick route to even the loftiest floors.

Streets of several American port cities lengthened spectacularly from urban to metropolitan by hurdling rivers and bays to new land for suburbs. The magnificent suspension bridges were born when John A. Roebling, who would later design the Brooklyn Bridge, in 1841 applied for a patent on his method of twisting wire cables together into strands strong enough to hold up the suspended span.

And sometimes the innovation has been a little masterpiece of common sense, as when Philadelphia in the mid-18th century began rounding its street surfaces slightly so water would drain sideways into gutters.

While our streets have been proving grounds for sundry items of innovation, they also have served as the conduits for whatever services city-dwellers need. It is useful in looking at today's city woes to recall that our set of municipal utilities—water system, sewers, paving, streetlights—did not come easy, and in fact were put together piecemeal through several urban generations. Compared with the transportation innovations backed by both private enterprise and government, utilities seem to have had a dolefully hard history. Amid our own problems of what to do with all the garbage and how to cleanse the gunk out of today's air and water, perhaps we should pause over a past priority to see what some of our civic initiative looks like from hindsight:

Troubled water was a commonplace of American cities until well into the 19th century. Until about 1800, cities depended almost entirely on springs, wells, and cisterns for water supply. With nearby privies and cemeteries seeping into the water table and with slop buckets and filthy streets substituting for efficient sewer systems, city water was suspected to be a hazard even before it was fully known that the germs of disease thrived in such circumstances. The engineering skills to do better did exist by then. For that matter, the example of the great Roman aqueducts bringing in pure streams had been around for many hundred years, and parts of London long had been using sizable waterworks. But American cities kept on drinking disgusting and dangerous water. In New York City, it was said even the horses balked at touching the stuff, and there was a thriving business by "tea water men" who went through the streets with casks of decent spring water to sell to the housewives.

It took the yellow fever epidemics of the 1790s, which raged through Philadelphia several times and also hit Baltimore, Boston, Charleston, New Haven, New York, Norfolk and Providence, to turn the cities toward new water resources. Since the epidemics were suspected to spring somehow from the widespread filth in the cities, demands grew for regular washing of the streets—and at least incidentally, for water which would look and taste more wholesome. Philadelphia promptly established a municipal water system, with a reservoir which drew from the Schuylkill River, but elsewhere the water problem was put in the hands of small private companies. Through the first decades of the 19th century, the private companies haphazardly sluiced water in from the country's copious sources of supply, but in effect they simply delayed an efficient municipal flow. Either unwilling or unable to invest the money needed for really large waterworks, the companies concentrated on furnishing water to the more prosperous neighborhoods. The continuing inadequacies gradually forced the cities wholesale into the water business. Reservoirs, aqueducts, pumping stations and water mains were installed in great quantities during the 1840s and 1850s. By 1860, the sixteen largest American cities, all with populations of more than 50,000, had waterworks, and all but four of the systems were municipally-owned.

The problems of water supply were not totally solved by the city projects; indeed, with our record of constantly using more and more water, some problems are not solved yet. Outbreaks of disease sometimes hit the cities in the last decades of the 19th century, and the new water supplies still were inadequate to quench historic fires such as Chicago's in 1871. Low pricing and lack of metering perhaps set us on our way to overly casual use of water. A very contemporary plaint can be heard in the claim by disgusted authorities in Boston in 1860 that their citizens were using an average of 97 gallons per person *every day*, "an amount believed to be without parallel in the civilized world." And while the well-to-do and middle class have enjoyed easy and safe water supply merely by paying for the plumbing, the poorest neighborhoods still lacked enough faucets and toilets.

Try to sum up the mixed record, and perhaps it comes to this: after neglect, false starts, and some bad habits, a utility was set up which bettered the safety and amenity of our city life. Maybe these days we could do better, faster. Maybe.

Besides the lines of history which stand out before us in the route and detail of our streets, there are lines harder for the eye to trace—the paths of political power. Even more than usual, history begins to sharpen into argument when it edges across the topic of politics. But in looking back down our streets, one long trend seems clear enough: distrust between rural America and city America.

From early on, the country has had to rely heavily on the city and its money. The fur trapper ranging the continent for pelts, the miner dealing in ore, the cattleman and farmer growing beef and wheat, these historical figures out beyond the city limits have worked for prices pegged on downtown streets. Besides the antagonism against the urban centers as the stronghold of the industrial barons and the gouging middlemen of commerce, the city was suspect as a strange and godless habitation, teeming with immigrants in one neighborhood and stilted with upper class snobbery in another. Small wonder that the 19th century, the span when our cities were growing to immensity, is bracketed by protests against the urban influence. At one end of the century is Thomas Jefferson, farmer-philosopher of the Virginia gentry that held the Presidency for 32 of the nation's first 36 years, warning that "the mobs of great cities add just so much to the support of pure government as sores do to the strength of the human body." At the other end, in the presidential election campaign of 1896 hear William Jennings Bryan, small-town lawyer of Nebraska, crying down a plague on all our rowhouses: "Burn down your cities and leave our farms, and your cities will spring up again as if by magic; but destroy our farms, and the grass will grow in the streets of every city in the country."

The city became a political stepchild in America very early. Read through the Constitution of the United States and you find that the federal government is defined in detail, the power of the states is discussed at length, and local government is nowhere. Trying to hold together a melee of states, sections, and economic interests, the Constitution writers spent not a word on how best to govern the communities —despite the prominent example of the New England town meetings, probably the most democratic invention of young America. The cities were left to their own devices, which usually turned out to be political machines run by crafty bosses.

Once the governing of the nation was apportioned by law this way, state after state tried to insure against future strength of the growing cities by putting the capital of government elsewhere, anywhere to keep it from the metropolitan grasp. Nine states followed the example of Washington, D.C., and built the capital city on a fresh site— Tallahassee, Florida; Indianapolis, Indiana; Jefferson City, Missouri; Jackson, Mississippi; Lincoln, Nebraska; Raleigh, North Carolina; Columbus, Ohio; Columbia, South Carolina; and Austin, Texas. Other times, the capital was deliberately placed in some lesser town away from the biggest city; where Pittsburgh and Louisville predominated along the Ohio River frontier, the state governments were tucked away at Harrisburg and Frankfort.

By and large, the efforts to keep state governments out of the big cities' embrace succeeded. A list of the twenty-five largest American cities in the 1970 census reveals only five—Boston, Columbus, Denver, Indianapolis, Phoenix—which are state capitals.* In the longer list when all fifty states are considered, only 16 of our state capitals are also the largest cities of their states. Once established, the small-town legislatures tried hard to hold on to power over the cities; by the end of the 19th century, the cities of only four states—California, Minnesota, Missouri and Washington—had been granted freedom from state interference in how they governed themselves.

Nor has the business of governing city streets been highly regarded as qualification for the White House. Of all our Presidents, only two ever had experience as a mayor: Grover Cleveland (1885-89 and 1893-97), who served in Buffalo on his way to becoming governor of New York, and Calvin Coolidge (1923-1929), who spent an inconsequential year as mayor of Northampton, Massachusetts, early in his political career. Of the total of 68 major contenders who have ever been nominated for the Presidency, only three more one-time mayors can be added to Presidents Cleveland and Coolidge: DeWitt Clinton (New York City), Horatio Seymour (Utica, New York), and Hubert H. Humphrey (Minneapolis). Perhaps a meager three other presidential candidates can be said to have made their reputations in big city jobs: Horace Greeley, editor of the New York *Tribune*; Thomas E. Dewey, as a New York district attorney; and Theodore Roosevelt, as a New York police commissioner. Overwhelmingly, most of our presidential nominees have come the route of the federal government—usually Congress—or from governorships. For that matter, we have nominated 15 generals for President, and elected ten of them.

This is not to say the American cities have entirely lacked potency in the running of the country. A number of urban legislators have been influential down through the decades in Congress, and the marriages of convenience between big city political machines and candidates for high office long have afforded the metropolitan areas some leverage. Yet, the ordinary city-dweller may wonder how much attention has ever

---

*These 25 largest cities, all of them more than half a million in population, were ranked as follows in the 1970 census: New York, Chicago, Los Angeles, Philadelphia, Detroit, Houston, Baltimore, Dallas, Cleveland, Indianapolis, Milwaukee, San Francisco, San Diego, San Antonio, Boston, Memphis, St. Louis, New Orleans, Phoenix, Columbus, Seattle, Jacksonville, Pittsburgh, Denver and Kansas City. Washington, D.C., ranked ninth in the census tabulation, is not included here because it is not within a state.

been paid to him. He might find it notable, for instance, that in 1862 the Homestead Act was passed to provide a rural method of homeowning, but it took the Depression of the 1930s to introduce a Home Owners Loan Corporation which urban residents could rely on.

Town planning and building, transportation systems, political structure—from all these sources some lasting concepts have coursed through our streets, have shaped the way we live. That imagined ancestor from several pages ago drifts close again. Last century's new city dweller learned the distance between the main avenue of illusion and the side street where reality dwells. We might better gauge our own routes if we recall where our steps began, back amid the deep imprints of the past.

Cincinnati

FRANCES TROLLOPE

What Frances Trollope (1780-1863) began as a trip from England to make money in the young United States produced instead a rich source of social history. Her venture as a merchant in Cincinnati flopped spectacularly, but the ensuing account in The Domestic Manners of the Americans *has been a classic of comeuppance ever since its publication in 1832.*

Though I do not quite sympathise with those who consider Cincinnati as one of the wonders of the earth, I certainly think it a city of extraordinary size and importance, when it is remembered that thirty years ago the aboriginal forest occupied the ground where it stands; and every month appears to extend its limits and its wealth.

Some of the native political economists assert that this rapid conversion of a bear-brake into a prosperous city, is the result of free political institutions; not being very deep in such matters, a more obvious cause suggested itself to me, in the unceasing goad which necessity applies to industry in this country, and in the absence of all resource for the idle. During nearly two years that I resided in Cincinnati, or its neighborhood, I neither saw a beggar, nor a man of sufficient fortune to permit his ceasing his efforts to increase it; thus every bee in the hive is actively employed in search of that honey of Hybla, vulgarly called money; neither art, science, learning, nor pleasure can seduce them from its pursuit . . . .

I never saw any people who appeared to live so much without amusement as the Cincinnatians. Billiards are forbidden by law, so are cards. To sell a pack of cards in Ohio subjects the seller to a penalty of fifty dollars. They have no public balls, excepting, I think, six, during the Christmas holidays. They have no concerts. They have no dinner parties.

They have a theatre, which is, in fact, the only public amusement of this triste little town; but they seem to care little about it, and either from economy or distaste, it is very poorly attended. Ladies are rarely seen there, and by far the larger proportion of females deem it an offence against religion to witness the representation of a play. It is in the churches and chapels of the town that the ladies are to be seen in full costume; and I am tempted to believe that a stranger from the continent of Europe would be inclined, on first reconnoitering the city, to suppose that the places of worship were the theatres and cafés of the place. No evening in the week but brings throngs of the young and beautiful to the chapels and meeting-houses, all dressed with care, and sometimes with great pretension; it is there that all display is made, and all fashionable distinction sought. The proportion of gentlemen attending these evening meetings is very small, but often, as might be expected, a sprinkling of smart young clerks make this sedulous display of ribbons and ringlets intelligible and natural. Were it not for the churches, indeed, I think there might be a general bonfire of best bonnets, for I never could discover any other use for them.

It seems hardly fair to quarrel with a place because its staple commodity is not pretty, but I am sure I should have liked Cincinnati much better if the people had not dealt so very largely in hogs. The immense quantity of business done in this line would hardly be believed by those who had not witnessed it. I never saw a newspaper without remarking such advertisements as the following:
"Wanted, immediately, 4,000 fat hogs."
"For sale, 2,000 barrels of prime pork."
But the annoyance came nearer than this; if I determined upon a walk up Main-street, the chances were five hundred to one against my reaching the shady side without brushing by a snout fresh dripping from the kennel; when we had screwed our courage to the enterprise of mounting a certain noble-looking sugar-loaf hill, that promised pure air and a fine view, we found the brook we had to cross, at its foot, red with the stream from a pig slaughter-house; while our noses, instead of meeting "the thyme that loves the green hill's breast," were greeted by odours that I will not describe, and which I heartily hope my readers cannot imagine; our feet, that on leaving the city had expected to press the flowery sod, literally got entangled in pigs' tails and jawbones: and thus the prettiest walk in the neighbourhood was interdicted for ever.

One of the sights to stare at in America is that of houses moving from place to place. We were often amused by watching this exhibition of mechanical skill in the streets. They make no difficulty of moving dwellings from one part of the town to another. Those I saw travelling were all of them framehouses, that is, built wholly of wood, except the chimneys; but it is said that brick buildings are sometimes treated in the same manner. The largest dwelling that I saw in motion was one containing two stories of four rooms each; forty oxen were yoked to it.

The first few yards brought down the two stacks of chimneys, but it afterwards went on well. The great difficulties were the first getting it in motion and the stopping exactly in the right place. This locomotive power was extremely convenient at Cincinnati, as the constant improvements going on there made it often desirable to change a wooden dwelling for one of brick; and whenever this happened, we were sure to see the ex No. 100 of Main-street or the ex No. 55 of Second-street creeping quietly out of town, to take possession of a humble suburban station on the common above it.

No one dreams of fastening a door in Western America; I was told that it would be considered as an affront by the whole neighbourhood. I was thus exposed to perpetual, and most vexatious interruptions from people whom I had often never seen, and whose names still oftener were unknown to me.

Those who are native there, and to the manner born, seem to pass over these annoyances with more skill than I could ever acquire. More than once I have seen some of my acquaintance beset in the same way, without appearing at all distressed by it; they continued their employment or conversation with me, much as if no such interruption had taken place; when the visitor entered, they would say, "How do you do?" and shake hands.

"Tolerable, I thank ye, how be you?" was the reply.

If it was a female, she took off her hat; if a male, he kept it on, and then taking possession of the first chair in their way, they would retain it for an hour together, without uttering another word; at length, rising abruptly, they would again shake hands, with, "Well, now I must be going, I guess," and so take themselves off, apparently well contented with their reception.

I could never attain this philosophical composure; I could neither write nor read, and I always fancied I must talk to them. I will give the minutes of a conversation which I once set down after one of their visits, as a specimen of their tone and manner of speaking and thinking. My visitor was a milkman.

"Well now, so you be from the old country? Ay—you'll see sights here, I guess."

"I hope I shall see many."

"That's a fact. I expect your little place of an island don't grow such dreadful fine corn as you sees here?"

"It grows no corn at all, sir."

"Possible! no wonder, then, that we reads such awful stories in the papers of your poor people being starved to death."

"We have wheat, however."

"Ay, for your rich folks, but I calculate the poor seldom gets a belly full."

"You have certainly much greater abundance here."

"I expect so. Why they do say, that if a poor body contrives to be smart enough to scrape together a few dollars, that your King George always comes down upon 'em, and takes it all away. Don't he?"

"I do not remember hearing of such a transaction."

"I guess they be pretty close about it. Your papers ben't like ourn, I reckon? Now we says and prints just what we likes."

"You spend a good deal of time in reading the newspapers."

"And I'd like you to tell me how we can spend it better. How should freemen spend their time, but looking after their government, and watching that them fellers as we gives offices to, doos their duty, and gives themselves no airs?"

"But I sometimes think, sir, that your fences might be in more thorough repair, and your roads in better order, if less time was spent in politics."

"The Lord! to see how little you knows of a free country! Why, what's the smoothness of a road, put against the freedom of a free-born American? And what does a broken zig-zag signify, comparable to knowing that the men what we have been pleased to send up to Congress, speaks handsome and straight, as we chooses they should?"

"It is from a sense of duty, then, that you all go to the liquor store to read the papers?"

"To be sure it is, and he'd be no true born American as didn't. I don't say that the father of a family should always be after liquor, but I do say that I'd rather have my son drunk three times in a week, than not look after the affairs of his country."

We quitted Cincinnati the beginning of March, 1830, and I believe there was not one of our party who did not experience a sensation of pleasure in leaving it. We had seen again and again all the queer varieties of it's little world; had amused ourselves with it's consequence, it's taste, and it's ton, till they had ceased to be amusing. Not a hill was left unclimbed, nor a forest path unexplored; and, with the exception of two or three individuals, who bore heads and hearts peculiar to no clime, but which are found scattered through the world, as if to keep us every where in good humour with it, we left nought to regret at Cincinnati. The only regret was, that we had ever entered it; for we had wasted health, time, and money there.

Letter from the North

CHARLES C. JONES, JR.

Charles C. Jones, Jr., (1831-1893) was the eldest son in a Georgia family of plantation owners. Educated at Princeton and Harvard, he contributed extensively to the immense correspondence among members of the Jones family. This historical trove of letters from 1855-1867 has been edited by Robert Manson Myers into a volume called The Children of Pride.

Galt House, Louisville, Kentucky, *Wednesday*, July 12th, 1854

My dear Father and Mother,

I had hoped long before this to have written you at length, but a succession of novelties, each attracting attention, and also the daily routine of travel, each evening finding me wearied with the dust and fatigue of the day, have thus far prevented. Before retiring this evening, however, I am resolved to send you at least a few hasty lines, acquainting you with my journeyings hitherto.

You will perceive from the date of this letter that I am again on Southern soil, and although many hundred miles away from you, feel more at home than I have done for some time. From the bird's-eye view of Louisville which we had in crossing the river from Jeffersonville and in passing through to this hotel, it is not the elegant city which I had anticipated. Probably this is the most unfavorable season of the year for one to form his ideas and gather first impressions of the thrift, business, and neatness of the place. The river is quite low, business matters seem quite dull, and there is very little activity in the streets. On my right, through an open window, I have a fine view of the Ohio and the Indiana shore. Ferryboats are crossing and recrossing, and the heavy cough of large steamers is heard now and then ascending and descending the river. It must be a noble stream in the spring of the year, when its swollen waters are even with the banks. Louisville is situated upon a sandy bluff of perhaps some fifteen feet in height, seems to be pretty regularly laid out, but many of the buildings present an old and

---

dingy appearance. Tomorrow morning, D.V.,[1] I expect to leave at four o'clock in the stage for Elizabethtown, near which place Governor Helm and family reside.

Let me recur to a few of the scenes and localities through which I have passed since leaving Cambridge. From Buffalo I wrote Brother and Sister, just after I reached the city, before I had noted its situation and appearance, giving them a running account of my trip thus far. The next morning my young friend and myself hired a buggy and rode all over the city. It is, you may say, regularly laid out, and advantageously situated upon Lake Erie, whose waters, like those of the sea, stretch far away in the distance until they seem limited by the horizon alone. Upon its broad bosom the white sails of commerce were widely spread, and were you not intellectually apprised of the fact that this was indeed a lake, you could not otherwise have refrained from believing that you were indeed viewing the blue waters of the Atlantic. The wharves were crowded with steamers for all parts of its enlarged domains, while canalboats without number, with vessels of every description, were discharging their respective cargoes and receiving others. Dutch and German emigrants seem now to form a principal article of import and export. You are surrounded with them on every hand, and sometimes it is with difficulty that you can under some circumstances address yourself to an assemblage with any degree of certainty that you will receive an English reply.

This influx of foreign population forms a prominent and in some respects a dangerous feature in the present history and condition of the West. I have seen in the past week a far greater number of Germans, Dutch, Irish, and other emigrants than in all the former portion of my life. It is among this class principally that the cholera occurs on the lakes and rivers here. And no wonder that they are affected with that terrible disease. Often, debilitated with the sea voyage, they land in some large city, are huddled together in narrow quarters by hundreds, indulge to an enormous extent in salt cabbage and other kindred cheap articles of food, sleep in rooms badly ventilated, thence spend days and sometimes weeks upon steamboats where they are generally treated no better than so many beasts. And thus in consequence of bad food, bad air, and bad attention, hundreds of them fall victims to disease while seeking their fortunes and a home in this western world. I have been among them and observed their habits, their modes of travel, of diet, etc., and can well comprehend the hardships and inconveniences which induce this mortality among them. The only wonder is that more do not perish. They can thank Heaven, however, for their originally excellent constitutions.

---

[1] D.V.—Deo volente, Latin for "God willing."

Buffalo in that part which looks towards the lake must be rather unhealthy. The shores are low, and that portion of the city is intersected by numerous canals, which are filled with water by no means the clearest and purest in the world. Here also are large manufacturing establishments, ironworks, tanyards, etc. Its commercial relations must be extensive. In the suburbs and in the country part of the city there are many beautiful residences with fine open lots and luxuriant trees and gardens. The National Hotel there is well kept, and is the best in the city. . . .

I . . . proceeded to Cleveland, which seemed beautiful indeed as the last rays of the sun fell upon its pretty houses and the deep blue expanse of the lake, which extended far away in the distance as far as the eye could reach, blue as the azure vault of heaven, calm and quiet in the evening air, the white sail contrasting charmingly with its placid bosom. The cars for some distance just before we entered Cleveland skirted along the edge of the lake, thus affording us an admirable view of its beautiful expanse. "The lake! The lake!" involuntarily burst from the lips of the passengers, and that side of the cars which was nearest to it was thronged with persons eager to gaze upon the attractions of the scene.

Cleveland stands upon a high bluff, and you do not see much of the city until you ascend from the level of the lake. As we passed up the bluff, numbers were sitting upon benches upon the edge, watching the last rays of the sun as they sported with a few fleecy clouds in the sky and kissed the glassy bosom of Erie. Cleveland is well laid out, and appears to be a very thriving place. In fact, its happy location would insure it much business in a commercial point of view. Put up at the Weddell Hotel. Did not find it the hotel I expected, or was led to believe it from report. Food covered with flies, waiters inattentive, and house dirty. Should I pass through Cleveland again I should stop at the American or Angier. The latter, I think, would be the preferable one of the two.

During our ride from Buffalo to Cleveland the road ran for many miles parallel with the lake, every now and then affording us a most beautiful glimpse of its blue waters through opening trees and the streets of the towns at which the iron horse paused to drop his passengers, or himself to take his frugal yet substantial meal of wood and water. Hence the road from Buffalo to Cleveland is called the "Lake Shore Railroad Route," passing through Erie, etc.

Left Cleveland for Cincinnati at 8 A.M., and arrived at the latter city at 6 P.M. The country through which we passed this day is the most beautiful I have ever seen in my life if viewed with reference to agricultural purposes. Level, rich, and thickly wooded, it apparently possesses a fertility which will richly repay the labors of the farmer; and judging from the character of the crops, such is undoubtedly the case. Ohio is indeed a noble state in her internal resources. The road between Cleveland and Cincinnati via Columbus is also the finest I have ever traveled upon. The cars themselves are well furnished and softly cushioned, and there is no motion at all, so accurately are the rails laid. The speed is also rapid. I was much pleased with Ohio, and am happy that I have had an opportunity of acquainting myself with the character of this part of our country.

Arrived at Cincinnati, and having dressed and supped at the Burnet House, which by the way is one of the finest hotels I have ever seen, I called upon Dr. Law. He was unfortunately not at home. Conversed with Mrs. Law, however, for more than an hour. She seemed pleased to see me, and inquired very particularly concerning you both, my dear parents. Gave her all the Liberty news of which I was possessed. Much that was very old was quite new to her. . . . Dr. Law is in the insurance business and succeeds well. Mrs. Law is pleased with Cincinnati, and feels perfectly at home. Returned to the hotel before ten. Horrible smells in some parts of the city: cholera among the Irish and emigrants.

Leaving Cincinnati at six this morning, we took the cars for Louisville, which city we reached at one o'clock. Road miserable: almost jolted to death. Indiana a poor state except along the river bottoms. Corn there not tasseling as yet. The railroad runs from Cincinnati to Seymour; there you change cars and come to Jeffersonville opposite Louisville on the Indiana shore.

And now, my dear father and mother, regretting that my letter has necessarily been so hastily penned, I must bid you good night as, D.V., I have to be up at three o'clock tomorrow morning for the stage. With warmest love to you both, Aunt Susan, Sister, Cousin Laura, Brother, and all relatives and friends, I remain

Your ever affectionate son,
Charles C. Jones, Jr.

Howdy for the servants.

I Pray Thee Ask No Questions, This Is That Golden Land

HENRY ROTH

---

*Sixteen million people came to America through Ellis Is-
land, the floodgate of immigration in New York harbor.
Many of them stayed on in the city, and Henry Roth grew
up among them, on the streets of those newest Americans in
New York's Lower East Side. During the Depression he
wrote the experience of slum life into an intense novel,* Call
It Sleep *(which belatedly became a bestseller when reissued
as a paperback in the 1960s), and then abandoned writing.
What follows is the Prologue of* Call It Sleep.

The small white steamer, Peter Stuyvesant, that delivered the immigrants from the stench and throb of the steerage to the stench and
the throb of New York tenements, rolled slightly on the water beside
the stone quay in the lee of the weathered barracks and new brick
buildings of Ellis Island. Her skipper was waiting for the last of the officials, laborers and guards to embark upon her before he cast off and
started for Manhattan. Since this was Saturday afternoon and this the
last trip she would make for the week-end, those left behind might
have to stay over till Monday. Her whistle bellowed its hoarse warning.
A few figures in overalls sauntered from the high doors of the immigration quarters and down the grey pavement that led to the dock.

It was May of the year 1907, the year that was destined to bring
the greatest number of immigrants to the shores of the United States.
All that day, as on all the days since spring began, her decks had been
thronged by hundreds upon hundreds of foreigners, natives from almost every land in the world, the joweled close-cropped Teuton, the
full-bearded Russian, the scraggly-whiskered Jew, and among them
Slovack peasants with docile faces, smooth-cheeked and swarthy Ar-
menians, pimply Greeks, Danes with wrinkled eyelids. All day her
decks had been colorful, a matrix of the vivid costumes of other lands,
the speckled green-and-yellow aprons, the flowered kerchief, embroi-
dered homespun, the silver-braided sheep-skin vest, the gaudy scarfs,
yellow boots, fur caps, caftans, dull gabardines. All day the guttural,

---

From CALL IT SLEEP by Henry Roth. Reprinted with permission of Cooper
Square Publishers, Inc.

the high-pitched voices, the astonished cries, the gasps of wonder, reiterations of gladness had risen from her decks in a motley billow of sound. But now her decks were empty, quiet, spreading out under the sunlight almost as if the warm boards were relaxing from the strain and the pressure of the myriads of feet. All those steerage passengers of the ships that had docked that day who were permitted to enter had already entered—except two, a woman and a young child she carried in her arms. They had just come aboard escorted by a man.

About the appearance of these late comers there was very little that was unusual. The man had evidently spent some time in America and was now bringing his wife and child over from the other side. It might have been thought that he had spent most of his time in lower New York, for he paid only the scantest attention to the Statue of Liberty or to the city rising from the water or to the bridges spanning the East River—or perhaps he was merely too agitated to waste much time on these wonders. His clothes were the ordinary clothes the ordinary New Yorker wore in that period—sober and dull. A black derby accentuated the sharpness and sedentary pallor of his face; a jacket, loose on his tall spare frame, buttoned up in a V close to the throat; and above the V a tightly-knotted black tie was mounted in the groove of a high starched collar. As for his wife, one guessed that she was a European more by the timid wondering look in her eyes as she gazed from her husband to the harbor, than by her clothes. For her clothes were American—a black skirt, a white shirt-waist and a black jacket. Obviously her husband had either taken the precaution of sending them to her while she was still in Europe or had brought them with him to Ellis Island where she had slipped them on before she left.

Only the small child in her arms wore a distinctly foreign costume, an impression one got chiefly from the odd, outlandish, blue straw hat on his head with its polka dot ribbons of the same color dangling over each shoulder.

Except for this hat, had the three newcomers been in a crowd, no one probably could have singled out the woman and child as newly arrived immigrants. They carried no sheets tied up in huge bundles, no bulky wicker baskets, no prized feather beds, no boxes of delicacies, sausages, virgin-olive oils, rare cheeses; the large black satchel beside them was their only luggage. But despite this, despite their even less than commonplace appearance, the two overalled men, sprawled out and smoking cigarettes in the stern, eyed them curiously. And the old peddler woman, sitting with basket of oranges on knee, continually squinted her weak eyes in their direction.

The truth was there was something quite untypical about their behavior. The old peddler woman on the bench and the overalled men in the stern had seen enough husbands meeting their wives and children after a long absence to know how such people ought to behave. The most volatile races, such as the Italians, often danced for joy, whirled each other around, pirouetted in an ecstasy: Swedes sometimes just looked at each other, breathing through open mouths like a panting dog; Jews wept, jabbered, almost put each other's eyes out with the recklessness of their darting gestures; Poles roared and gripped each other at arm's length as though they meant to tear a handful of flesh; and after one pecking kiss, the English might be seen gravitating toward, but never achieving an embrace. But these two stood silent, apart; the man staring with aloof, offended eyes grimly down at the water—or if he turned his face toward his wife at all, it was only to glare in harsh contempt at the blue straw hat worn by the child in her arms, and then his hostile eyes would sweep about the deck to see if anyone else were observing them. And his wife beside him regarding him uneasily, appealingly. And the child against her breast looking from one to the other with watchful, frightened eyes. Altogether it was a very curious meeting.

They had been standing in this strange and silent manner for several minutes, when the woman, as if driven by the strain into action, tried to smile, and touching her husband's arm said timidly, "And this is the Golden Land." She spoke in Yiddish.

The man grunted, but made no answer.

She took a breath as if taking courage, and tremulously, "I'm sorry, Albert, I was so stupid." She paused waiting for some flicker of unbending, some word, which never came. "But you look so lean, Albert, so haggard. And your mustache—you've shaved."

His brusque glance stabbed and withdrew. "Even so."

"You must have suffered in this land." She continued gentle despite his rebuke. "You never wrote me. You're thin. Ach! Then here in the new land is the same old poverty. You've gone without food. I can see it. You've changed."

"Well that don't matter," he snapped, ignoring her sympathy. "It's no excuse for your not recognizing me. Who else would call for you? Do you know anyone else in this land?"

"No," placatingly. "But I was so frightened, Albert. Listen to me. I was so bewildered, and that long waiting there in that vast room since morning. Oh, that horrible waiting! I saw them all go, one after the other. The shoemaker and his wife. The coppersmith and his children from Strij. All those on the Kaiserin Viktoria. But I—I remained. Tomorrow will be Sunday. They told me no one could come to fetch me. What if they sent me back? I was frantic!"

"Are you blaming me?" His voice was dangerous.

"No! No! Of course not, Albert! I was just explaining."

"Well then let me explain," he said curtly. "I did what I could. I took the day off from the shop. I called that cursed Hamburg-American Line four times. And each time they told me you weren't on board."

"They didn't have any more third-class passage, so I had to take the steerage—"

"Yes, now I know. That's all very well. That couldn't be helped. I came here anyway. The last boat. And what do you do? You refused to recognize me. You don't know me." He dropped his elbows down on the rail, averted his angry face. "That's the greeting I get."

"I'm sorry, Albert," she stroked his arm humbly. "I'm sorry."

"And as if those blue-coated mongrels in there weren't mocking me enough, you give them that brat's right age. Didn't I write you to say seventeen months because it would save the half fare! Didn't you hear me inside when I told them?"

"How could I, Albert?" she protested. "How could I? You were on the other side of that—that cage."

"Well why didn't you say seventeen months anyway? Look!" he pointed to several blue-coated officials who came hurrying out of a doorway out of the immigration quarters. "There they are." An ominous pride dragged at his voice. "If he's among them, that one who questioned me so much, I could speak to him if he came up here."

"Don't bother with him, Albert," she exclaimed uneasily. "Please, Albert! What have you against him? He couldn't help it. It's his work."

"Is it?" His eyes followed with unswerving deliberation the blue-coats as they neared the boat. "Well he didn't have to do it so well."

"And after all, I did lie to him, Albert," she said hurriedly trying to distract him.

"The truth is you didn't," he snapped, turning his anger against her. "You made your first lie plain by telling the truth afterward. And made a laughing-stock of me!"

"I didn't know what to do." She picked despairingly at the wire grill beneath the rail. "In Hamburg the doctor laughed at me when I said seventeen months. He's so big. He was big when he was born." She smiled, the worried look on her face vanishing momentarily as she stroked her son's cheek. "Won't you speak to your father, David, beloved?"

The child merely ducked his head behind his mother.

His father stared at him, shifted his gaze and glared down at the officials, and then, as though perplexity had crossed his mind he frowned absently. "How old did he say he was?"

"The doctor? Over two years—and as I say he laughed."

"Well, what did he enter?"

"Seventeen months—I told you."

"Then why didn't you tell them seventeen—" He broke off, shrugged violently. "Baah! You need more strength in this land." He paused, eyed her intently and then frowned suddenly. "Did you bring his birth certificate?"

"Why—" She seemed confused. "It may be in the trunk—there on the ship. I don't know. Perhaps I left it behind." Her hand wandered uncertainly to her lips. "I don't know. Is it important? I never thought of it. But surely father could send it. We need only write."

"Hmm! Well, put him down." His head jerked brusquely toward the child. "You don't need to carry him all the way. He's big enough to stand on his own feet."

She hesitated, and then reluctantly set the child down on the deck. Scared, unsteady, the little one edged over to the side opposite his father, and hidden by his mother, clung to her skirt.

"Well, it's all over now." She attempted to be cheerful. "It's all behind us now, isn't it, Albert? Whatever mistakes I made don't really matter any more. Do they?"

"A fine taste of what lies before me!" He turned his back on her and leaned morosely against the rail. "A fine taste!"

They were silent. On the dock below, the brown hawsers had been slipped over the mooring posts, and the men on the lower deck now dragged them dripping from the water. Bells clanged. The ship throbbed. Startled by the hoarse bellow of her whistle, the gulls wheeling before her prow rose with slight creaking cry from the green water, and as she churned away from the stone quay skimmed across her path on indolent, scimitar wing. Behind the ship the white wake that stretched to Ellis Island grew longer, raveling wanly into melon-green. On one side curved the low drab Jersey coast-line, the spars and masts on the waterfront fringing the sky; on the other side was Brooklyn, flat, water-towered; the horns of the harbor. And before them, rising on her high pedestal from the scaling swarmy brilliance of sunlit water to the west, Liberty. The spinning disk of the late afternoon sun slanted behind her, and to those on board who gazed, her features were charred with shadow, her depths exhausted, her masses ironed to one single plane. Against the luminous sky the rays of her halo were spikes of darkness roweling the air; shadow flattened the torch she bore to a black cross against flawless light—the blackened hilt of a broken sword. Liberty. The child and his mother stared again at the massive figure in wonder.

The ship curved around in a long arc toward Manhattan, her bow sweeping past Brooklyn and the bridges whose cables and pillars superimposed by distance, spanned the East River in diaphanous and rigid waves. The western wind that raked the harbor into brilliant clods blew fresh and clear—a salt tang in the lull of its veerings. It whipped the polka-dot ribbons on the child's hat straight out behind him. They caught his father's eye.

"Where did you find that crown?"

Startled by his sudden question his wife looked down. "That? That was Maria's parting gift. The old nurse. She bought it herself and then sewed the ribbons on. You don't think it's pretty?"

"Pretty? Do you still ask?" His lean jaws hardly moved as he spoke. "Can't you see that those idiots lying back there are watching us already? They're mocking us! What will the others do on the train? He looks like a clown in it. He's the cause of all this trouble anyway!"

The harsh voice, the wrathful glare, the hand flung toward the child frightened him. Without knowing the cause, he knew that the stranger's anger was directed at himself. He burst into tears and pressed closer to his mother.

"Quiet!" the voice above him snapped.

Cowering, the child wept all the louder.

"Hush, darling!" His mother's protecting hands settled on his shoulders.

"Just when we're about to land!" her husband said furiously "He begins this! This howling! And now we'll have it all the way home, I suppose! Quiet! You hear?"

"It's you who are frightening him, Albert!" she protested.

"Am I? Well, let him be quiet. And take that straw gear off his head."

"But Albert, it's cool here."

"Will you take that off when I—" A snarl choked whatever else he would have uttered. While his wife looked on aghast, his long fingers scooped the hat from the child's head. The next instant it was sailing over the ship's side to the green waters below. The overalled men in the stern grinned at each other. The old orange-peddler shook her head and clucked.

"Albert!" his wife caught her breath. "How could you?"

"I could!" he rapped out. "You should have left it behind!" His teeth clicked, and he glared about the deck.

She lifted the sobbing child to her breast, pressed him against her. With a vacant stunned expression, her gaze wandered from the grim smouldering face of her husband to the stern of the ship. In the silvery-green wake that curved trumpet-wise through the water, the blue hat still bobbed and rolled, ribbon stretched out on the waves. Tears sprang to her eyes. She brushed them away quickly, shook her head as if shaking off the memory, and looked toward the bow. Before her the grimy cupolas and towering square walls of the city loomed up. Above the jagged roof tops, the white smoke, whitened and suffused by the slanting sun, faded into the slots and wedges of the sky. She pressed her brow against her child's, hushed him with whispers. This was that vast incredible land, the land of freedom, of immense opportunity, that Golden Land. Again she tried to smile.

"Albert," she said timidly, "Albert."

"Hm?"

"Gehen vir voinen du? In New York?"

"Nein. Bronzeville. Ich hud dir schoin geschriben."[1]

She nodded uncertainly, sighed . . .

Screws threshing, backing water, the Peter Stuyvesant neared her dock—drifting slowly and with canceled momentum as if reluctant.

---

[1] "Are we going to live here? In New York?" "No. Brownsville. I already wrote you so."

George Washington Plunkitt of New York: Diary of a Tammany Boss

George Washington Plunkitt (1842-1924) was a ward boss in New York City's Democratic political machine, the durable organization called Tammany Hall. As this account of a typical day among his constituents illustrates, he was highly skilled in the care and feeding of voters.

2 a.m. Wakened by a boy with message from a bartender to bail him out of jail.

3 a.m. Back to bed.

6 a.m. Fire-engines, up and off to the scene to see my election district captains tending the burnt-out tenants. Note names for new homes.

8:30 to police court. Six drunken constituents on hand. Got four released by a timely word to the judge. Paid the others' fines.

Nine o'clock to Municipal Court. Told an election district captain to act as lawyer for a widow threatened with dispossession.

11 to 3 p.m. Found jobs for four constituents.

3 p.m. An Italian funeral, sat conspicuously up front.

4 p.m. A Jewish funeral—up front again, in the synagogue.

7 p.m. Meeting of district captains and reviewed the list of all voters, who's for us, who's agin.

8 p.m. Church fair. Bought ice-creams for the girls; took fathers for a little something round the corner.

9 p.m. Back to club-house. Heard complaints of a dozen pushcart pedlars.

10:30 A Jewish wedding. Had sent handsome present to the bride.

Midnight—to bed.

Abraham Ruef of San Francisco:
Learning the Business of Boss

*Abraham Ruef (1864-1936) in the early years of this century
controlled San Francisco's city hall through hand-picked
candidates and an alliance with labor unions. His power
ended in 1908 with a jail sentence for bribery. These scenes
of Ruef's political education are from* Boss Ruef's San Francisco, *by Walton Bean.*

Ruef first took part in real politics, according to his memoirs, in
the primaries of the Republican party of San Francisco in the elections
of 1886. He had just opened his law office, and it was the first year in
which he was old enough to vote. Attracted by a newspaper announce-
ment of a meeting of the Republican club of his district, he made his
way at eight in the evening to the advertised address on Sansome
Street. This proved to be a dark and dangerous-looking three-story
boarding house for sailors, under the cliffs of Telegraph Hill. It was a
district where shanghaiing was still practiced, and it took all Ruef's
courage to knock. The boarding house keeper led him with a lantern to
an upstairs room and introduced him to the only person present, a
saloonkeeper. The two men said that a meeting of more than a
hundred and fifty Republicans had already adjourned, having elected
these two as officers with unanimity and enthusiasm. As the disap-
pointed Ruef turned to leave, he was asked, "Young man, can you
write?" Giving an affirmative answer, he was designated secretary of
the district Republican club and furnished with a vivid account of the
meeting, which he wrote down and carried to the office of a newspaper.
His glowing account of a large and intelligent gathering was published
the next morning just as he had written it. Not until later, he asserted,
did he realize that there had been no such meeting, and that so forbid-
ding a place had been scheduled in order that no one would attend and
his two hosts might elect each other. . . .

In his own right, Ruef became boss of the "Latin Quarter," where
he was soon a familiar and popular figure. In the school of ward politics, he mastered the various methods of garnering votes. He was active

From BOSS RUEF'S SAN FRANCISCO by Walton Bean. Originally published
by the University of California Press, 1952; reprinted by permission of the University of California.

in every possible social organization. He studied the strange psychology of patronage, the moth-like fascination of the job seeker with the glamor of even the lowliest and least secure public office. It was, he observed, "a craze . . . as enslaving as the drink or drug habit," and he marveled at the often repeated pattern of a young man ruining his life by deserting a safe and promising trade or business for the mirage of a poorly paid and temporary political job. Even minor political office holders were subject to endless demands for charity, and Ruef learned that a successful boss could never refuse aid to the needy or decline to purchase tickets to a benefit. Ruef discovered, also, that one special favor bound the recipient and his friends "more tightly than a dozen general benefits to the community." Influence with police-court judges on behalf of an arrested person could produce a release form signed in blank by the judge. Friends in the assessor's office could overlook gross undervaluations of the taxable property of corporations and wealthy individuals, and cement their support for the boss. The auditor's office could expedite payment of a bill or approval of a doubtful claim. The coroner's office could modify the circumstances entered in a report of death, relating to culpability or damages. There were as many opportunities for favors as there were functions of city government.

As a platform speaker at political meetings Ruef learned to capture the most hostile and unruly audience with a combination of humor, courage, and tact. Once, when he arrived at a rally, the platform was already dotted with "uncooked omelettes," and more were obviously being reserved for him. "Throw all the rest of those eggs at one time, so that we can get down to business," Ruef suggested. "They look like good fresh eggs. That egg man cheated you if you bought them for rotten ones." The audience laughed and cheered, and a deluge of eggs soared to the platform, spattering against posts, onto coats, and even into the band's brass horns. "Are they all in?" They were. Then, without interruption, Ruef managed a speech that ended in goodnatured applause.

Edward H. Crump of Memphis: The Boss as a Party Man

Edward H. Crump (1874-1954) served two terms as mayor of Memphis, but most of his 40-year span of power in western Tennessee was spent behind the scenes as a political king-maker. This sample of his local savvy is from Mr. Crump of Memphis, *by William D. Miller.*

. . . Rural immigrants. . . . looked upon him as their patron and protector. He possessed an easy affability that enabled him to speak their language—perhaps to discourse upon their ailments and to suggest valued remedies his mother had used when he was a boy. He knew their names and in many instances an amazing amount of their personal history. As they repeated among themselves the numerous stories that circulated about Crump's timely intervention in the affairs of one of their number to set aright some fearful problem, they developed an unshakable faith in "Mr. Crump," and to fail to vote his ticket on election day was a betrayal of a trust.

In his role as patron Crump would sometimes have a "possum" hunt, barbecue, or some other festive event, and very often he would invite representatives of the humbler segments of society to attend. There were also his boatrides for the shut-ins, theater parties for orphans, and later the benefit football game for the blind, all of which contributed to the image of Crump as a great benefactor.

One of the largest Crump parties took place in September, 1935, when the whole populace was invited to a "Crump Day at the Fair." Children were given free rides on all the midway devices; there was dancing, old-fashioned community singing, boxing, wrestling, and track contests to entertain the older folks. When the fairground gates were opened at 3:30 on September 23, Crump was there in front of the band on the midway, wearing a brown plaid coat, brown and white striped pants, white shoes, and a bronze dahlia the size of a saucer. As the people entered, he bowed and smiled while organization personnel passed out paper hats with the label: "Mr. Crump's Party." Then, with Mrs. Crump and his three sons and their wives marching with him, he twirled his cane and led the band up and down the midway. It was estimated that over fifty thousand people attended the event.

From MR. CRUMP OF MEMPHIS by William Miller. Reprinted by permission of the Louisiana State University Press.

Richard J. Daley of Chicago:
Another Workday for The Boss

Richard J. Daley (1902-   ) rose through a number of posts in Cook County Democratic politics to emerge as mayor of Chicago in 1953. Term after term, the vote-pulling power of his cohorts in the precincts has returned him to office, and made him influential even in national politics. This account of a Daley day is from Mike Royko's biography, Boss.

. . . at 9 A.M. he, Richard Joseph Daley, is in his office and behind the big gleaming mahogany desk, in a high-backed dark green leather chair, ready to start another day of doing what the experts say is no longer possible—running a big American city. But as he, Daley, has often said to confidantes, "What in hell do the experts know?" He's been running a big American city for fifteen of the toughest years American cities have ever seen. He, Daley, has been running it as long or longer than any of the other famous mayors—Curley of Boston, LaGuardia of New York, Kelly of Chicago—ran theirs, and unless his health goes, or his wife says no, he, Daley, will be running it for another four years. Twenty is a nice, round figure. They give soldiers pensions after twenty years, and some companies give wristwatches. He'll settle for something simple, like maybe another jet airport built on a man-made island in the lake, and named after him, and maybe a statue outside the Civic Center, with a simple inscription, "The greatest mayor in the history of the world." And they might seal off his office as a shrine.

It's a business office. Like the man, the surroundings have no distracting frills. He wears excellently tailored business suits, buying six a year from the best shop on Michigan Avenue. The shirt is always radiant white, the tie conservative. Because his shoulders are narrow, he never works in his shirt sleeves, and is seldom seen publicly in casual clothes. The businesslike appearance carries through the office. The carpets, furniture, and walls are in muted shades of tan and green. The only color is provided by the flags of the United States and the city of Chicago, and a color photograph of his family. When a prominent cultural leader offered to donate some paintings for the office, an aide said, "Please, no, he can't accept them. People would think he's going high-hat."

. . . One of his visitors will be a city official unique to Chicago city government: the director of patronage. He brings a list of all new city employees for the day. The list isn't limited to the key employees, the professional people. All new employees are there—down to the window washer, the ditch digger, the garbage collector. After each person's name will be an extract of his background, the job, and most important, his political sponsor. Nobody goes to work for the city, and that includes governmental bodies that are not directly under the mayor, without Daley's knowing about it. He must see every name because the person becomes more than an employee: he joins the political Machine, part of the army numbering in the thousands who will help win elections. They damn well better, or they won't keep their jobs.

He scans the list for anything unusual. A new employee might be related to somebody special, an important businessman, an old political family. That will be noted. He might have been fired by another city office in a scandal. That won't keep him from being put to work somewhere else. Some bad ones have worked for half the governmental offices in the city. There might be a police record, which prompts a call to the political sponsor for an explanation. "He's clean now." "Are you sure?" "Of course, it was just a youthful mistake." "Three times?" "Give him a break, his uncle is my best precinct captain." "Okay, a break, but keep your eye on him." As he has said so often, when the subject of ex-cons on the city payroll comes up, "Are we to deny these men honest employment in a free society . . . are we to deprive them of the right to work . . . to become rehabilitated. . . ." He will forgive anything short of Republicanism.

. . . He has many requests from neighborhood people. And when a group is admitted to his office, most of them nervous and wide-eyed, he knows who they are, their leaders, their strength in the community. They have already been checked out by somebody. He must know everything. He doesn't like to be surprised. Just as he knows the name of every new worker, he must know what is going on in the various city offices. If the head of the office doesn't tell him, he has somebody there who will. In the office of other elected officials, he has trusted persons who will keep him informed. Out in the neighborhoods his precinct captains are reporting to the ward committeemen, and they in turn are reporting to him.

His police department's intelligence-gathering division gets bigger and bigger, its network of infiltrators, informers, and spies creating massive files on dissenters, street gangs, political enemies, newsmen, radicals, liberals, and anybody else who might be working against him. If one of his aides or handpicked officeholders is shacking up with a woman, he will know it. And if that man is married and a Catholic, his political career will wither and die. That is the greatest sin of all. You can make money under the table and move ahead, but you are forbidden to make secretaries under the sheets. He has dumped several party members for violating his personal moral standards. If something is leaked to the press, the bigmouth will be tracked down and punished. Scandals aren't public scandals if you get there before your enemies do.

So when the people come in, he knows what they want and whether it is possible. Not that it means they will get it. That often depends on how they act.

He will come out from behind his desk all smiles and handshakes and charm. Then he returns to his chair and sits very straight, hands folded on his immaculate desk, serious and attentive. To one side will be somebody from the appropriate city department.

Now it's up to the group. If they are respectful, he will express sympathy, ask encouraging questions, and finally tell them that everything possible will be done. And after they leave, he may say, "Take care of it." With that command, the royal seal, anything is possible, anybody's toes can be stepped on.

But if they are pushy, antagonistic, demanding instead of imploring, or bold enough to be critical of him, to tell him how he should do his job, to blame him for their problem, he will rub his hands together, harder and harder. In a long, difficult meeting, his hands will get raw. His voice gets lower, softer, and the corners of his mouth will turn down. At this point, those who know him will back off. They know what's next. But the unfamiliar, the militant, will mistake his lowered voice and nervousness for weakness. Then he'll blow, and it comes in a frantic roar:

"I want *you* to tell *me* what to do. *You* come up with the answers. *You* come up with the program. Are we perfect? Are *you* perfect? We all make mistakes. We all have faults. It's easy to criticize. It's easy to find fault. But *you* tell me what to do. This problem is all over the city. We didn't create these problems. We don't want them. But we are doing what we can. *You* tell me how to solve them. *You* give me a program." All of which leaves the petitioners dumb, since most people don't walk around with urban programs in their pockets. It can also leave them right back where they started.

They leave and the favor seekers come in. Half of the people he sees want a favor. They plead for promotions, something for their sons, a chance to do some business with the city, to get somebody in City

Hall off their backs, a chance to return from political exile, a boon. They won't get an answer right there and then. It will be considered and he'll let them know. Later, sometimes much later, when he has considered the alternatives and the benefits, word will get back to them. Yes or no. Success or failure. Life or death.

Some jobseekers come directly to him. Complete outsiders, meaning those with no family or political connections, will be sent to see their ward committeemen. That is protocol, and that is what he did to the tall young black man who came to see him a few years ago, bearing a letter from the governor of North Carolina, who wrote that the young black man was a rising political prospect in his state. Daley told him to see his ward committeeman, and if he did some precinct work, rang doorbells, hustled up some votes, there might be a government job for him. Maybe something like taking coins in a tollway booth. The Rev. Jesse Jackson, now the city's leading black civil rights leader, still hasn't stopped smarting over that.

Others come asking him to resolve a problem. He is the city's leading labor mediator and has prevented the kind of strikes that have crippled New York. His father was a union man, and he comes from a union neighborhood, and many of the union leaders were his boyhood friends. He knows what they want. And if it is in the city's treasury, they will get it. If it isn't there, he'll promise to find it. He has ended a teachers' strike by promising that the state legislature would find funds for them, which surprised the Republicans in Springfield, as well as put them on the spot. He is an effective mediator with the management side of labor disputes, because they respect his judgment, and because there are few industries that do not need some favors from City Hall.

There are disputes he won't bother with, such as that between two ranking party members, both lawyers, each retained by a rival business interest in a zoning dispute. That was the kind of situation that can drive judges, city agencies, and functionaries berserk. He angrily wiped his hands off the matter, bawled the lawyers out for creating the mess, and let them take their chances on a fair decision. There are so many clients, peace should exist among friends.

The afternoon is almost gone, but they still keep coming in the front door and those he summons through the side. The phone keeps ringing, bringing reports from his legislators in Springfield, his congressmen in Washington, and prominent businessmen, some of whom may waste a minute of his time for the status of telling dinner guests, "I mentioned that to Dick and he likes the idea. . . ."

Finally the scheduled appointments have been cleared, the unscheduled hopefuls told to come back again, and a few late calls made to his closest aides. It's six o'clock, but he is still going, as if reluctant to stop. The workdays have grown longer over the years, the vacations shorter. There is less visible joy in it all, but he works harder now than ever before. Some of his friends say he isn't comfortable anywhere but in the office on five.

The bodyguards check the corridor and he heads downstairs to the limousine. Most of the people in the Hall have left, and the mop crews are going to work, but always on the sidewalk outside will be the old hangers-on, waiting to shout a greeting, to get a nod or a smile in return.

On the way out, his press secretary hands him a speech. That's for the next stop, a banquet of civic leaders, or a professional group, or an important convention. The hotel grand ballroom is a couple of minutes away and he'll speed-read the speech just once on the way, a habit that contributes to his strange style of public speaking, with the emphasis often on the wrong 'words, the sentences overlapping, and the words tumbling over each other. Regardless of where he goes, the speech will be heavy in boosterism, full of optimism for the future, pride in the city, a reminder of what he has done. Even in the most important of gatherings, people will seek out his handshake, his recognition. A long time ago, when they opposed him, he put out the hand and moved the few steps to them. Now they come to him. He arrives after dinner, in time to be introduced, speak, and get back to the car.

The afternoon papers are on the back seat and he reads them until the limousine stops in front of a funeral home. Wakes are still part of political courtesy and his culture. Since he started in politics, he's been to a thousand of them. On the way up, the slightest connection with the deceased or his family was enough reason to attend a wake. Now he goes to fewer, and only to those involving friends, neighbors. His sons fill in for him at others. Most likely, he'll go to a wake on the South Side, because that's where most of his old friends are from. The funeral home might be McInerney's, which has matchbooks that bear a poem beginning, "Bring out the lace curtains and call McInerney, I'm nearing the end of life's pleasant journey." Or John Egan's, one of the biggest, owned by his high school pal and one of the last of the successful undertaker-politicians. The undertaker-politicians and the saloon keeper-politicians have given way to lawyer-politicians, who are no better, and they don't even buy you a drink or offer a prayer.

He knows how to act at a wake, greeting the immediate family, saying the proper things, offering his regrets, somberly and with dignity. His arrival is as big an event as the other fellow's departure. Before leaving, he will kneel at the casket, an honor afforded few of the living, and sign the visitor's book. A flurry of handshakes and he is back in the car.

It's late when the limousine turns toward Bridgeport. His neighbors are already home watching TV or at the Pump Tavern having a beer, talking baseball, race or politics. His wife Eleanor, "Sis" as he calls her, knows his schedule and will be making supper. Something boiled, meat and potatoes, home-baked bread. She makes six loaves a week. His mother always made bread. And maybe ice cream for dessert. He likes ice cream. There's an old ice cream parlor in the neighborhood, and sometimes he goes there for a sundae, as he did when he was a boy.

The limousine passes Comiskey Park, where his beloved Sox play ball. He goes to Wrigley Field, too, but only to be seen. The Sox are his team. He can walk to the ball park from the house. At least he used to be able to walk there. Today it's not the same. A person can't walk anywhere. Maybe someday he'll build a big superstadium for all the teams, better than any other city's. Maybe on the Lake Front. Let the conservationists moan. It will be good for business, drawing conventioneers from hotels, and near an expressway so people in the suburbs can drive in. With lots of parking space for them, and bright lights so they can walk. Some day, if there's time, he might just build it.

Across Halsted Street, then a turn down Lowe Avenue, into the glow of the brightest street lights of any city in the country. The streets were so dark before, a person couldn't see who was there. Now all the streets have lights so bright that some people have to lower their shades at night. He turned on all those lights, he built them. Now he can see a block ahead from his car, to where the policeman is guarding the front of his home.

He tells the driver that tomorrow will require an even earlier start. He must catch a flight to Washington to tell a committee that the cities need more money. There are so many things that must be built, so many more people to be hired. But he'll be back the same day, in the afternoon, with enough time to maybe stop at the Hall. There's always something to do there. Things have to be done. If he doesn't do them, who will?

How the Other Half Lives

JACOB A. RIIS

Jacob Riis (1849-1914) came to the United States from his native Denmark in 1869. He would retain a passionate interest in how America's "other half," the immigrants, were housed; the muckraking reporting in his 1890 book How the Other Half Lives *made him a nationally known crusader against the scandal of overcrowding in the tenement slums.*

GENESIS OF THE TENEMENT

The first tenement New York knew bore the mark of Cain from its birth, though a generation passed before the writing was deciphered. It was the "rear house," infamous ever after in our city's history. There had been tenant-houses before, but they were not built for the purpose. Nothing would probably have shocked their original owners more than the idea of their harboring a promiscuous crowd; for they were the decorous homes of the old Knickerbockers, the proud aristocracy of Manhattan in the early days.

It was the stir and bustle of trade, together with the tremendous immigration that followed upon the war of 1812 that dislodged them. In thirty-five years the city of less than a hundred thousand came to harbor half a million souls, for whom homes had to be found. Within the memory of men not yet in their prime, Washington had moved from his house on Cherry Hill as too far out of town to be easily reached. Now the old residents followed his example; but they moved in a different direction and for a different reason. Their comfortable dwellings in the once fashionable streets along the East River front fell into the hands of real-estate agents and boarding-house keepers; and here, says the report to the Legislature of 1857, when the evils engendered had excited just alarm, "in its beginning, the tenant-house became a real blessing to that class of industrious poor whose small earnings limited their expenses, and whose employment in workshops, stores, or about the warehouses and thoroughfares, render a near residence of much importance." Not for long, however. As business increased, and the city grew with rapid strides, the necessities of the poor became the opportunity of their wealthier neighbors, and the stamp was set upon the old houses, suddenly become valuable, which the best thought and effort of a later age has vainly struggled to efface. Their "*large* rooms were partitioned into *several smaller ones*, without regard to light or ventilation, the rate of rent being lower in proportion to space or height from the street; and they soon became filled from cellar to garret with a class of tenantry living from hand to mouth, loose in morals, improvident in habits, degraded, and squalid as beggary itself." It was thus the dark bedroom, prolific of untold depravities, came into the world. It was destined to survive the old houses. In their new role, says the old report, eloquent in its indignant denunciation of "evils more destructive than wars," "they were not intended to last. Rents were fixed high enough to cover damage and abuse from this class, from whom nothing was expected, and the most was made of them while they lasted. Neatness, order, cleanliness, were never dreamed of in connection with the tenant-house system, as it spread its localities from year to year; while reckless slovenliness, discontent, privation, and ignorance were left to work out their invariable results, until the entire premises reached the level of tenant-house dilapidation, containing, but sheltering not, the miserable hordes that crowded beneath smouldering, water-rotted roofs or burrowed among the rats of clammy cellars." Yet so illogical is human greed that, at a later day, when called to account, "the proprietors frequently urged the filthy habits of the tenants as an excuse for the condition of their property, utterly losing sight of the fact that it was the tolerance of those habits which was the real evil, and that for this they themselves were alone responsible."

Still the pressure of the crowds did not abate, and in the old garden where the stolid Dutch burgher grew his tulips or early cabbages a rear house was built, generally of wood, two stories high at first. Presently it was carried up another story, and another. Where two families had lived ten moved in. The front house followed suit, if the brick walls were strong enough. The question was not always asked, judging from complaints made by a contemporary witness, that the old buildings were "often carried up to a great height without regard to the strength of the foundation walls." It was rent the owner was after; nothing was said in the contract about either the safety or the comfort of the tenants. The garden gate no longer swung on its rusty hinges. The shell-paved walk had become an alley; what the rear house had left of the garden, a "court." Plenty such are yet to be found in the Fourth Ward, with here and there one of the original rear tenements.

Worse was to follow. It was "soon perceived by estate owners and agents of property that a greater percentage of profits could be realized by the conversion of houses and blocks into barracks, and dividing their space into smaller proportions capable of containing human life within four walls. . . . Blocks were rented of real estate owners, or 'purchased on time,' or taken in charge at a percentage, and held for under-letting." With the appearance of the middleman, wholly irresponsible, and utterly reckless and unrestrained, began the era of tenement building which turned out such blocks as Gotham Court, where, in one cholera epidemic that scarcely touched the clean wards, the tenants died at the rate of one hundred and ninety-five to the thousand of population; which forced the general mortality of the city up from 1 in 41.83 in 1815, to 1 in 27.33 in 1855, a year of unusual freedom from epidemic disease, and which wrung from the early organizers of the Health Department this wail: "There are numerous examples of tenement-houses in which are lodged several hundred people that have a *pro rata* allotment of ground area scarcely equal to two square yards upon the city lot, court-yards and all included." The tenement-house population had swelled to half a million souls by that time, and on the East Side, in what is still the most densely populated district in all the world, China not excluded, it was packed at the rate of 290,000 to the square mile, a state of affairs wholly unexampled. The utmost cupidity of other lands and other days had never contrived to herd much more than half that number within the same space. The greatest crowding of Old London was at the rate of 175,816. Swine roamed the streets and gutters as their principal scavengers.[1] The death of a child in a tenement was registered at the Bureau of Vital Statistics as "plainly due to suffocation in the foul air of an unventilated apartment," and the Senators, who had come down from Albany to find out what was the matter with New York, reported that "there are annually cut off from the population by disease and death enough human beings to people a city, and enough human labor to sustain it." And yet experts had testified that, as compared with uptown, rents were from twenty-five to thirty per cent higher in the worst slums of the lower wards, with such accommodations as were enjoyed, for instance, by a "family with boarders" in Cedar Street, who fed hogs in the cellar that contained eight or ten loads of manure; or "one room 12 x 12 with five families living in it, comprising twenty persons of both sexes and all ages, with only two beds, without partition, screen, chair, or table." The rate of rent has been successfully maintained to the present day, though the hog at least has been eliminated.

Lest anybody flatter himself with the notion that these were evils of a day that is happily past and may safely be forgotten, let me men-

---

[1] It was not until the winter of 1867 that owners of swine were prohibited by ordinance from letting them run at large in the built-up portions of the city.

tion here three very recent instances of tenement-house life that came under my notice. One was the burning of a rear house in Mott Street, from appearances one of the original tenant-houses that made their owners rich. The fire made homeless ten families, who had paid an average of $5 a month for their mean little cubby-holes. The owner himself told me that it was *fully* insured for $800, though it brought him in $600 a year rent. He evidently considered himself especially entitled to be pitied for losing such valuable property. Another was the case of a hard-working family of man and wife, young people from the old country, who took poison together in a Crosby Street tenement because they were "tired." There was no other explanation, and none was needed when I stood in the room in which they had lived. It was in the attic with sloping ceiling and a single window so far out on the roof that it seemed not to belong to the place at all. With scarcely room enough to turn around in they had been compelled to pay five dollars and a half a month in advance. There were four such rooms in that attic, and together they brought in as much as many a handsome little cottage in a pleasant part of Brooklyn. The third instance was that of a colored family of husband, wife, and baby in a wretched rear rookery in West Third Street. Their rent was eight dollars and a half for a single room on the top-story, so small that I was unable to get a photograph of it even by placing the camera outside the open door. Three short steps across either way would have measured its full extent.

There was just one excuse for the early tenement-house builders, and their successors may plead it with nearly as good right for what it is worth. "Such," says an official report, "is the lack of house-room in the city that any kind of tenement can be immediately crowded with lodgers, if there is space offered." Thousands were living in cellars. There were three hundred underground lodging-houses in the city when the Health Department was organized. Some fifteen years before that the old Baptist Church in Mulberry Street, just off Chatham Street, had been sold, and the rear half of the frame structure had been converted into tenements that with their swarming population became the scandal even of that reckless age. The wretched pile harbored no less than forty families, and the annual rate of deaths to the population was officially stated to be 75 in 1,000. These tenements were an extreme type of very many, for the big barracks had by this time spread east and west and far up the island into the sparsely settled wards. Whether or not the title was clear to the land upon which they were built was of less account than that the rents were collected. If there were damages to pay, the tenant had to foot them. Cases were "very frequent when property was in litigation, and two or three different parties were collecting rents." Of course under such circumstances "no repairs were ever made."

The climax had been reached. The situation was summed up by the Society for the Improvement of the Condition of the Poor in these words: "Crazy old buildings, crowded rear tenements in filthy yards, dark, damp basements, leaking garrets, shops, outhouses, and stables[2] converted into dwellings, though scarcely fit to shelter brutes, are habitations of thousands of our fellow-beings in this wealthy, Christian city." "The city," says its historian, Mrs. Martha Lamb, commenting on the era of aqueduct building between 1835 and 1845, "was a general asylum for vagrants." Young vagabonds, the natural offspring of such "home" conditions, overran the streets. Juvenile crime increased fearfully year by year. The Children's Aid Society and kindred philanthropic organizations were yet unborn, but in the city directory was to be found the address of the "American Society for the Promotion of Education in Africa."

THE AWAKENING

The dread of advancing cholera, with the guilty knowledge of the harvest field that awaited the plague in New York's slums, pricked the conscience of the community into action soon after the close of the war. A citizens' movement resulted in the organization of a Board of Health and the adoption of the "Tenement-House Act" of 1867, the first step toward remedial legislation. A thorough canvass of the tenements had been begun already in the previous year; but the cholera first, and next a scourge of small-pox, delayed the work, while emphasizing the need of it, so that it was 1869 before it got fairly under way and began to tell. The dark bedroom fell under the ban first. In that year the Board ordered the cutting of more than forty-six thousand windows in interior rooms, chiefly for ventilation—for little or no light was to be had from the dark hallways. Air-shafts were unknown. The saw had a job all that summer; by early fall nearly all the orders had been carried out. Not without opposition; obstacles were thrown in the way of the officials on the one side by the owners of the tenements, who saw in every order to repair or clean up only an item of added expense to diminish their income from the rent; on the other side by the tenants themselves, who had sunk, after a generation of unavailing protest, to the level of their surroundings, and were at last content to remain there. The tenements had bred their Nemesis, a proletariat ready and able to avenge the wrongs of their crowds. Already it taxed the city heavily for the support of its jails and charities. The basis of opposition, curiously enough, was the same at both extremes; owner and

---

[2] "A lot 50 x 60, contained twenty stables, rented for dwellings at $15 a year each; cost of the whole $600."

tenant alike considered official interference an infringement of personal rights, and a hardship. It took long years of weary labor to make good the claim of the sunlight to such corners of the dens as it could reach at all. Not until five years after did the department succeed at last in ousting the "cave-dwellers" and closing some five hundred and fifty cellars south of Houston Street, many of them below tide-water, that had been used as living apartments. In many instances the police had to drag the tenants out by force.

The work went on; but the need of it only grew with the effort. The Sanitarians were following up an evil that grew faster than they went; like a fire, it could only be headed off, not chased, with success. Official reports, read in the churches in 1879, characterized the younger criminals as victims of low social conditions of life and unhealthy, overcrowded lodgings, brought up in "an atmosphere of actual darkness, moral and physical." This after the saw had been busy in the dark corners ten years! "If we could see the air breathed by these poor creatures in their tenements," said a well-known physician, "it would show itself to be fouler than the mud of the gutters." Little improvement was apparent despite all that had been done. "The new tenements, that have been recently built, have been usually as badly planned as the old, with dark and unhealthy rooms, often over wet cellars, where extreme overcrowding is permitted," was the verdict of one authority. These are the houses that to-day perpetuate the worst traditions of the past, and they are counted by thousands. The Five Points had been cleansed, as far as the immediate neighborhood was concerned, but the Mulberry Street Bend was fast outdoing it in foulness not a stone's throw away, and new centres of corruption were continually springing up and getting the upper hand whenever vigilance was relaxed for ever so short a time. It is one of the curses of the tenement-house system that the worst houses exercise a levelling influence upon all the rest, just as one bad boy in a schoolroom will spoil the whole class. It is one of the ways the evil that was "the result of forgetfulness of the poor," as the Council of Hygiene mildly put it, has of avenging itself.

The determined effort to head it off by laying a strong hand upon the tenement builders that has been the chief business of the Health Board of recent years, dates from this period. The era of the air-shaft has not solved the problem of housing the poor, but it has made good use of limited opportunities. Over the new houses sanitary law exercises full control. But the old remain. They cannot be summarily torn down, though in extreme cases the authorities can order them cleared. The outrageous overcrowding, too, remains. It is characteristic of the tenements. Poverty, their badge and typical condition, invites—compels it. All efforts to abate it result only in temporary relief. As long as they exist it will exist with them. And the tenements will exist in New York forever.

To-day, what is a tenement? The law defines it as a house "occupied by three or more families, living independently and doing their cooking on the premises; or by more than two families on a floor, so living and cooking and having a common right in the halls, stairways, yards, etc." That is the legal meaning, and includes flats and apartment-houses, with which we have nothing to do. In its narrower sense the typical tenement was thus described when last arraigned before the bar of public justice: "It is generally a brick building from four to six stories high on the street, frequently with a store on the first floor which, when used for the sale of liquor, has a side opening for the benefit of the inmates and to evade the Sunday law; four families occupy each floor, and a set of rooms consists of one or two dark closets, used as bedrooms, with a living room twelve feet by ten. The staircase is too often a dark well in the centre of the house, and no direct through ventilation is possible, each family being separated from the other by partitions. Frequently the rear of the lot is occupied by another building of three stories high with two families on a floor." The picture is nearly as true to-day as ten years ago, and will be for a long time to come. The dim light admitted by the air-shaft shines upon greater crowds than ever. Tenements are still "good property," and the poverty of the poor man his destruction. A barrack down town where he *has to live* because he is poor brings in a third more rent than a decent flat house in Harlem. The statement once made a sensation that between seventy and eighty children had been found in one tenement. It no longer excites even passing attention, when the sanitary police report counting 101 adults and 91 children in a Crosby Street house, one of twins, built together. The children in the other, if I am not mistaken, numbered 89, a total of 180 for two tenements! Or when a midnight inspection in Mulberry Street unearths a hundred and fifty "lodgers" sleeping on filthy floors in two buildings. Spite of brownstone trimmings, plate-glass and mosaic vestibule floors, the water does not rise in summer to the second story, while the beer flows unchecked to the all-night picnics on the roof. The saloon with the side-door and the landlord divide the prosperity of the place between them, and the tenant, in sullen submission, foots the bills.

Where are the tenements of to-day? Say rather: where are they not? In fifty years they have crept up from the Fourth Ward slums and the Five Points the whole length of the island, and have polluted the Annexed District to the Westchester line. Crowding all the lower wards, wherever business leaves a foot of ground unclaimed; strung along both rivers, like ball and chain tied to the foot of every street, and filling up Harlem with their restless, pent-up multitudes, they hold within their clutch the wealth and business of New York, hold them at their mercy in the day of mob-rule and wrath. The bullet-proof shutters, the stacks of hand-grenades, and the Gatling guns of the Sub-Treasury are tacit admissions of the fact and of the quality of the mercy expected. The tenements to-day are New York, harboring three-fourths of its population. When another generation shall have doubled the census of our city, and to that vast army of workers, held captive by poverty, the very name of home shall be as bitter mockery, what will the harvest be?

Homestead, Incorporated

FRANK R. KRAMER

Wisconsin-born, Frank R. Kramer brought the insights of a professor of classics to the legends and folkways of his native region. His book Voices in the Valley *carries the study of Midwestern folk beliefs from the arrival of the "magnificently mad" French explorers to the precision-tooled advent of Detroit's automotive kingdom.*

The plant superintendent at Highland Park in 1914 stood watching an intricate maze of overhead trolleys, chain-driven assemblies, and moving platforms converging with measured pace.[1] As he watched, a new automobile every twenty-four seconds rolled off the terminal—the product of a synchronized magic the like of which had not been seen before. There were others, too, with an eye for mass technique—within this plant, in Chicago, Pittsburgh, in cities across the continent—who watched as invisible lines of assembly, carrying precisely interchangeable units, converged upon the production of a simplified, standardized myth.

The specifications for the myth had been drawn up by amateur and professional "engineers" scattered from farm to factory office. They ran as follows:

Motor:
An individual free to act in accordance with his own view of his
    interests and so
responsible for his own economic fate in a land of equal opportu-
    nity . . .
self-reliant . . .
working with initiative and reason (practical realism)
    to win (in wages or capital) the rewards of work . . . .

Chassis (of standard "natural law" steel):
Free enterprise operating in accordance with the competitive in-
    stinct of all mankind . . .

From Frank R. Kramer, VOICES IN THE VALLEY (Madison: The University of Wisconsin Press; copyright © 1964 by the Regents of the University of Wisconsin), pp. 163-172.

[1] Henry Ford's automobile factory near Detroit helped to revolutionize industry with mass production and assembly-line techniques.

as inexorably as the law of gravity (provided that there was no interference from government)
to achieve production regulated by supply and demand . . .

Body (from rolling-mill stock of logical argument):
Industry the source of wealth (other institutions being derivative
of industry) . . .
prime indicator of national progress (its labors, like Hercules',
performed in the service of mankind) . . .
engaged in the pursuit of self-interest and at one with the goals of
the human race (human rights are at bottom property
rights) . . .
its harmonious relations like those of the American family, its essential nature like that of the common man . . .
born with democracy in the days of the Founding Fathers and
growing side by side with freedom from that time to this . . .
in corporate form, the key to order in society; in its consistent
wholeness, the one reality in the modern world . . . valid for
all societies . . .
through its mission of raising standards of living, through its conviction that its self-interest serves the community interest, and
through its identity with democratic goals the core of American society and the most representative American way of
life . . . .

As it rolled off the assembly line, the myth gleamed in the national sunlight. There was a fascination in the myth itself; but there
was more in the factory that produced it—in the raw materials of reality, in the shapes of power forged from them, and in the folk techniques
of ideological assembly.

Above the din of the lathes and the chomp of the presses rose the
gritty hum of a remarkable machine, a drill that punctured a cylinder
block simultaneously with forty-five holes in ninety seconds. Machines
like this, said the master of Highland Park,[2] "multiply the power of
the hand"; and he had a passion for them born of the discovery of Truth.
The machine was a catalyst of freedom: it could lift "farm drudgery
off flesh and blood and lay it on steel and motors"; it gave "refine-
ments to colleges and homes; man's rise in intelligence [could] be
charted by this machine civilization."

The machines at Highland Park were stretched out as in a vast
stable—powerful organisms with a long evolution, a gestation period, a

---

[2] Henry Ford (1863-1947), whose methods of design and manufacture made his
company the first colossus of the auto industry.

dramatic birth. If they were not "the only absolute truth in the possession of mankind," they were solid segments of material reality, with "an elemental force, blindly creative, like nature."

In these Augean stables stacks of heavy castings, motor fittings, chassis frames, axles—parts for the 182,000 automobiles completed within the year—stood in endless stalls. To set them moving, as King Expansion had ordered, was a labor beyond anything the brute efficiency of machines could accomplish. Now it happened that there were two rivers flowing near Highland Park. The River of Interchangeability actually coursed through the plant itself; nearby was the River of Automatic Sequence, a smoothly flowing stream that rose in the land of flour milling and meandered through harvests of wheat fields. In a matter of months these rivers were channelled together and loosed upon the stables. They began slowly—a trickle of magneto assemblies; then a flood of steel strips and automobiles poured out.

Here, as it seemed to the men at Highland Park, and as some philosophers had always insisted, was a different kind of reality. It was not the reality made up of things: raw materials, machines, and even men (since they were interchangeable now) were no longer real in themselves but only in so far as they were channelled into an automatic pattern. The new reality was Process, a technique with incredible power. "It [was] this pattern that [was] actually productive, not the individual." The man who installed it in his plant called it the "New Messiah," a power that would change the world.

It was the pattern that was productive. But to the plant superintendent charged with seeing that each belt and trolley ran at precisely the right speed, that the assembly line reached each station at precisely the right moment, the pattern itself rested on the exact, inexorable cycles of time. Six feet every sixty seconds: that was the ultimate arbiter, and every operation in the plant was geared to it. Like a mammoth clock, Highland Park was the embodiment of the greatest of abstract symbols.

In the drafting room, in the pattern and experimental departments, men were busily manipulating other symbols. These symbols had no weight, shape, color, or extension, though they stood for things that did. They were self-contained essences having no necessary connection even with the things they stood for, things that might rot or rust. They were like letters of a word: the letters were everlastingly good though the word might change or die. There had to be symbols before there could be machines and assembly lines.

Highland Park was sailing, as once Hercules had sailed in quest of the fat cattle of Geryon, in Apollo's golden bowl. Now of all the symbols that made up the bowl, the cleverest was the stock certificate, a symbol of two other symbols—currency and certificates of ownership. With a paper properly marked with these abstractions "a man who had never seen a locomotive could say that he had a railroad in his pocket." Last year a man had died who had in his pocket not only railroads but steel mills, a legend whose international influence proved just how powerful these abstractions could be.[3] This year they were turning out an ominous flood of Chevrolets.

But enterprises like railroads, said the directors of Highland Park, were too often "factors in the stock market"; they were "run . . . from banking offices." And having a railroad in one's pocket was of small value unless it hauled supplies to the plant. Stock symbols could tie a company up with banking corporations or with other companies, and that must never be. The directors had only to look around them to see the potentialities of concentrated power. They could see it in general motors combinations, in steel, lumber, meat packing, and flour milling —combinations that were closing the frontiers of enterprise so rapidly that Congress had become alarmed and, in the last two years, had tried grimly to curb them. But there were other ways of organizing them than by weaving a horizontal network of interests. They had organized step by vertical step—making their own parts, treating the ore in their own furnaces, buying their own coal and iron mines—moving steadily through every stage of production in a vast spiral of integration.

Highland Park was an ascending ring of production, an inverted pyramid of departmental divisions. But it was immensely more: it was a coiled synthesis—machines, symbols, process—of realities and powers. Watching the growth of this automatic, autonomous structure with its own laws of being, men noted that it was a state within a state.

> Another plant on a somewhat larger scale is in building at Flat Rock. . . . We have dammed the river. The dam also serves as a bridge for the Detroit, Toledo & Ironton Railway, which was in need of a new bridge at that point, and a road for the public—all in one construction. We are going to make our glass at this point. The damming of the river gives sufficient water for the floating to us of most of our raw material. It also gives us our power through a hydro-electric plant. . . . The men will have plots of ground or farms as well as their jobs in the factory, and these can be scattered over fifteen or twenty miles surrounding—for of course nowadays the workingman can come to the shop in an automobile.

---

[3] J.P. Morgan, financier and industrial magnate, died in March, 1913.

On a stretch of farm land fifteen miles from Detroit an industrial homestead would soon be springing up—like many other factory communities except, perhaps, that the Engineer at Highland Park had carefully planned it. He had selected the land ("everything," he said, "is produced from the earth"); then he had dammed the river and bridged it to bring in materials and generate power for manufacturing. "There we shall have the combination of agriculture and industrialism," he promised; these two, along with transportation, "hold the world together."

The homestead at Flat Rock would be a little world in itself, held together by growing things, making things, and carrying things. The men would have farms as well as their jobs in the factory: farms, after all, were the greatest of factories—no mere rural occupation but the business of raising food. On idyllic acres reaching out fifteen or twenty miles from the glass plant, the Engineer could see men "working with material which we did not and could not create, but which was presented to us by Nature," putting into their farms "the human element which makes the fruitful seasons of the earth useful to men." He could see them unconsciously working out the economic and the moral fundamentals:

> For the day's work is a great thing—a very great thing! It is at the very foundation of the world. . . . Work is our sanity, our self-respect, our salvation. . . .

They would be driving in from their farms as the morning sun glinted off the bridge over the dam and taking their places at the machines. The machines would be spaced with ultimate precision—no space, no time wasted. "The most beautiful things in the world," said the Engineer, "are those from which all excess . . . has been eliminated"; "cut out useless parts and simplify necessary ones." And this, too, was an economic and moral fundamental.

The Engineer studied the blueprints of his industrial homestead. The plans were as steely bright as the rails of the Toledo and Ironton Railway; they had all the concentrated economy of the dam that was also a road and a bridge, that provided both draft for transportation and power for production; they were as translucent as the glass that would soon be moving in continuous sheets over semi-automatic rollers. Here as at Highland Park ("a department is a little factory in itself") men and machines would be perfectly synchronized; in an organization in which "one part is so dependent upon another," the men would move in a tightly disciplined, coolly impersonal pattern. No stubborn Dionysius stood in the way of realizing this industrial Republic. On the farmland at Flat Rock its logistical precision of work and technique would presently be emerging, clean and clear as a mathematician's dream, on the foundation of economic and moral certainties. It would be a world complete and self-contained, a rational homestead.

Cut out useless parts and simplify necessary ones. In the Engineer's homestead there was nothing that did not reduce to the great One of production, to making and transporting things. This was the dam that supplied the power, the machines that, like books, gave men ideas, the awesome precision of symbols; the continuity of assembly— "a lever to move the world"; the mainspring of integration. There were moments when the Engineer seemed to see human nature itself as a creative power. A man's "personality" had little to do with whether he had "been in Sing Sing or at Harvard," whether he had come from Chicago or Czechoslovakia; its essence was his "rate of production." This was his guide in his work, his status in the shop, the ratio of his intrinsic value. Symbols, too, whatever their original shade, took on the same productive coloration: "time is money," money is a "part of our transportation system," an "engine of production." Even the necessary parts had been simplified in the industrial homestead at Flat Rock.

The elements of the Engineer's Republic now building here were meticulously tooled: they were interchangeable with Flat Rock or Highland Park plants anywhere—or even, the Engineer thought, with the structure of society itself. He could see the nation tooled on the pattern of Flat Rock: "We want those who can mould the political, social, industrial, and moral mass into a sound and shapely whole. . . . We want men who can create the working design for all that is right and good and desirable in our life," men who can plan the nation's progress with the logic of plant management ("each step has to be regulated"), whose dream of universal justice can be realized by perfecting the wage system.

In the Engineer's eyes, the good society was simply an extension of the carefully regulated power and process that hummed so smoothly in the plant, the "working design" of the truths he had discovered there. For these revelations were not only for Flat Rock; they were universally true.

> There is something sacred about wages [the myth was moving in absolutes]—they represent homes and families and domestic destinies. . . . Wages are bread boxes and coal bins, babies' cradles and children's education—family comforts and contentment. . . . There is something just as sacred about capital which is used to provide the means by which work can be made productive. . . .

This was no part of the blueprint, a design that stripped human nature to the productive bone. But the Engineer (as makers of rational myths have always done) was putting back the flesh—cradles, education, contentment—on the skeleton he had constructed. The pulse of life was the reward of work—wages and capital; they were the primal urge, and they were sacred.

"Every spirit builds itself a house," another individualist had said. The rational homestead that the Engineer was building seemed to him "the mainstay of all the finer things which the home represents"; there was "something just as sacred about a shop that employs thousands of men as there is about a home."

> When one looks about . . . at the young workingmen who, on the strength of their jobs are marrying and setting up for themselves, at the thousands of homes that are being paid for on installments . . . when one looks at a great productive organization that is enabling all these things to be done, then the continuance of that business becomes a holy trust.

The myth was complete—a sound and shapely whole. The Engineer's horological soul had discovered its chronometrical truth, and upon it he was building his industrial homestead. It was a homestead in which young men who were expressing their essential natures in productive work might live in exact social justice among the comforts that spilled out of the cornucopia of the shop, fired with the fervor of keeping as a holy trust the business that made these bounties possible. It was a world in which these young men might rest secure in the realization that "business is a reality" with its own immutable laws ("the laws of business are like the laws of gravity") or, rather, a synthesis of realities, each with its special form of power. These were the logical absolutes—the steel frame of a chassis that would support the body not alone of industry but of the nation itself.

The Engineer's ideas had been born on a Michigan farm; they had grown up in the myth of valley and prairie—the myth that machines were "hired hands" to lighten the work, that they were created to increase the yield and the market, that they were the natural fulfillment of the promise of the homestead. But the articles of the myth had been transferred one by one from the vignette of the farm to the panorama of the factory. The change was embodied in the workman at Flat Rock whose shoes carried the soil of his farm plot into the plant. It was not on his farm that he symbolized the genuine American. It was the synchronized pattern of his work at the plant that made him the prime producer of the wealth that built homes, schools, and churches. The homestead had been incorporated.

The process of incorporation was the classic one of rational myth-making. The Engineer had Yankee notions; reason was at the root of things; the world was made up of rational units condensed in rational symbols. He had Emerson's horological soul, and the world was made in its image. He had the Platonic vision of society as a rational One like free enterprise, a "tightly integrated, consistent system" . . . "homogeneous in time and space."

This was the rational myth, as remote from other myths as a Yankee peddler's cart from a Conestoga wagon, or as an anemoscope from an Indian's finger moistened to the wind. And yet all mythmaking—from the Hurons' forest lore to the creed of a Detroit industrialist—follows the same folk trails; and the same winds blow spring on all men's dreams. The Engineer, like a Mennonite farmer, made of his world a simple, understandable whole; like a Southern Appalachian settler, he fitted together facts—and ideas—by analogy.

It would not be long before this folk "science" would reduce the life of every American—whether he was buying and selling, marking a ballot, enjoying his home and friends, or worshipping Providence—to the pattern and principles of free enterprise. Business would soon become one with progress, with freedom and patriotism, with the family and "the people," and finally with the divine plan for a happier humanity. What was true of each of these would be true of business, and what belonged to the nature of business would belong to each of these. And soon this streamlined System would be extended, as once farmers had extended the ideal of the homestead to include the nation, to every crosspath of American life. The blood of business would seem to run through the body of the nation; its ideals would be those of society itself, its way "the American way."

The way of business would come to appear to the men of business as immutable as the path of the stars; it would appear to follow orbits of economics and of human nature, to gleam for all men in every century. It would seem to rest on a self-adjusting equilibrium, to be, in a word, "natural." And the nature of business—a rationally ordered System homogeneous in space and time—would emerge as "reality," a System releasing the tremendous power of technology and technological integration. In the naves of banquet halls, in the pulpits of public forums and the choir lofts of the press, the liturgy of the myth would give homage to the glory of reality and to its all-embracing power.

QUESTIONS

1a. Ivan Doig's article argues that there has been a historical pattern of distrust of the cities. What evidence is there of such distrust today, or is there any?

  b. The United States still is one of the least densely populated nations of the Western world. With our expanse of territory, why do you think we have become such an urban civilization? What is there about cities that makes people crowd into them?

  c. Two criticisms sometimes made about the American grid pattern of streets are that it breaks up neighborhoods with artificial lines and that traffic is impeded by its numerous intersections. What are some arguments in favor of the grid pattern? Do you think this pattern and others discussed in the Doig article have made life easier or harder for today's city dwellers? Why?

2a. What good and bad qualities does Mrs. Trollope find in the Americans she encounters? What features of Cincinnati life seem most unusual to her?

  b. Do you find anything in today's city life that seems to agree with Mrs. Trollope's assessment of American character and behavior, or have citified Americans changed dramatically? In what ways do you yourself fit or not fit her view of Americans?

3a. How does "Letter from the North" compare with Mrs. Trollope's viewpoint?

  b. What urban features described by Jones would be different today? Which ones would be similar?

  c. If you live in or near a city, or have visited one lately, write your own analysis, in the manner of Trollope or Jones, of what you think "Americans" are like. Like the two authors, don't hesitate to use sweeping generalizations as well as specific details.

4a. In 1907, the year of Henry Roth's vignette, a record million immigrants came ashore to the "golden land." Thousands who arrived at Ellis Island stayed on to live in New York. What details used by the author show the strangeness of the new land for the immigrants? How much is it the city itself that overwhelms the newcomers he describes?

  b. What tensions seem to be in the newcomers on the dock? Why does Albert act the way he does? Why does his wife?

5a. The four examples of big-city political bosses are spaced across nearly a century, yet they have many similarities. What are the continuing features of city life that have enabled them to hold power?

b. One theme of Mike Royko's article is the gathering and wielding of power. From his description of Mayor Daley's day, which of the mayor's uses of power would you approve of as a resident of his city, and which wouldn't you? In each case, explain why.

6. Earlier in the book, articles by Claude Brown and James Baldwin described aspects of modern tenement life. Compare Riis's description with theirs, or with some other contemporary view such as Michael Harrington's in his book *The Other America* (see ch. 8, "Old Slums, New Slums"). What details of life in each case seem to you similar, or significantly different? Now compare your own neighborhood and way of life with those you have just examined. Again, what details do you think similar or significantly different?

7. Frank R. Kramer shows that an era's myths grow out of its past experiences, as with the beliefs carried over from the homestead to the factory. What are our current beliefs about work and opportunity? How do they compare with those described by Kramer?

FURTHER SOURCES

A number of helpful books about urban history are available. Arthur M. Schlesinger, Sr., is notable for being one of the earliest historians to focus on urban America; see his *The Rise of the City, 1878-1898* (The Macmillan Co., 1933). Two studies of the era when our cities were growing into metropolises are *The Response to Industrialism, 1885-1914*, by Samuel P. Hays (University of Chicago Press, 1957) and *The Search for Order, 1877-1920*, by Robert H. Wiebe (Hill and Wang, 1967). An excellent study of how American town sites originated is *The Making of Urban America*, by John W. Reps (Princeton University Press, 1965); a shorter version by the same author is *Town Planning in Frontier America* (Princeton University Press, 1969). A fine television documentary series on the growth of the United States is *America: A Personal History of the United States, by Alistair Cooke* (Time-Life Films, 100 Eisenhower Drive, Paramus, N.J. 07652). A documentary which could be used to compare modern tenement life with the past is *The Tenement* (Carousel Films, 1501 Broadway, New York, N.Y. 10036).

Street of Dreams, Street of Life *Ivan Doig* For a careful, detailed study of the growth of a single city, see *A History of Chicago*, by Bessie L. Pierce (3 volumes, Alfred A. Knopf, 1937-1957). A good study of early frontier cities is *The Urban Frontier*, by Richard C. Wade (Harvard University Press, 1959). Vivid description of 19th century city life can be found in *Immigrant Life in New York City, 1825-1863*, by Robert Ernst (Columbia University Press, 1949).

Cincinnati *Frances Trollope* Perhaps the most famous observations of America by a foreign visitor are in Alexis de Tocqueville, *Democracy in America* (available in many editions; an abridged version is the Washington Square Press edition, 1964, in paperback).

Letter from the North *Charles C. Jones, Jr.* The letters of the Jones family make a remarkable source of social history from 1854 to 1867. They have been painstakingly collected and edited by Robert Manson Myers in the massive volume *The Children of Pride* (Yale University Press, 1972).

I Pray Thee Ask No Questions, This Is That Golden Land *Henry Roth* The story begun on the docks of New York continues in the novel *Call It Sleep* (Avon Books, 1965). For an article about Roth's unusual writing career, see "The Belated Success of Henry Roth," by Jane Howard, *Life*, Jan. 8, 1965, pp. 75-76. A general history of immigration is *The Uprooted*, by Oscar Handlin (Little, Brown, 1951). "The Huddled Masses," episode 9 of the Alistair Cooke series mentioned above, is an excellent documentary on this topic.

The Bosses Each of these political figures is featured in at least one book. See: *Plunkitt of Tammany Hall*, recorded by William L. Riordon (E.P. Dutton & Co., 1963); *Boss Ruef's San Francisco*, by Walton Bean (University of California Press, 1967); and *Boss*, Mike Royko's book on Mayor Richard J. Daley of Chicago (New American Library, 1971). Numerous articles about Daley are indexed in *Readers' Guide to Periodical Literature* over the past twenty years. A famous exposé of bossism at the turn of the century is *The Shame of the Cities*, by Lincoln Steffens (Hill and Wang, 1963).

How the Other Half Lives *Jacob A. Riis* Many articles by Riis can be found in magazines of the 1890s and the first decade of this century. For a biography, see *Jacob A. Riis*, by Louise Ware (Appleton-Century, 1938). A vivid book about growing up in a tenement district is Michael Gold's *Jews Without Money* (Tower Publications, 1930).

Homestead, Incorporated *Frank R. Kramer* A critical biography of Henry Ford and the automobile empire he founded is *Ford*, by Booton Herndon (Weybright and Talley, 1969). Also see: *The Reputation of the American Businessman*, by Sigmund Diamond (Harvard University Press, 1955), and *The American Business Creed*, by Francis X. Sutton et al. (Harvard University Press, 1956).

PART 4

WHERE NEXT?

INTRODUCTION

Guessing ahead about urban life is a game with plenty of defeats guaranteed. Whenever grandiose visions of the city of the future are pronounced, it should be recalled that the learned among us have been trying to outguess tomorrow for a very long time. Consider the first Europeans to make a broad mark on this continent—the Spaniards, with their long sweep of influence across the southern reaches of this continent from St. Augustine to San Francisco. They came and planted their communities according to the first great master plan of the New World: the Laws of the Indies proclaimed by King Philip II in 1573. The Laws were a meticulous "how to" guide for selecting town sites, even for where and why to place the important buildings. (In coastal towns the church should be near the harbor to double as fortification against attack from the sea; at inland sites the church should be high on a hill to command respect.) The lasting glory of the Laws, surviving even yet to grace many of the towns laid out by the Spaniards some centuries ago, is the central plaza. Long and roomy, a fine centerpiece for downtown life, it stands as lovely testimony to the foresight of those original wise planners. That is, until you read closely in the Laws of the Indies to check on precisely what the omniscient Spaniards had in mind with such spacious plazas: ". . . this proportion is the best for festivals in which horses are used."

It is a reminder that we need some wariness about the profession of looking ahead. Besides the possibility of being wrong, the expert may turn out to have been right for some wrong reason—which is not very reassuring about the process of prediction. Accordingly, the future-watchers chosen here have been selected for the amounts of yesterday and today they straightforwardly include in their crystal-balling, and the skepticism is to be added in whatever amounts seem needed. Part Four, predictably, gathers observations about where the cities may be trending, and advice about how some matters might be made better.

Tomorrow comes faster these days than it did yesterday, Alvin Toffler advises us, and the quickened pace puts us off stride. In "New York Faces Future Shock" he discusses the anxieties which continual change inflicts on the city-dweller.

Eopolis, polis, metropolis, megalopolis, tyrannapolis, nekropolis. Village community to the city of death. Lewis Mumford takes a long historical look at the urban "Cycle of Growth and Decay," and offers a few "possibilities of renewal."

But what does the individual do in the enormous hive of humanity? Is there virtue in anonymity and balm in mobility? Harvey Cox discusses the privacy of multitudes and other angles in "The Shape of the Secular City."

The message from Jane Jacobs is simple: stop thinking huge. Stop tinkering neighborhoods into high-rise sameness like rows of giant suitcases. In "The Generators of Diversity," she lists the four conditions needed so "city life will get its best chances."

Edward C. Banfield poses the radical idea that our cities are doing okay, and that in fact the metropolitan citizenry is better off than ever. Attacking the cries of crisis, he sets out to tell us what's right about "The Unheavenly City."

"What if" is one of the incessant little haunts which keeps residence in the human head. In his short story "The Law," Robert M. Coates offers us a tongue-in-cheek "what if" about our urban behavior.

New York Faces Future Shock

ALVIN TOFFLER

As a writer interested in social trends, Alvin Toffler put the phrase "future shock" front and center in the America of the 1970s. His best-selling book of that title helped to focus dismay about the tempos of change in our more and more urban society.

"Hey, there's a naked man on the street corner!" And so there was, 8:30 in the morning, a Monday in June. Right there at the corner of 77th and Madison where Parke-Bernet stares blankly across the street at the Carlyle Hotel. My daughter Karen and I peered out our fifth-story window, blinking with amusement and disbelief at the sounds rising from below. Not from the naked man. (He was tall, rather handsome from the distance, light-brown in color, and stark to the soles of his feet.) But the screams emanating from some little old dowagers. The fingers pointing in horror. A Lord & Taylor lady standing directly alongside him at the traffic light, looking straight ahead, but stealing little glances out of the corners of her eyes. The three pubescent Puerto Rican girls who ran to a police cruiser and who, as the man strode majestically east toward Park Avenue, could be heard telling the cops, amid little gasps of pleasure, that "He went that way!"

A little piece of the future arrived in New York that morning. Not the nudity, but the novelty. For if one thing can be safely predicted about the coming years, it is that our lives will be subjected to an accelerating stream of surprises—including some big ones. Millions of perfectly normal people are going to be jolted out of their jobs, their neighborhoods, their daily routines. New values, vocabularies, sights, sounds, crises and lifestyles are going to test our capacity for coping.

New York, where the Hard Hats are edgier, the cabbies more frazzled, the kids more strung out, and the smell of nervous breakdown pervades the air, is also the place where the future arrives ahead of schedule, and there is a distinct connection between this fact and our burgeoning civic troubles. Whatever its other problems may be, New York is an early victim of future shock.

Future shock is not listed in any of the orthodox catalogues of physical or social ills. It is still too new. Yet it may well turn out to be the most devastating urban disease of tomorrow, and millions of New Yorkers are first in line, as usual. They display confusional breakdown, mounting anxiety, erratic swings of purpose, and a panicky urge to escape from it all, to cop out, opt out, get out. They complain that they "can't cope." Some also exhibit the "paradoxical" behavior that Pavlov reported in his famous experiments: they produce a mushroom cloud of emotion to deal with a molehill of inconvenience. Bus drivers, storekeepers, strap-hangers, politicians, police and teenagers all too often fly into senseless rage.

Anthropologists know that unprepared travelers who find themselves suddenly plunged into an alien culture often break out in a rash of physical and psychological problems. Linguist Robert Maston, who has worked in dozens of countries and trained Peace Corps volunteers, tells of a girl who arrived on an island in the Far East and, within a few hours, found herself unable to breathe, eat or drink. She had to be shipped right back home.

"Culture shock" is what happens when the individual suddenly finds himself in an environment in which things no longer make sense, in which the signs, customs, cues and rules are all switched. The impact of sudden change leaves the person anxious, bewildered and apathetic. According to psychologist Sven Lundstedt, he begins to long desperately for "an environment in which the gratification of important psychological and physical needs is predictable."

It is hard to read formal descriptions of this malady without instantly recognizing how well they apply to millions of New Yorkers. The construction workers who marched down Wall Street, it seems reasonable to believe, also wanted a more "predictable environment." Their neighborhoods, jobs, and kids are changing rapidly—pumping unwelcome novelty into their lives.

The fact is that you don't need to travel to Baluchistan to suffer from an overdose of newsness anymore. You can stay right in Sheepshead Bay or the Upper East Side or Pelham and the novelty comes at you. Indeed, the future is arriving so swiftly that, for all practical purposes, we are superimposing a new, alien culture, with new values, esthetics, politics, sexual roles, on top of the old one—Baluchistan in Bensonhurst, if you will. And we are doing it so fast that we are creating culture shock in our own society—future shock.

Three powerful forces are changing New York, altering the psychological landscape of the city. Until we learn to recognize them, we won't be able to make sense of, let alone solve, our urban crises. These three powerful forces are: acceleration, novelty, and diversity.

The first of these, the accelerative thrust, has to do with the pace at which we New Yorkers live our lives, which is to say, faster than anyone else. All of us know in the pit of our stomach that the pace of life is quickening. We seldom stop, however, to correlate this fact with some of the larger-than-life forces loose in the world as a whole.

In 1850 there were only four cities on earth with a population in excess of 1 million. By 1900, the number had increased to 19. By 1960, it had skyrocketed to 141. World urban population has been estimated to be rising since then at a rate of 6.5 per cent annually. This doesn't seem like much, unless you happen to be familiar with the compound interest tables, in which case you know that anything increasing at that rate doubles in 11 years.

One way to grasp the meaning of change on so phenomenal a scale is to imagine what would happen if all existing cities—including New York—were to retain their present size. If this were so, in order to accommodate the new urban millions we would have to build a duplicate city for each of the hundreds that already dot the globe. A new New York, Tokyo, London, a new Rome and Rangoon—all in 11 years.

If we look at rates of population-increase and knowledge-acquisition, the same powerful accelerative trend is evident. The pace at which new chemical elements are discovered, the pace at which books and scientific papers are published, are both curving up and off the graph. The figures for consumption of energy, for speeds of transport, for explosive power—all, once more, show exponential rates of increase.

Even more dramatic is the escalation of the pace at which new technology floods into the environment. It is true, of course, that "90 per cent of all the scientists who ever lived are now alive" and that the laboratories are pumping out breakthroughs by the bushel. What is more important, however, is that those discoveries are diffused more swiftly so that the lead time for adjustment to them is slashed.

Robert B. Young of the Stanford Research Institute studied the history of several familiar household appliances. He measured the span of time between the moment an appliance was first introduced and the time when the industry manufacturing it reached peak production of the item. He found that, for a group of appliances introduced in the U.S. before 1920—including the vacuum cleaner, the electric range and the refrigerator—the average span between introduction and peak production was 34 years. But for a group that appeared between 1929 and 1959—including the electric frying pan, television and the washer-dryer combination—the span of time was sliced to eight years. The spread of the transistor radio, tape cassettes and more recent technical innovations has been even faster.

The accelerative thrust forces *time* into a new prominence in our lives. It compels us to make and break our relationships with the environment at a faster and faster tempo. It telescopes the duration of our relationships with things, places, and people—and this, as we shall see, provides a vital clue to the sources of future shock.

When we speak of the pace of daily life, what we actually mean is the rate at which things, places, people and other components of the environment turn over in our lives. It is the duration of our relationships with each of these that, in fact, determines the pace of life, and New Yorkers tend to have shorter, more temporary links with the environment than anyone else.

This becomes clear if we start by looking at our relationship with *things.* Even our ties with architecture, precisely that part of the physical environment that in the past contributed most heavily to man's sense of permanence, are now more short-lived. We tear down neighborhoods and put up new ones at a mind-numbing rate.

A few years ago my wife sent my daughter, then 12, to an A & P supermarket a few blocks from our East Side apartment. Our little girl had been there only once or twice before. Half an hour later she returned, perplexed. "It must have been torn down," she said. "I couldn't find it." It hadn't been. New to the neighborhood, Karen had merely looked on the wrong block. But she is a child of the Age of Transience, and her assumption—that the building had been razed and replaced—was a natural one for a 12-year-old growing up in New York at this time.

That the duration of our ties with the physical environment is shrinking is also underscored by the rise of the whole throwaway economy. Technology leads to physical objects that are cheaper to throw away than to repair, so that a child growing up in America today, especially New York, finds himself surrounded by all kinds of things that pass into and out of his life at a rapid clip. Diapers, bibs, paper napkins, Kleenex, towels, non-returnable soda bottles are all used up quickly in the home and ruthlessly eliminated. The child quickly learns that home is a processing machine through which objects flow, entering and leaving at a faster and faster rate of speed. From birth on, he is embedded inextricably in a throwaway culture. We have throwaway paper wedding gowns to go with throwaway marriages. Our links with things are telescoped in time.

The rental revolution goes hand in hand with the trend toward disposability. The link between disposable diapers, apartments by Lefrak and cars by Hertz may seem obscure at first glance, but rentalism, too, intensifies the transience of our environmental relationships.

Apartment living, the standard in New York, is now, for a variety of reasons, "in" elsewhere. (In 1969, for the first time in the United States, more building permits were issued for apartment construction than for private homes.) It is particularly in among young people, who, in the words of M.I.T. Professor Burnham Kelly, want "minimum-involvement housing."

At the same time, the spectacular rise of auto rentals telescopes the duration of the average relationship between driver and car. And the rise of auto rentals has been paralleled by the emergence of a new kind of general store—one which sells nothing but rents everything. In New York, consumers now rent gowns, crutches, jewels, TV sets, camping equipment, air conditioners, wheelchairs, linens, skis, tape recorders, champagne fountains and silverware, and the East Side is dotted with "swinging pads" filled with rented furniture.

Just as we are speeding up the turnover of things in our lives, we are also ephemeralizing our connections with *places*. The average rural person, even the average New Yorker in the past, used to stay very much put. Today most of us are moving around at high speed, like particles in an accelerator, so that our psychological and physical ties with any one place grow less and less durable. New York is filled with executive "high-mobiles" for whom repeated residential relocation is simply an accepted part of the job. The *Wall Street Journal* refers to "corporate gypsies" in an article headlined HOW EXECUTIVE FAMILY ADAPTS TO INCESSANT MOVING ABOUT COUNTRY. It describes the life of M.E. Jacobson, an executive with Montgomery Ward. He and his wife, both 46 at the time the story appeared, had moved 28 times in 26 years of married life. "I almost feel like we're just camping," his wife tells her visitors. Their case is atypical, but in 70 major U.S. cities, including New York, average residence in one place is less than four years. Contrast this with the lifelong residence in one place characteristic of the rural villager. Moreover, residential relocation is critical in determining the duration of many other place relationships, so that when a New Yorker terminates his ties with one apartment or home, he usually also terminates his relationship with all kinds of "satellite" places in the neighborhood. He changes his supermarket, gas stations, bus stop and barbershop, cutting short a lot of other place links at the same time. Across the board, therefore, we not only experience more places in the course of a lifetime, but, on the average, maintain our links with each place for a shorter and shorter interval.

Here we begin to see more clearly how the accelerative thrust in society, and particularly in the mega-cities of the technologically hot nations, affects the individual. For this telescoping of man's relationship with place precisely parallels the truncation of his relationship with things. In both cases, the individual is compelled to forge and fracture ties more rapidly. In both cases he experiences a quickening of the pace of life. In both cases, for reasons that will become apparent, the risk of future shock rises.

If the typical New Yorker is making and breaking his ties with things and places more rapidly than, say, a typical resident of Springfield, Missouri, he also is making and breaking ties with *people* at a faster clip. Urban sociologists from Weber to Wirth have talked about the impersonality of human ties in the city. Contemporary behavioral scientists worry about crowding. The problem, however, may not lie in urbanism or in population density, as such. If we want to understand impersonality and alienation in the city, it may be we ought to focus on the rates of turnover involved. For the shortening *duration* of our ties has a hidden, powerful impact on the emotional quality of these ties. Indeed, it may be impossible to understand what is happening to human relationships in America—and New York in particular—unless we examine their duration.

The fact is that the average urban person today deals with more people in the course of a month than a feudal peasant dealt with in a lifetime, and, as the number of different people we deal with grows, the average duration of a relationship shrinks. This doesn't mean that city people don't have old friends, college buddies, or long-lasting ties of other kinds. But these are no longer typical; they are exceptions to the rule.

The greater the mobility of the individual, the greater the number of brief, face-to-face encounters, human contacts—each one a relationship of sorts, fragmentary and, above all, compressed in time. (Such contacts appear natural and unimportant to us. We seldom stop to consider how few of the 66 billion human beings who preceded us on this planet experienced this high rate of transience in their human ties.)

Job mobility is another force increasing the turnover of people in our lives. Even with the present recession, and in some cases because of it, people are switching jobs at a frantic rate. One big management research firm recently estimated that 85 per cent of the nation's executives are "on the prowl." A survey of 209 U.S. banks indicated that virtually half of the college graduates they hire leave within five years. Head-hunters swap stories about job-hopping M.B.A.s, and down at less skilled levels of labor, the turnover rate in some companies is awesome. *Fortune* reports that at Ford Motor Company, the quit-rate last year was 25.2 per cent. In the Bronx the figure for operators in the traffic department of New York Telephone is 66 per cent.

The epitome of job transience is found in a novel industry that has grown up alongside the Hertzes and Avises. For we now rent not only things, but people as well. Something like 500 companies in the U.S. now "rent" workers to industry—laborers, secretaries, engineers, models—people who step into a new job for a few hours or a few weeks, then plug out. S.A. Russo, Jr., president of American Girl Service, one of the larger "temp" companies, says, "A successful temporary worker not only has to have ordinary job skills, or learn them fast, but must know how to make and break relationships with other people rapidly."

Throughout the high-technology nations, but particularly in the mega-cities like New York, we find, therefore, the same relentless pressure toward temporary human ties. And so it goes, a process of continual temporal contraction. Instead of conversations, we send high-speed communiqués back and forth among ourselves, and we search for all sorts of magic to accelerate friendship: encounter groups, sensitivity training, group-grope, sex-on-the-run, all intended to produce instant intimacy in a high-transience environment.

Transience is the psychological counterpart of, the necessary consequence of, the accelerative thrust. The more temporary our ties, whether with things, places, or people, the faster the daily pace becomes. Some people, of course, are deeply attracted to this quicker, more active pace. In fact, some go far out of their way to bring it about and feel anxious, tense or uncomfortable when the pace slows. They want desperately to be "where the action is." (Some hardly care what the action is, so long as it occurs at a rapid clip.)

But if some people thrive on the new, rapid pace, many are fiercely repelled by it. For a long time the hunger for a faster pace of life— more turnover—made New York the mecca for executives on the make. Today many of them would rather be fired than relocate here, partly for precisely the reason that the pace has gotten too fast for sanity. Jay Perry, the whiz-kid block trader at Salomon Brothers & Hutzler, tells of a $40,000-a-year financial executive from Atlanta who was offered a job in New York at twice the pay with a promise of another doubling within a year or two. He flatly refused. Perry himself, sitting alongside you on the TWA flight from London (he's almost a regular commuter), will complain feelingly about the way the pace is getting out of control.

The quickening pace of life, however, is not felt by the upper middle class or the rich alone. The same pressure to hurry up—adapt quickly to novelty—is felt by the secretary, the salesman, the garment worker, and the Staten Island housewife. The hustle and bustle is intensifying, and it is more and more difficult to escape.

If squares in New York are beginning to resent or resist the constant speed-up, they are only discovering what the longhairs seem to have discovered a few years earlier. Thus the quietism and search for new ways to "opt out" or "cop out" that characterize certain (though not all) hippies may be less motivated by their loudly expressed aversion to the values of a technological civilization than by an unconscious effort to escape from a pace of life that many find intolerable. It is not accidental that they describe society as a "rat race"—a term that refers quite specifically to pacing.

What the accelerative thrust adds up to, therefore, in the life of the average New Yorker is not only a high level of transience or impermanence, but a demand for faster and faster adaptation, an ability to handle crises faster than other people, a constant pressure to make decisions faster. The accelerative thrust is felt soonest in New York and it has its most powerful impact here. But it is only the first component of the adaptive crisis called future shock.

If New Yorkers only had to cope with a speed-up in the pace of decision-making, the problems of living here would be much simpler. Speed by itself, however, is not the crusher. It is the combination of acceleration plus another environmental characteristic—*novelty*—that intensifies the stress of urban life. Novelty is the second ingredient in the combustible mix of forces that is now producing future shock in our midst.

It is one thing to cope with routine or familiar situations and crises at a faster tempo. It is quite another to cope with non-routine, strange, unfamiliar, even bizarre, situations and crises—and that is what, increasingly, we are forced to do. The environment is always a balance of old and new, familiar and unfamiliar. Today, however, in New York, as in most of the other technology-rich urban centers, the level of novelty is rising. The novelty-ratio is changing.

This is true at the level of technology, for example, so that New York, as a city, is now compelled to adapt itself in rapid succession to jumbo jets (it hasn't even digested the ordinary jets yet), nuclear power generators, and to a blazing stream of equally important innovations. Computers are revolutionizing Wall Street. Communications companies, from CBS and NBC to ITT and AT&T, are desperately trying to cope with advances in satellite technology and other transmission systems. Industries like printing, publishing and apparel manufacture are undergoing similarly rapid technological change, with upsetting consequences for the various unions involved. The fashion industry has to deal not merely with sudden new tastes and trends, many of them self-generated, but with new materials that simply never existed before—new plastics and fibers with strange and novel qualities.

All this directly influences the daily life of ordinary people, presenting them with new products to be marketed or bought, new forms of competition, new roles, new patterns of organization. For one thing, the rising level of novelty threatens every bureaucracy and leads to a shift toward a totally new form of organization in business and government, a kinetic form that I call "adhocracy." It also translates into a new job picture. A look at the help-wanted pages of any New York newspaper brings home the fact that novel occupations are emerging at a rapid rate. Systems analyst, console operator, coder, tape librarian, tape handler, are only a few of those recently created by the computer revolution.

When *Fortune* in the mid-sixties surveyed 1,003 young executives employed by major corporations, it found that fully one out of three held a job that simply had not existed until he stepped into it. Another large group held positions that had been filled by only one incumbent before them. Even when the name of the occupation stays the same, the content of the work is frequently transformed and the people filling the job change or do a fantastic amount of learning and relearning.

But the exploding novelties that confront New Yorkers every day of the week are not limited to their jobs. Strange new events and dilemmas spring at us out of the social setting itself, invading our private micro-environments, demanding attention and rational explanation. New social forms erupt into being—urban communes like the one run by some Jesuit friends of mine on upper Broadway, free universities, guerrilla theatres, Black Panther-run nurseries. New movements, each shorter-lived than the last, leap into the headlines, from the Young Lords and Red Stockings to the Italian American Civil Rights League. We are constantly forced to rearrange the image-structures in our heads to make sense of the swirling phantasmagoria around us.

One day it is the naked man on the street corner, the next it is a washline of blue nurses' uniforms strung from building to building in the Cornell medical complex, part of the anti-war protest. ("Never seen nothing like it," my cabdriver grumbles, and he is not amused at the task of trying to understand what he sees. He is too busy dodging around a new construction site that wasn't there yesterday.) Another day it is a girl with supermammaries who creates a traffic-stopping crowd on Wall Street by simply strolling through the lunchtime snarl. Or it is a postal strike, a telephone crisis, a gay-in, a bomb scare, a black-out or a black-in—the first black family on lily-white block. Blue Cross covers abortion. The city's principal product is not rags, words or money. It is novelty.

All this gives New York its surrealistic, carnival-like atmosphere, the "never-a-dull-moment" quality that makes it sparkle with excitement. But it carries dangerous side effects with it. For life in a full-time, 365-days-a-year carnival has its drawbacks. It forces us to operate at higher levels of unpredictability than most people find tolerable.

It is precisely here that rising novelty collides with the accelerative thrust in our lives. Low-novelty neighborhoods, jobs or cities permit the individual to cope with much of his daily life by means of behavioral routines—programmed decisions, as it were—leaving him time and mental energy enough for other, more important things. A high-novelty environment, such as that in New York, compels people to process vastly greater amounts of information than a low-novelty environment.

When the novelty level rises too high, however, when you can no longer count on certain regularities, when you can't be reasonably sure the LIRR[1] will run today, or the power will be available, or the building will not have to be evacuated, or the mail will arrive and the garbage will leave, when you can't be sure that the schools will be open, or that they will do their job if they are, when you can't be sure you won't see a naked man on your street corner, you begin to devote a great deal of precious mental energy to revising your behavior with regard to relatively unimportant matters. Even getting little things done requires tremendous amounts of stamina. As the novelty level rises, rules break down. In organizations, the bureaucratic machinery, beautifully designed to make routine decisions in slower, more stable surroundings, suddenly finds itself inept, incapable of coping with the strange new crises that present themselves. A calcified bureaucracy like the Board of Education simply does not know how to—and, given its structure, cannot—cope with black militancy, white parent revolts, the demand for decentralization, drugs, angry teachers, sex education, not to mention educationally crucial issues like long hair and midi-skirts. Doing things according to the rules no longer works, because the rules don't cover all the startling, upsetting, kooky, novel situations that confront us. Similarly, in our personal lives, novelty demands that we break our own rules, that we continually re-program our daily habits.

This has always been difficult for men to do. What makes it doubly difficult today, what lays the groundwork for the explosive adaptive breakdown, future shock, is the convergence of novelty with acceleration. For we now have not only to make more and more decisions of the most difficult and costly kind, we have to make them at a faster and faster clip.

The situation is intensified still further by *diversity*—the third environmental force fundamentally altering the quality of city life and challenging our adaptive responses and decision-making ability.

To understand how diversity affects us, we have to set aside a lot of what we have learned from social critics in the last 75 years. We have been told that technology brings with it ever more standardization and choicelessness, that we are heading for a terrible homogenization of our lives. We have been told it so often we believe it. And, in fact, industrialism, with its emphasis on the production of millions of

---

[1] Long Island Rail Road

identical items by millions of interchangeable men, *did* thrust in that direction.

What is happening now, however, is a revolution. What we are undergoing is not simply a linear extension of the same old industrialism. We are creating a radically new society that does not depend upon industrial-type technologies, on factory-style bureaucracies, or on mass men. This is not the place to sketch the full scope of the Super Industrial Revolution—how it will alter our values and family forms, how it will restructure the economy and the business world, how it changes even the rules by which we choose our lifestyles. What is significant here is that part of the Super Industrial Revolution is an enormously powerful push, just now beginning, toward differentiation and diversity.

We are beginning to feel it in student demands for individualized instruction. In black demands for ethnic independence, even separatism. In the emergence in our midst of new, ephemeral sub-cultures from hippies and motorcyclists to surfers and skindivers. In the consumer marketplace, where the housewife who visits Grand Union or the A & P, whether in Riverdale or Ridgewood, faces a dazzling array of gastronomic choices, from fried eggrolls to frozen pizza.

Diversity, like novelty, is a mixed blessing. It, too, collides frontally with the accelerative pressures that demand speed in decision-making. Every psychological experiment on this subject indicates that decisions slow down as the number of options increases. Reaction time is longer when you have to choose between 100 alternative striped ties at Macy's instead of the 25 at the neighborhood haberdasher. It takes longer to decide among the varieties of shrimp available at Sea Fare than at Schrafft's. And there is a perfectly normal and understandable reason for this, if we recognize that what is involved is the scanning, processing and evaluation of more information. This is at the heart of decision-making, not merely in the executive suite of General Electric or in the corridors of City Hall, but in the private adaptive choices made by all of us every day as we attempt to cope with our environment. And it is precisely at our ability to make rational decisions that future shock strikes.

Future shock is the outcome of a concealed, yet crucial, conflict in our lives. It is the head-on collision between an accelerative push forever pressuring us to live faster, to adapt more quickly, to make and break our environmental ties more frequently, to make speedier decisions, and the equally powerful counter-pressures of novelty and diversity which demand that we process more data, that we break out of our old, carefully honed routines, that we examine each situation anew before we make a decision.

In this struggle of psycho-environmental forces, acceleration, more often than not, wins out. We may make decisions faster—but we make them less well. Thus, if we examine the scientific evidence about what happens to men when they are forced to cope with high levels of novelty and choice at extremely high speeds, we find a consistent pattern summarized by the phrase "breakdown of performance." Accuracy declines. Thoughtfulness, the ability to anticipate consequences, all fall by the wayside as the time pressures mount.

The blunt fact is that there are certain upper limits on how much sensory input we can handle, how much information we can process, the number and kind of decisions we can make in a given interval. Today, as change escalates out of all proportion, we are forcing millions of human beings to operate above their adaptive range. We are throwing them into future shock.

Future shock already accounts for much of the psychosomatic illness in our midst. It is apparent in the tenseness, anxiety and confusion around us; in the notorious irritability of the change-frazzled New Yorker; in the analysands who trek to their Park Avenue couch-sessions in search of ways to "cope"; in the corporate cadets who live in dread of a stress coronary; in the junkies and potheads who seek surcease from external stimulation by turning on, off, or in.

Politically, we see it in the Procaccino voters[2] and the Hard Hats, for many of whom the gut issue is not so much race, war, or long hair, but the rate at which novelty explodes into their lives, smashing their lifelong routines and values. We see it also in the super-simplification practiced by the extremists and terrorists who can release a lot of pressure by phoning in a bomb warning or by actually planting a bomb.

Our biggest corporations, organizations and city agencies also evince the dizzying disorientation that is the hallmark of the future-shock victim. Consolidated Edison is reeling as people fearful of blackouts clamor for increased capacity, and, at the same time, protest whenever it tries to build a new generating plant. City officials charged with cleaning up air pollution and slums are staggered to learn that they themselves are the biggest polluters and slumlords of all. Firemen risk their lives and expect to be rewarded for it; they are, with rocks. The teachers' union, once a paragon of integrationist virtue, stands accused of racism. The reversals of position, the shifts, twists and upsets, stun even the most stolid bureaucrats as the surrealistic becomes commonplace.

Pressed for instant action on all sides, the basic organizations of the city, like future-shocked individuals, find themselves punch-drunk,

---

[2] Procaccino voters: Mario Procaccino was the unsuccessful Democratic candidate for mayor of New York in 1969.

hopelessly bewildered about their goals. Like adolescents caught up in identity crises, they stumble about asking, "What are we doing?" "Who are we, anyhow?" And there is no time to stop and think deeply about the answer. This is why so many companies and government agencies seem out of control. For all intents and purposes, they are.

None of this is an argument against change. Change is life itself, and New York in particular stands in desperate need of certain changes. Its ghettos remain a tragic insult to the mind and heart. Its educational system is a farce. Its old people are left to fester in misery and isolation. Its children are cheated of the right to a functional role in the community. Its number of deaths attributable to narcotics over-dose continues to spiral grimly upward. Change is needed—radical change—and fast.

But what we have today is non-selective, across-the-board change, without direction, without regulation, reflecting such a welter of con-fused goals that even the best-intentioned programs prove self-can-celing. We are experiencing what the scientists call Brownian motion, rather than anything remotely resembling progress. And if this churn-ing, mindless, self-contradictory, continually accelerating change—forcing the pace of life to pathological levels, attacking the precondi-tions of rationality—is permitted to continue, it will destroy us. We must somehow capture control of the basic change processes in the urban environment, decelerating some of them while we intelligently accelerate others.

We are going to need, therefore, a whole new set of strategies—collective ones—to make the environment livable. Some of these are psychological. New kinds of counseling services for people caught up in transitions. A lot of people who complain to their shrinks that they can't "cope" aren't neurotic. They don't need to have their ids and egos extruded. They need to analyze the life changes they are passing through; they need a chance to talk to other people who are in the same fix. I don't mean group therapy, either. Therapy implies someone is sick. Rather, I think, we are going to see more and more use of "sit-uational groups"—people brought together in the form of future-oriented temporary groups to discuss impending changes in their lives. People who have moved for the 17th time have some wisdom to impart to those who have only relocated once or twice. People who have under-gone divorce can help those who are still caught in the painful process. People who are promoted, demoted, who have gained a child or lost a spouse, can be helped to make the adaptive transition by simply being able to talk with others who have been there before them. "Parents Without Partners" may be the forerunner of a range of new "situa-tional" organizations.

Other strategies involve the creation of what I have elsewhere called "enclaves of the past" and "enclaves of the future"—specially designed environments to help us de-fuse or, on the other hand, to give us an advance sense of what the future will smell, feel and taste like, so that we can plan our adjustments to it—or our resistance.

Even without attempting to spell out all the possibilities we can be sure of several things: traditional approaches are not terribly effective anymore, and anything that works is likely to look strange, even weird, to us. Furthermore, whatever we do to support crisis-caught individuals or to enhance the adaptivity of large numbers of people (e.g., through future-oriented education) is not going to be enough if the accelerative thrust itself is uncontrolled.

This, then, is the new name of the political game—control of change—and we are going to hear a lot more about it as the squeeze gets tighter. We are not going to solve our other problems or moderate the tensions between Hard Hat and student, black militant and scared liberal, Staten Islander and Manhattanite, until we find ways to depressurize the city.

To do this, we are going to need a whole new political vocabulary, attention to all sorts of aches and pains, psychological and otherwise, that have until now been ignored by politics. No one has any blueprint for how to proceed, but there are many different things that a city, especially one as creative and venturesome as New York, might do to protect its psycho-social environment, to make life a little less pointlessly hectic, a little less aggravating, a little more livable.

We might create "social future assemblies"—neighborhood groups devoted to the examination of alternative futures and strategies for managing change. We might set up "imaginetic centers"—new organizations intended to draw on the problem-solving ideas and talents of non-experts. We might consciously design high- or low-stimulation sub-centers in the city itself, so that people who want something less than total and unremitting bombardment of their senses and brains don't have to move away.

Once we start thinking outside the usual political categories, however, there is one need so urgent that it ought to be singled out for special, immediate attention. If the city is to survive its collision with the future, it is going to have to exert some control over that future. This will require New York to do something that no major city in the world has yet done—something that, once done, could become a pattern all over the technological world, something that would place cities in a new relationship to their federal or national governments, something in which New York, of all cities, can exhibit leadership.

The people of the city have an enormous stake in keeping it going and growing. But the surest way to destroy it is to let outside forces, more or less at random, shake and shatter it. For example, the forces of technology. New York has the right to determine the kinds of technology that it will permit to operate in the city limits and the rate at which it will allow technological innovations to infuse novelty into its environment. In fact, if it does not have and exercise this right, it cannot influence the single most powerful determinant of the quality of life within its boundaries.

One would have to be stupid and immoral to want to stop the advance of technology in a world in which hundreds of millions still suffer from malnutrition and disease. But one has to be either selfish or irresponsible to want the technological juggernaut to roll on unmanaged, unguided, in a witless, short-sighted and life-imperiling fashion. We do not need a Luddite[3] attack on that favorite scapegoat of today, The Machine. But we similarly do not need a blind acceptance of every technical innovation that comes along simply because it is possible and profitable, especially when technology is one of the hidden driving forces behind the acceleration of daily life.

The truth is that New York and other cities have more power to influence technology than they suspect. In recent years a loud but ineffectual drive has been conducted in Washington to stop the development of supersonic jet transports. I am not sure we *should* kill the SST. Maybe we should merely delay it. Whatever the objective, the place to apply pressure may not be Washington but Kennedy Airport. If New York banned SSTs from its airports (and if, say, San Francisco joined with it), it could do more to influence the project than all the campaigning in the capital. No airline is likely to buy SSTs unless it is reasonably sure it can operate them in the major urban markets. I use this only as an example of how a city might bring power to bear on the future of technological development.

The time has come for New York to consider creating its own "Technological Assessment Agency"—some group charged with worrying about the impact of new technologies still on the horizon. If our people and organizations show signs of future shock now, what is going to happen in the next few years, as even faster, more powerful technologies begin to pour into our lives? Somebody ought to be worrying about the long-term effects on the city of cable television—not merely now, but when it begins to make possible shopping and banking in the home. About the changes that electronic video recording will trigger in

---

[3] Luddite: The Luddites were English workmen of the early 19th century who rebelled against machinery by destroying it.

New York's entertainment industry and educational system. How will early efforts at weather modification affect the city's snow-removal problem? What will the development of ultralight building materials, such as "whisker-reinforced" composites, do to construction work in the city? How will the ability to predetermine the sex of babies affect the ratio of boys to girls in our schools? The spread of drug usage is only beginning: what will the highly sophisticated mood-modifying chemicals of tomorrow do to us? Most important, how will these innovations influence one another and the environment?

Somebody, somewhere in the city, ought to be worrying now about these problems, for they are closer to us in time than most people suspect—in some cases only months away. Such an agency ought to employ the most advanced methods—poor as yet, but not by any means useless—to assess in advance the potential impact of these mechanical innovations. It ought to anticipate at least some of tomorrow's urban problems, so that we do not have to wait for a crisis before facing up to them (or, better yet, averting them).

Whether such an agency ought to be purely advisory or whether it should have the muscle to ban, delay, or set preconditions for the diffusion of new technologies is open to fierce and legitimate debate. Whether there ought to be just one or many such technology assessment centers in the city is another open issue. How such an agency ought to relate to industry in the city (and before long corporations will be busy setting up their own technology assessment operations) needs to be thought out carefully, if such an agency is not to stifle beneficial developments. Whether the task of technology assessment ought to be left to the "experts" or ought to involve large masses of lay citizens can and should be argued. Whether it should report to the mayor or the City Council or the public at large—all these need to be considered. The problems are towering.

But that New York must begin to exert some influence over its own technological (and hence social, cultural and psychological) destiny, and over the pace at which major new technologies stream into the environment—this seems to me to be beyond reasonable argument, unless we are all prepared to pack up and move out.

Beginning to act consciously, and perhaps in concert with other cities, on the technological revolution churning and chopping our lives is only the first of many necessary steps toward rational new urban policies. But it is a crucial step out of the present bog of tired, irrelevant city politics. It strikes at the problem festering just below the surface of our political consciousness—the sickening spread of future shock.

Cycle of Growth and Decay

LEWIS MUMFORD

The history and future of cities became Lewis Mumford's main topic early in his immense career as a thinker, writer and teacher. At least three of his books have become classics of modern urban study: The Culture of Cities *(1938),* The City in History *(1961), and* The Pentagon of Power *(1971).*

. . . There have been numerous attempts to summarize the course of city development and to correlate this with the rise and fall of civilizations. One of the best-known of these interpretations is that of Oswald Spengler in the book euphemistically translated as *The Decline of the West.* He traced the development of the community from "culture" to "civilization": from its beginnings as the living expression of a people, harmoniously interacting upon a certain soil and swayed by a common feeling toward life and the earth and the universe, not yet formulated as philosophic vision, to the final stage, that which he called civilization, with its hard mechanistic organization of men and goods and ideas: rootless, spiritless, ultimately lifeless and hopeless: concentrated in a few world capitals that were no longer related to the land, where the malleable and changeable forms of earlier cultures were made over into dead stereotypes.

According to Spengler's early scheme, the process of mastery, which begins with agriculture, ends with a predominance of the machine: a contrivance in which there is for him something infernal, inimical to life. The business man and the engineer and the industrialist displace the artist and the peasant. But mechanism, tied to a ruthless scheme of exploitation, leads into savagery: Spengler acknowledged that fact and in his later formulations he even boasted of man's being a carnivore in order to justify the conclusion that the men of our time must heartily embrace savagery: submit to the lash of a Caesar and take part in his brutal machinations. There is of course a serious contradiction between Spengler's romantic belief in the predatory carnivore and the historic facts of rural domestication and urbane culture; but one may pardon Spengler's barbarous solecisms if only because he was one of the first in our generation to grasp the critical significance of the city in the development of culture.

A later interpretation of this cycle of development and deterioration is that of Arnold J. Toynbee, in his monumental survey, *A Study of History.* Toynbee's study is more profound than Spengler's, is based on a much richer grasp of historic facts, and does not neglect empirical evidence for the sake of preserving intact a literary figure. Unfortunately, Toynbee's theory of the development of civilization does not embrace the special function of the city, as both the instrument and the symbol of this process; and although he rediscovers the function of the cloister, in his conception of withdrawal-and-return as necessary for the process of renewal, he does not connect this with the process of urban development itself. Hence Toynbee is weak precisely at the point where Spengler is strongest: though his division of the component cultures into societies, and his schematic cycle of development rest on a closer reading of the historical evidence.

The most significant summary of all, from the point of view being developed here, is likewise the earliest: that put forward by Patrick Geddes early in this century in his outline of the six stages of city development, from polis to nekropolis. Like a true disciple, I have modified Geddes's scheme. . . . Thus I propose to insert an earlier stage that he left out of the picture, and I have combined two of his later stages, those of Parasitopolis and Patholopolis into a single stage, since there is no observable time-interval between them. These modifications, made after his death, too late for his sanction, have the merit of placing the first three stages of the cycle on the rising curve, and the last three on the descending side; and this, I believe, is more in line with his essential views than his own original diagram.

First Stage: Eopolis. Rise of the village community. Development of permanent habitation and permanent external organs of association through the domestication of plants and the ensurance of a balanced food supply by the domestication of animals. Cultivation of the hard grains and legumes: also deliberate tree and vine culture: plentiful supply of proteins, vegetable fats, and fermented liquors. Surplus production in agriculture smooths over seasonal and cyclical irregularities and ensures an orderly routine of life: security and continuity. Permanent utilities for storage: translation of kinetic energy into potential energy (food storage) brings vast increase in power, economic and cultural.

Differentiation of the permanent dwelling house, and regular outlines of the village through systematic layout and orderly apportionment of land: pile villages, plains villages, etc. Important technical advances, especially in development of utensils and agricultural tools:

basketwork, pottery, hoe, beginnings of systematic mining and tool-working: dawn of metallurgy. Fire as symbol of advance: hearth and altar. Oral transmission of tradition through occupational groups and through close companionship of senescents and youths. Association on basis of blood and neighborhood: predominance of primary groups. Culture continuous with life but limited by arbitrary restriction of experience (taboos), fear of departure from magical formulae, submissive respect for ancestral wisdom as transmitted by priesthood, and lack of stimulating intercourse with other cultures. First crude differentiation of villages on basis of topographic facts, local resources, indigenous occupations: mining villages, fishing villages, agricultural villages.

Arising probably in neolithic culture, the village remains the most enduring of collective forms. Its life underlies all subsequent transformations of civilization; and although villages that continue as such never climb more than part of the cycle upward and never participate except by adaptive infiltration in the advances made in the city, they likewise tend to escape the worst defects of decay. The agricultural village, not the market, is the prototype of the city: its utilities for protection, storage, and life-maintenance are the essential nucleus of the city: they become "etherealized" in culture-forms, at the same time as they are finally given concrete expression in the form of collective art: altar becomes temple: planting and harvest rituals become drama and theater, granary bin and cellar are village prototypes of library, archive, museum and vault. The village remains the essential root from which fresh urban shoots from time to time thrust upward: its form and content persist long after more differentiated urban types have flourished and disappeared. Hence the truth in the boast of the little village near Edinburgh:

> *Musselburgh was a borough when Edinburgh was none,*
> *And Musselburgh will be a borough when Edinburgh is gone.*

Second Stage: Polis. An association of villages or blood-groups having a common site that lends itself to defense against depredation: a common deity with a common shrine or temple, usually on or near the defensive site: a common meeting place where the special products and skills of the larger community may be interchanged in periodical markets. Rise in industrial productivity through the more systematic division of labor and the partial specialization of functions: development of trades and crafts: surplus of manufactured goods as well as surplus of food. Beginnings of mechanization: stamping, molding, casting, in the early river-civilizations, the watermill, the paved road, the general use of wheeled vehicles in Graeco-Roman civilization: special instruments of power and precision in addition to the above in modern civilization in its eotechnic phase.

Free energy: free time: release from incessant preoccupation with physical survival. Opportunity for further nurture of the family, for education, for the cultivation of the body in military and athletic exercise, for the discipline of the mind in contemplation and dialectics and science, and for the practice of the humane arts. Systematic medicine and health-culture. Further development of social division of labor through multiplication of purposive associations and organizations. Differentiation of theoretic from empiric knowledge: beginnings of mathematics, astronomy, philosophy: increased scope of a special class, immune to obligations of practical labor, devoted to preserving and extending the cultural heritage. Erection of special buildings that collectively embody new cultural and political functions: temple, stadium, theater, guildhall, cathedral. Rise of the school, as the organ for systematically transmitting elements of social heritage to the young; and further differentiation of the cloister from the school: grove, shaded walk, porch, cloister, study, studio, laboratory. Civic unity and common vision of life symbolized in Temple or Cathedral. Increase of cultural storage by means of sculptured figures, painted images, monuments, books.

Preservation of rural occupations and rural customs, including the practice of piety toward ancestors and ancestral rites: the polis remains a collection of families; family organization tends to prevail in industry no less than in agriculture; and seasonal and other migrations between village and polis preserve and renew rural connections. Dependence upon the local region for water, building materials, food, and main industrial resources. Transformation of structures in impermanent materials into more durable ones: refinement of architectural detail: formal modifications of shrines and important buildings so as to reflect collective sentiments about life and the universe. Pervasiveness of esthetic and moral culture through all ranks of society: expression of a differentiated but still homogeneous way of life.

Third Stage: Metropolis. Within the region one city emerges from the less differentiated groups of villages and country towns. Taking advantage of a strategic location, a larger supply of potable water, a more defensible site, better land for agriculture, easier command of land routes or water routes, a safer harbor—usually with a number of these advantages coming together—one city succeeds in attracting larger numbers of inhabitants: it becomes the metropolis or "mother-city." In heaping up these advantages, the command of transportation routes probably marks the critical change: compare the Hittites with the Egyptians, or the land-locked Spartans with the adventurous, mobile, water-borne Athenians.

With a surplus of regional products, a specialized trade develops with other regions. This brings to the growing metropolis the necessary food supply, which can no longer be raised in the immediate vicinity, along with a host of stimulating goods from other regions: special fabrics, special forms, even esthetic patterns, unused by the traditional industries of the local region. Cross-fertilization of culture takes place: stimulus to fresh invention: stimulus to departures from routine. Long distance trading and long distance administration help further invention and create a necessity for abstract symbols: pictorial signs, numerical tables, alphabets. A foreign population of traders and students enters the metropolis: unabsorbed as citizens at first, since blood and neighborhood may still count, they bring the shock of fresh habits and ideas: challenges to old ways. Further specialization of economic and social functions: the specialized workshop: the specialized trading class: subdivisions of these. Large-scale development of library and university as storehouse and powerhouse of ideas. Development of more effective organs of centralized administration, apart from primitive courts and assemblies. Agriculture tends to be secondary to manufacture: manufacture in turn becomes an instrument of trade. Rivalry between patricians of the soil and new trades and industrialists of the metropolis: splitting off of landless workers, selling their labor, with no prospect of rise in economic rank. Also migration of an élite within the polity.

Religion, literature, the drama reach the stage of self-conscious criticism and expression: the systematic-rational grows at the expense of organic and instinctive modes of expression. Every part of the environment and the culture is deliberately remolded: written law supplements custom and common law, written language helps to shape the labile dialects of the surrounding regions and gives them a common medium of secondary intercourse: rational inquiry challenges customary acceptance. The representatives of religion, philosophy, and science, no longer united as a single priestly hierarchy, pursue separate paths: the gap between sacred knowledge and secular knowledge, between empiricism and theory, between deed and idea, tends to widen; but out of these oppositions and likenesses, out of these hostilities and wider friendships, new syntheses come forth. A similar refocusing takes place in every other department of life: emancipation from fixed patterns and stereotyped routine. Fusion of the instinctive, the imaginative, and the rational in great philosophies and works of art: maximum release of cultural energy: Platonic Athens: Dantean Florence: Shakespearean London: Emersonian Boston.

Signs of weakness appear beneath the surface. Increasing failure to absorb and integrate disparate cultural elements: beginnings of an individualism that tends to disrupt old social bonds without creating new order on a higher plane. Professionalizing of war, already differentiated as a culture-trait, acquires new energy through increasing technical equipment, and new impetus from economic rivalry. Opening up of a grave breach between the owners of the machinery of production and the workers, whether slave or free: beginning of the class struggle in active form. Fixation on pecuniary symbols of gain, as the growing class of merchants and bankers begin to exercise greater influence.

Fourth Stage: Megalopolis. Beginning of the decline. The city under the influence of a capitalistic mythos concentrates upon bigness and power. The owners of the instruments of production and distribution subordinate every other fact in life to the achievement of riches and the display of wealth. Physical conquest by military means: financial domination by trade and legal processes: loans, mortgages, speculative enterprises. The agricultural base extends: the lines of supply become more tenuous: the impulse to aggressive enterprise and enterprising aggression grows as the lust for power diminishes the attraction of all other attributes of life: as the moral sense becomes more callous and the will-to-culture increasingly impotent. Standardization, largely in pecuniary terms, of the cultural products themselves in art, literature, architecture, and language. Mechanical reproduction takes the place of original art: bigness takes the place of form: voluminousness takes the place of significance. Triumph of mechanism in every department: passivity: manual helplessness: bureaucratism: failure of direct action.

Megalopolis ushers in an age of cultural aggrandizement: scholarship and science by tabulation: sterile research: elaborate fact-finding apparatus and refined technic with no reference to rational intellectual purpose or ultimate possibilities of social use: Alexandrianism. [1] Belief in abstract quantity in every department of life: the biggest monuments, the highest buildings, the most expensive materials, the largest food supply, the greatest number of worshipers, the biggest population. Education becomes quantitative: domination of the cram-machine and the encyclopedia, and domination of megalopolis as concrete encyclopedia: all-containing. Knowledge divorced from life: industry divorced from life-utility: life itself compartmentalized, dis-specialized, finally disorganized and enfeebled. Representatives: Alexandria, third century B.C.; Rome, second century A.D.; Byzantium, tenth century; Paris, eighteenth century; New York, . . . twentieth century.

Over-investment in the material apparatus of bigness. Diversion of energy from the biological and social ends of life to the preparatory physical means. Outright exploitation of the proletariat and increasing conflict between organized workers and the master classes. Occasional attempts at insurance by philanthropy on the part of the possessing

---

[1] Alexandrianism: overly derivative or artificial.

classes: justice in homeopathic doses. Occasional outbursts of savage repression on the part of frightened bourgeoisie, employing basest elements in the city. As conflict intensifies rise of a coalition between landed oligarchy, trained in combat, and a megalopolitan rabble of speculators, enterprisers, and financiers who furnish the sinews of war and profit by all the occasions for class-suppression, price-lifting, and looting that it gives. The city as a means of association, as a haven of culture, becomes a means of dissociation and a growing threat to real culture. Smaller cities are drawn into the megalopolitan network: they practice imitatively the megalopolitan vices, and even sink to lower levels because of lack of higher institutions of learning and culture that still persist in bigger centers. The threat of widespread barbarism arises. Now follow, with cumulative force and increasing volume, the remaining downward movements of the cycle.

Fifth Stage: Tyrannopolis. Extensions of parasitism throughout the economic and social scene: the function of spending paralyzes all the higher activities of culture and no act of culture can be justified that does not involve display and expense. Politics becomes competition for the exploitation of the municipal and state exchequer by this or that class or group. Extirpation of organs of communal and civic life other than "state." Caesarism. Development of predatory means as a substitute for trade and give-and-take: naked exploitation of colonies and hinterland: intensification of the cycles of commercial depression, following overexpansion of industry and dubious speculative enterprise, heightened by wars and war-preparations. Failure of the economic and political rulers to maintain the bare decencies of administration: place-hunting, privilege-seeking, bonus-collecting, favor-currying, nepotism, grafting, tribute-exacting become rife both in government *and* business. Widespread moral apathy and failure of civic responsibility: each group, each individual, takes what it can get away with. Widening of the gap between producing classes and spending classes. Multiplication of a *Lumpenproletariat*[2] demanding its share of bread and shows. Overstress of mass-sports. Parasitic love of sinecures in every department of life. Demand for "protection money" made by armed thugs and debased soldiery: organized looting, organized blackmail are "normal" accompaniments of business and municipal enterprise. Domination of respectable people who behave like criminals and of criminals whose activities do not debar them from respectability.

Imperialistic wars, internal and external, result in starvation, epidemics of disease, demoralization of life: uncertainty hangs over every prospect of the future: armed protection increases all the hazards of

---

[2]Lumpenproletariat: a degraded group of the working class.

life. Municipal and state bankruptcy. Drain of local taxes to service increasing load of local debt. Necessity to appeal to the state for further
aid in periods of economic disorganization: loss of autonomy. Drain of
national taxes to support the growing military establishment of the
state. This burden penalizes the remnants of honest industry and agriculture, and further disrupts the supply of elementary material goods.
Decrease in agricultural production by soil-mining and erosion,
through falling off in acreage, through the withholding of crops from
the city by resentful husbandmen. Decline in rate of population-
increase through birth control, abortion, mass slaughter, and suicide:
eventual absolute decline in numbers. General loss of nerve. Attempt
to create order by external military means: rise of gangster-dictators
(Hitler, Mussolini) with active consent of the bourgeoisie and systematic terrorism by pretorian guards. Recrudescence of superstition and
deliberate cult of savagery: barbarian invasions from within and without. Beginnings of megalopolitan exodus. Material deficiencies and
lapses of cultural continuity: repression and censorship. Cessation of
productive work in the arts and sciences.

Sixth and Final Stage: Nekropolis. War and famine and disease
rack both city and countryside. The physical towns become mere
shells. Those who remain in them are unable to carry on the old municipal services or maintain the old civic life: what remains of that life
is at best a clumsy caricature. The names persist; the reality vanishes.
The monuments and books no longer convey meaning; the old routine
of life involves too much effort to carry on: the streets fall into disre-
pair and grass grows in the cracks of the pavement: the viaducts break
down, the water mains become empty; the rich shops, once looted,
remain empty of goods by reason of the failure of trade or production.
Relapse into the more primitive rural occupations. The historic culture
survives, if at all, in the provinces and the remote villages, which share
the collapse but are not completely carried down by it or submerged in
the debris. First the megalopolis becomes a lair: then its occupants are
either hunted out by some warrior band, seeking the last remnants of
conquest in gold or women or random luxuries, or they gradually fall
away of their own accord. The living forms of the ancient city become a
tomb for dying: sand sweeps over the ruins: so Babylon, Nineveh,
Rome. In short, Nekropolis, the city of the dead: flesh turned to ashes:
life turned into a meaningless pillar of salt.

POSSIBILITIES OF RENEWAL

History is full of burying grounds: the dead forms and deserted
shards of communities that had not learned the art of living in harmonious relations with nature and with other communities. The end

stage, over which Spengler gloated, is an undeniable reality that has overtaken many civilizations: dead-food for the vulturelike imagination.

But one must not, like a Spengler or a Sorokin,[3] make the mistake of identifying the *logical* stages of a process, as discovered and systematized by intellectual analysis, with the living reality. For in real life, in real cultures, history does not present a solid laminated block of uniform dimensions that one may break down into smaller blocks, each unified within itself to form part of a consistent whole. End-processes often occur in the middle of a culture; accidental mischances and injuries may bring to the middle-aged the normal deteriorations of senescence. Likewise early processes or rejuvenating reactions may be noted in the final phases of the most mechanized civilization. In short, time as experience and duration upsets this logical order, which is based chiefly on time as an attribute of spatial movement. Mutations arise in human communities from unexpected sources: the social heritage makes society much less of a unity than we are compelled to conceive it, by the nature of language, when we interrupt the complex stream of actual life in order to take account of it in thought. Out of these mutations, a new social dominant may arrive: veritably a saving remnant.

To take the simplest point of all: the final stage in civilization is often reached at an intermediate point in urban development. Witness fourteenth century Rome. It exhibited most of the characteristics of a Nekropolis, including a loss, not alone of the single title to papal supremacy, but of a good part of its population. Yet, after that nadir had been reached, a renewal took place: two centuries later its ruins stimulate Brunelleschi and its new buildings offer a challenge to the genius of Michelangelo. The other point to remember is that civilization is not, even in its utmost megalopolitan phase, confined to the world-cities alone. Though they cast their shadows over the farthest territories, neither their governments nor their armies nor their culture institutes can embrace with any degree of thoroughness the provinces they lay claim to: part of their dominion is mere bluff and pretense, unchallengeable until actually challenged.

Even in the ultimate stage of Tyrannopolis, the tyranny is only partly effective: Krilov[4] contrives to tell his satirical fables and Epictetus,[5] the slave, thinks his own thoughts and preserves autonomy within his soul. At this stage there still remain regions and cities and vil-

---

[3] P.A. Sorokin (1889-1968), a leading sociologist and theoretician, was best known for his 4-volume work, *Social and Cultural Dynamics.*

[4] Ivan A. Krilov (1769-1844), Russian author known for clever fables.

[5] Epictetus (born about 50 A.D.), influential Greek philosopher who began life as a slave.

lages with other memories, other backgrounds, other hopes: though in shackles to the external dictatorship, they remain essentially withdrawn. In the heyday of the megalopolitan economy, such regional centers remain partly outside the cycle: some failure of enterprise, some lack of opportunity, or some sturdier sense of life-values keeps them from sharing the delusive growth and splendor of the metropolis.

When, through the processes of decay and destruction hastened by Tyrannopolis, the great cities sink into ruin, these other centers, though they may stagger from the blow, will nevertheless continue to live: indeed, they may live more intensely once the incubus of the big city and its tyrannous system of political and financial administration is removed. Marseilles and some of the other towns of Provence had such a function after the disintegration of the old Roman civilization in Italy: this fact, along with their closer contact with Byzantium and the Arabic possessions, played a significant part, no doubt, in that brilliant outburst of Provencal culture in the early Middle Ages. On the other hand, to face the blacker side of the picture, the reverse process may happen: a process that doubly demands our watchful care today: that is, a deteriorative phase of culture may prolong its existence by capturing the fresh energies of a younger growth. In this fashion, Byzantium reached up to paralyze the "young" culture of sixteenth century Russia; and in similar fashion, again, the Tyrannopolis of the Czars in Russia, which exhibited many of the symptoms of the end-process by the close of the nineteenth century, has left its cruel mark on the fresh beginnings made by the Soviet regime: furthering that aimless centralization and that rigid bureaucratism and that habit of systematic repression of valid differences which leaves no place for young initiative, or for those forms of co-operation which, to be whole-hearted, must be voluntary.

In other words, the life course of cities is essentially different from that of most higher organisms. Cities exhibit the phenomena of broken growth, of partial death, of self-regeneration. Cities and city cultures may have sudden beginnings from remote gestations; and they are capable of prolongations as *physical organizations* through the life-spans of more than one culture: witness Damascus, most ancient of surviving towns, already venerable in St. Paul's day. It is only a parable rather than as scientific statement that one may talk of the spring or winter of a civilization as if the cycle had a climatic inevitability, or of the birth and death of a culture-phase, as if any contemporary observer could confidently recognize either the birth-cry or the death rattle.

Cities can take on new life by a transplantion of tissues from healthy communities in other regions or civilizations: a few hundred people, like the Huguenots in Scotland or Germany, or the Jews in almost every civilization, may have a profoundly stimulating effect. In the 1930s, the dispersal of the élite from Germany and Italy and in some degree from Russia may have been one of the elements that will compensate for the growing elements of barbarism within those countries. And these transplanted tissues need not even be in the form of living people: the collective organs of culture, signs, symbols, forms, the abstract and etherealized essences, may likewise exercise a decisive effect: witness the powerful influence of Roman monuments and Greek literature in temporarily supplementing the spent energies of the Middle Ages. All that is necessary is that the organism which receives these new tissues shall be in a state of readiness.

In short: the roots of a culture are deep. If the crown is blighted by disease, it may still put forth new shoots at the base; and in time these shoots may flourish and provide a new trunk and crown. All these are of course figures of speech: but they are means of counteracting and truing up analogies that are even more abstract, figures that are even more fanciful: the curve of a cycle, the succession of the seasons. Social life has its own laws and rhythms: much remains hidden or irrational: much escapes empiric observation and still more escapes statistical analysis. All one can say with any surety is this: when a city has reached the megalopolitan stage, it is plainly on the downward path: it needs a terrific exertion of social force to overcome the inertia, to alter the direction of movement, to resist the immanent processes of disintegration. But while there is life, there is the possibility of counter-movement, fresh growth. Only when the big city has finally become wasteland must the locus of life be elsewhere.

The Shape of the Secular City

HARVEY COX

Harvey Cox is a professor at the Harvard Divinity School and an ordained Baptist minister. His 1965 book, The Secular City, *gained widespread attention by discussing what Cox calls the two main hallmarks of the modern era: "the rise of urban civilization and the collapse of traditional religion."*

What comes to mind when we think of the *shape* of technopolis? We visualize contours. We envisage networks of radial and circumferential thoroughfares, grids of disparate but interlocking land-use regions, a profile carved out by the city's natural topography—a mountain range, a lakefront, a river. We also see buildings, short and squat, tall and erect. Terminals, stations, offices, residences jostle each other for space. These are the physical shapes of the city.

But what about the social shape of the secular metropolis, its human silhouette, the institutional basis for its culture? The shape of the secular city, along with its style, comprises its *maniere d'etre.*[1] Its shape is its social system as distinguished from its cultural system. The distinction is of course merely analytic. In reality shape and style merge, but for purposes of discussion, . . . we shall focus on the shape of the secular city. . . .

Let two images drawn from the physical setting of technopolis suggest the elements of its social shape on which we wish to concentrate. The first is the *switchboard,* the key to communication in the city, linking human beings to one another through modern electronic magic. The next is the highway *cloverleaf,* the image of simultaneous mobility in many different directions. These symbols suggest both possibility and problems. They illustrate two characteristic components of the social shape of the modern metropolis: *anonymity* and *mobility.* But why focus on them?

Not only are anonymity and mobility central. They are also the two features of the urban social system most frequently singled out for attack by both religious and nonreligious critics. How often has one

---

[1]maniere d'etre: condition

heard that urban man's existence has been depleted and despoiled by the cruel anonymity and ceaseless mobility of the city? How frequently is urban man depicted by his detractors as faceless and depersonalized, rushing to and fro with no time to cultivate deeper relationships or lasting values? It is in part because anonymity and mobility have been made into antiurban epithets that we need to examine them and to point out the positive side. We shall do this first by showing how both anonymity and mobility contribute to the sustenance of human life in the city rather than detracting from it, why they are indispensable modes of existence in the urban setting. . . .

THE MAN AT THE GIANT SWITCHBOARD

Technopolitan man sits at a vast and immensely complicated switchboard. He is *homo symbolicus*, man the communicator, and the metropolis is a massive network of communications. A whole world of possibilities for communication lies within his reach. The contemporary urban region represents an ingenious device for vastly enlarging the range of human communication and widening the scope of individual choice. Urbanization thus contributes to the freedom of man. This is perfectly evident when we think for example of cinema theatres and restaurants. Residents of a city of 10,000 may be limited to one or two theaters, while people who live in a city of a million can choose among perhaps fifty films on a given night. The same principle holds for restaurants, schools, and even in some measure for job opportunities or prospective marriage partners. Urban man is free to choose from a wider range of alternatives. Thus his manhood as *homo symbolicus* is enhanced.

But freedom always demands discipline. The mere availability of such a wide spectrum of possibilities requires an adjustment of urban man's behavior. He must exercise choice more frequently, and choice always means exclusion. He doesn't just "go to the movies" on a free evening, as his more rural counterpart might; he must choose one from among the fifty films now showing. This means a conscious decision *not* to see the other forty-nine.

In the area of personal relationships this selectivity becomes more demanding. Urban man has a wider variety of "contacts" than his rural counterpart; he can choose only a limited number for friends. He must have more or less impersonal relationships with most of the people with whom he comes in contact precisely in order to choose certain friendships to nourish and cultivate. This selectivity can best be symbolized perhaps by the unplugged telephone or the unlisted number. A person does not request an unlisted number to cut down on the depth of his relationships. Quite the opposite; he does so to guard and deepen the worthwhile relationships he has against being dissolved in the deluge of messages that would come if one were open on principle and on an equal basis to anyone who tried to get through, including the increasing army of telephone salesmen who violate one's privacy so arrogantly. Those we want to know have our number; others do not: We are free to use the switchboard without being victimized by its infinite possibilities.

Urban man must distinguish carefully between his private life and his public relationships. Since he depends on such a complex net of services to maintain himself in existence in a modern city, the majority of his transactions will have to be public and will be what sociologists call functional or secondary. In most of his relationships he will be dealing with people he cannot afford to be interested in as individuals but must deal with in terms of the services they render to him and he to them. This is essential in urban life. Supermarket checkers or gas-meter readers who became enmeshed in the lives of the people they were serving would be a menace. They would soon cause a total breakdown in the essential systems of which they are integral parts. Urban life demands that we treat most of the people we meet as persons—not as things, but not as intimates either. This in turn produces the kind of "immunization" against personal encounters which Louis Wirth explains this way:

> Characteristically, urbanites meet one another in highly segmental roles. They are, to be sure, dependent upon more people for the satisfactions of their life-needs than are rural people and thus are associated with a greater number of organized groups, but they are less dependent upon particular persons, and their dependence upon others is confined to a highly fractionalized aspect of the other's round of activity. This is essentially what is meant by saying that the city is characterized by secondary rather than primary contacts. The contacts of the city may indeed be face to face, but they are nevertheless impersonal, superficial, transitory, and segmental. The reserve, the indifference, and the blasé outlook which urbanites manifest in their relationships may thus be regarded as devices for immunizing themselves against the personal claims and expectations of others.

This immunization results in a way of life which often appears cold and even heartless to those unfamiliar with the dynamics of urban living. Here both writers and sociologists have missed the point. Cultural romantics such as Rilke and Ortega recoiled in distaste at what they took to be the cruelty of the city. In sociology a similar criticism was also voiced. Relationships in the city, it was complained, tended to be divested of their really human substance and made mechanical and lifeless.

One of the most influential sociological critics of the shape of urban life was a German scholar named Ferdinand Tönnies (1855-1936), whose work has continued to exert a considerable influence on modern sociology and cultural analysis. In 1887 Tönnies published a book in which he contrasted the coherent, organic togetherness of *Gemeinschaft* (community) with the more rational, planned, and partial nexus of the *Gesellschaft* (society). Kaspar Naegele summarizes Tönnies' distinction:

> Relations of the *Gemeinschaft* type are more inclusive; persons confront each other as ends, they cohere more durably. . . . In *Gesellschaft* their mutual regard is circumscribed by a sense of specific, if not formal obligation. . . . A transaction can occur without any other encounters, leaving both parties virtually anonymous.

Tönnies is talking about what some sociologists describe as "primary" versus "secondary" relationships, or "organic" versus "functional" relationships. Having lived both as a villager and as an urbanite I know just what these terms mean. During my boyhood, my parents never referred to "the milkman," "the insurance agent," "the junk collector." These people were, respectively, Paul Weaver, Joe Villanova, and Roxy Barazano. All of our family's market transactions took place within a web of wider and more inclusive friendship and kinship ties with the same people. They were never anonymous. In fact, the occasional salesman or repairman whom we did not know was always viewed with dark suspicion until we could make sure where he came from, who his parents were, and whether his family was "any good." Trips to the grocery store, gasoline station, or post office were inevitably social visits, never merely functional contacts.

Now, as an urbanite, my transactions are of a very different sort. If I need to have the transmission on my car repaired, buy a television antenna, or cash a check, I find myself in functional relationships with mechanics, salesmen, and bank clerks whom I never see in any other capacity. These "contacts" are in no sense "mean, nasty or brutish," though they do tend to be short, at least not any longer than the time required to make the transaction and to exchange a brief pleasantry. Some of these human contacts occur with considerable frequency, so that I come to know the mannerisms and maybe even the names of some of the people. But the relationships are unifaceted and "segmental." I meet these people in no other context. To me they remain essentially just as anonymous as I do to them. Indeed, in the case of the transmission repairman, I hope I never see him again—not because he is in any way unpleasant, but because my only possible reason for seeing him again would be a new and costly breakdown in my car's gear box. The important point here is that my relationships with bank clerks and garagemen are no less human or authentic merely because we both prefer to keep them anonymous. Here is where much theological analysis of urbanization has gone hopelessly astray.

Theologians have spent themselves in well-intentioned forays against the "depersonalization of urban life," often fed by a misunderstanding of Martin Buber's philosophy of "I and Thou" relationships. In contrast to those who utilize his categories in a different manner, Buber himself never claimed that *all* our relationships should be of the deep, interpersonal I—Thou variety. He knew this experience was a rich and rare one. But Buber did open the door for misunderstanding by neglecting to study with sufficient thoroughness the place of types of relationships which actually constitute most of our lives, a point to which we shall return shortly.

A recent survey by some Protestant ministers in a new urban highrise apartment area where they intended to establish house church groups illustrates the misplaced emphasis on I—Thou relationships that has marked modern Christian theology. In conducting their study, the pastors were shocked to discover that the recently arrived apartment dwellers, whom they expected to be lonely and desperate for relationships, did not want to meet their neighbors socially and had no interest whatever in church or community groups. At first the ministers deplored what they called a "social pathology" and a "hedgehog" psychology. Later, however, they found that what they had encountered was a sheer survival technique. Resistance against efforts to subject them to neighborliness and socialization is a skill apartment dwellers must develop if they are to maintain any human relationships at all. It is an essential element in the shape of the secular city.

In condemning urban anonymity, the ministers had made the mistake of confusing a preurban ethos with the Christian concept of *koinonia*. [2] The two are not the same. The ministers had wanted to develop a kind of village togetherness among people, one of whose main reasons for moving to high-rise apartments is to escape the relationships enforced on them by the lack of anonymity of the village. Apartment dwellers, like most urbanites, live a life in which relationships are founded on free selection and common interest, usually devoid of spatial proximity. Studies have shown that even friendship patterns within a large apartment complex follow age, family-size, and

---

[2] *Koinonia:* sharing a common religious commitment and spiritual community.

personal-interest lines. They do not ordinarily spring from the mere adjacence of apartments. Thus, to complain that apartment people often live for years just down the hall from another family but do not "really get to know them" overlooks the fact that many specifically choose *not* to "know" their spatial neighbors in any intimate sense. This allows them more time and energy to cultivate the friends they themselves select. This does not mean the apartment dweller cannot love his next-door neighbor. He can and often does so, certainly no less frequently than the small-town resident. But he does so by being a dependable fellow tenant, by bearing his share of the common responsibility they both have in that segment of their lives shaped by residence. This does not require their becoming cronies.

All this means that the urban secular man is summoned to a different *kind* of neighborliness than his town-dwelling predecessor practiced. Much like the Samaritan described by Jesus in the story he told in response to the question "Who is my neighbor?," his main responsibility is to do competently what needs to be done to assure his neighbor's health and well-being. The man who fell among thieves was not the next-door neighbor of the Samaritan, but he helped him in an efficient, unsentimental way. He did not form an I—Thou relationship with him but bandaged his wounds and made sure the innkeeper had enough cash to cover his expenses.

Urban anonymity need not be heartless. Village sociability can mask a murderous hostility. Loneliness is undoubtedly a serious problem in the city, but it cannot be met by dragooning urban people into relationships which decimate their privacy and reduce their capacity to live responsibly with increasing numbers of neighbors. The church investigators who shook their heads over the evasiveness of the apartment dwellers had forgotten this. They had come to the city with a village theology and had stumbled upon an essential protective device, the polite refusal to be chummy, without which urban existence could not be human. They had overlooked the fact that technopolitan man *must* cultivate and guard his privacy. He must restrict the number of people who have his number or know his name.

The small-town dweller, on the other hand, lives within a restricted web of relationships and senses a larger world he may be missing. Since the people he knows also know one another, he gossips more and yearns to hear gossip. His private life is public and vice versa. While urban man is unplugging his telephone, town man (or his wife) may be listening in on the party line or its modern equivalent, gossiping at the kaffee-klatsch.

Urban man, in contrast, wants to maintain a clear distinction between private and public. Otherwise public life would overwhelm and dehumanize him. His life represents a point touched by dozens of systems and hundreds of people. His capacity to know some of them better necessitates his minimizing the depth of his relationships to many others. Listening to the postman gossip becomes for urban man an act of sheer graciousness, since he probably has no interest in the people the postman wants to talk about. Unlike my parents, who suspected all strangers, he tends to be wary not of the functionaries he doesn't know but of those he does. . . .

MOBILITY

Every tendency in modern society points to accelerated mobility. Technology closes the saddlemaker's shop and opens electronic labs. Industrialization not only lures people off the farms and into the cities; it also invades the farms, transforming them into food factories and steadily diminishing the number of hands required to do the work. The modern city is a mass movement. It has been described by one writer as a kind of staging area where people pause in their complex movements from one place to another. Not only do we migrate between cities in search of improvement, but we migrate within cities to find more convenient or congenial surroundings. Commutation represents a small daily migration. We commute not only to work but also to play, to shop, to socialize. Everybody is going places, but what is happening to us as a people along the way?

Many view the high mobility of modern life in the most negative possible light. A whole literature of protest has grown up, much of it religious in nature, which bewails the alleged shallowness and lostness of modern urban man. Countless sermons deplore the "rush-rush of modern living" and the diminution of spiritual values supposed to accompany the loss of more sedentary cultural patterns. On a more serious level, themes of rootlessness and alienation constantly appear in contemporary literature. Indeed, the greatest novelists of our century have chosen to create heroes who wander far from home in the midst of strangers and foreigners. Thomas Mann's *Joseph in Egypt*, James Joyce's *Ulysses*, and Franz Kafka's *The Castle* come to mind immediately. Albert Camus and André Gide dealt with similar themes. Time and again there returns the image of man as a harried and homeless wanderer, frequently with absorbing artistic power. The question is, however: Must man necessarily be impoverished by mobility? Can he travel without getting lost? Can he move without meandering?

Before turning to these questions, it is worth pointing out that American men of letters have seldom taken such a cheerless view of mobility. Indeed, telling the stories of people on the go has been almost a speciality of American writers. Though *Moby Dick* has to do with more than whaling, it is impossible to read it, or Melville's other novels such as *Typee* or *Billy Budd*, without sensing his real fondness for ships and travel. In *Huckleberry Finn* Mark Twain tells of the complicated relationship between a white boy and a black man, but it is noteworthy that the characters find themselves riding a raft down the Mississippi. Joseph Conrad's settings were also the sea, while Thomas Wolfe, representing a younger generation, nourished a lifelong passion for railroads. Henry James is nearly as famous for his travel diaries as he is for his novels and essays. Hemingway, Steinbeck, and Dos Passos have all written with gusto about people on the move. Perhaps the fascination for automobiles one finds in John Updike and Jack Kerouac represents the newest phase of the American writer's traditional intoxication with going places.

America has produced a series of writers who tend to celebrate rather than denigrate mobility. But Americans have always been a mobile people. They had to be, even to come here. With one important exception, the Negroes, Americans all stem from people who voluntarily left home to come to a new land. Sociologists know that people who have already moved once are more likely to move again than are people who have never moved. They know also that mobile people are generally tolerant of new ideas and possibilities. Having entertained and acted on one big change already, they are never reticent to entertain the possibility of others. Let us examine how mobility lends a vital shape to modern urban life.

THE MAN IN THE CLOVERLEAF

Technopolitan man is on the go. In addition to the giant switchboard, he can be pictured as a driver in a cloverleaf intersection. Other images of the city include the airport control tower, high-speed elevators, and perpetually moving escalators in department stores and offices. The modern metropolis is a system of roads—thruways, subways, airways—linking the city to others and parts of the city to each other. It is also a system of vertical facilitators, snatching people from the street to the penthouse, from the janitor's basement to the executive suite and back again. Urban man is certainly in motion, and we can expect the pace and scope of mobility to increase as time goes on.

Analysts sometimes distinguish between two types of mobility—geographic and occupational. Sometimes status mobility, class mobility, and other forms of "social" mobility are added. But since these are so closely related to job and residence mobility, we shall restrict ourselves here to discussing the problems and possibilities of movement to new jobs and homes.

There are many critics of residential and occupational mobility. They use different rhetoric but quite frequently paint verbal landscapes of home and vocation which are laden with religious sentiments. For many people these images have a real appeal. To be born and reared in the same clapboard house where one may even grow old and die does have a certain cozy attractiveness. To work at the same job in the same place through all one's adult years might also provide elements of comfort. But those who bewail the passing of the era in which this stable, idyllic condition was supposed to have obtained forget one important fact: only a tiny minority of people ever really enjoyed such pastoral permanence. The majority of people in premobile societies lived and worked in ways we would not want to return to. Most of us today would vigorously object to living in the house or doing the job our great-grandfathers did. The fact is that most people's great-grandparents were dirt-poor and lived in hovels. Most of us are much better off today because our forebears *were* mobile. Mobility is always the weapon of the underdog. The desire to combat mobility, to encourage residential and occupational *im*mobility, is a romantic distortion which springs from a reactionary mentality.

Mobility is closely linked to social change; so guardians of the status quo have always opposed mobility. They are perfectly consistent in doing so. They sense that changes in one area of life—job or residence—will lead to other kinds of change; and they are against change. The conservatives in the polis of Athens were right in their fierce opposition to constructing a port at Piraeus. They knew that mixed with the exotic products of foreign shores there would come strange people with exotic ideas which would shake their security. Virulent opposition to the building of railroads was voiced by the lords of the English establishment in the early nineteenth century, not just because railroads were loud or dirty, but because even lowly villagers would now travel to other towns. There they could not be kept from coming under strange influences since they would wander about without the normal social controls. Worst of all, it was argued, they would meet people who had never heard of their local squires. They would see their own towns in perspective and might lose all respect for traditional authority.

The World War I song "How Ya Gonna' Keep 'Em Down on the Farm Now that They've Seen Paree?" illustrates the relationship between mobility, urbanization, and social change. Those who have been drawn into the tradition-demolishing orbit of urban life are never quite the same again. They will always know that things *could* be different; they will never again accept the farm as given; and this is the seedbed of revolution.

In our own country the emergence of the Negro Freedom Movement provides a particularly good example of the link between mobility and social change. Many observers believe that the movement of large numbers of Negroes out of rural areas in the South and into urban industrial centers, plus the experience of thousands of young Negroes in the military service, supplied the indispensable social exposure which has resulted in the civil rights revolution. Negroes discovered that things did not have to be the way they were. Those who acted against oppression were young, and they were geographically and occupationally mobile. Their battles, unlike those of the Civil War which took place at heretofore unknown villages—Bull Run and Gettysburg— now took place in urban centers such as Birmingham, and spread to the provinces. Mobility had unlocked the cage.

Geographic mobility always points to social or occupational mobility. Even in the storybooks, the son leaves the family homestead "to seek his fortune." Mobility in one area signifies mobility in another. People on the move spatially are usually on the move intellectually, financially, or psychologically. All of this naturally threatens those who already occupy the positions of power and influence in the society. It is the people on the bottom who have everything to gain and nothing to lose from a mobile society. . . .

The Generators of Diversity

JANE JACOBS

For several years an editor of Architectural Forum *magazine, Jane Jacobs emerged in 1962 as a devastating critic of huge urban renewal programs. Her book of that year,* The Death and Life of Great American Cities, *was a common sense plea against wiping out neighborhoods in the name of progress: "This is not the rebuilding of cities. This is the sacking of cities."*

Classified telephone directories tell us the greatest single fact about cities: the immense numbers of parts that make up a city, and the immense diversity of those parts. Diversity is natural to big cities.

"I have often amused myself," wrote James Boswell in 1791, "with thinking how different a place London is to different people. They, whose narrow minds are contracted to the consideration of some one particular pursuit, view it only through that medium. . . . But the intellectual man is struck with it, as comprehending the whole of human life in all its variety, the contemplation of which is inexhaustible."

Boswell not only gave a good definition of cities, he put his finger on one of the chief troubles in dealing with them. It is so easy to fall into the trap of contemplating a city's uses one at a time, by categories. Indeed, just this—analysis of cities, use by use—has become a customary planning tactic. The findings on various categories of use are then put together into "broad, overall pictures."

The overall pictures such methods yield are about as useful as the picture assembled by the blind men who felt the elephant and pooled their findings. The elephant lumbered on, oblivious to the notion that he was a leaf, a snake, a wall, tree trunks and a rope all somehow stuck together. Cities, being our own artifacts, enjoy less defense against solemn nonsense.

To understand cities, we have to deal outright with combinations or mixtures of uses, not separate uses, as the essential phenomena . . . the importance of this in the case of neighborhood parks is an example. Parks can easily—too easily—be thought of as phenomena in their own right and described as adequate or inadequate in terms, say, of acreage ratios to thousands of population. Such an approach tells us something about the methods of planners, but it tells us nothing useful about the behavior or value of neighborhood parks.

A mixture of uses, if it is to be sufficiently complex to sustain city safety, public contact and cross-use, needs an enormous diversity of ingredients. So the first question—and I think by far the most important question—about planning cities is this: How can cities generate enough mixture among uses—enough diversity—throughout enough of their territories, to sustain their own civilization?

It is all very well to castigate the Great Blight of Dullness and to understand why it is destructive to city life, but in itself this does not get us far. Consider the problem posed by the street with the pretty sidewalk park in Baltimore. . . . My friend from the street, Mrs. Kostritsky, is quite right when she reasons that it needs some commerce for its users' convenience. And as might be expected, inconvenience and lack of public street life are only two of the by-products of residential monotony here. Danger is another—fear of the streets after dark. Some people fear to be alone in their houses by day since the occurrence of two nasty daytime assaults. Moreover, the place lacks commercial choices as well as any cultural interest. We can see very well how fatal is its monotony.

But having said this, then what? The missing diversity, convenience, interest and vitality do not spring forth because the area needs their benefits. Anybody who started a retail enterprise here, for example, would be stupid. He could not make a living. To wish a vital urban life might somehow spring up here is to play with daydreams. The place is an economic desert.

Although it is hard to believe, while looking at dull gray areas, or at housing projects or at civic centers, the fact is that big cities *are* natural generators of diversity and prolific incubators of new enterprises and ideas of all kinds. Moreover, big cities are the natural economic homes of immense numbers and ranges of small enterprises.

The principal studies of variety and size among city enterprises happen to be studies of manufacturing, notably those by Raymond Vernon, author of *Anatomy of a Metropolis*, and by P. Sargant Florence, who has examined the effect of cities on manufacturing both here and in England.

Characteristically, the larger a city, the greater the variety of its manufacturing, and also the greater both the number and the proportion of its small manufacturers. The reasons for this, in brief, are that big enterprises have greater self-sufficiency than small ones, are able to maintain within themselves most of the skills and equipment they need, can warehouse for themselves, and can sell to a broad market which they can seek out wherever it may be. They need not be in cities, and although sometimes it is advantageous for them to be there, often it is more advantageous not to. But for small manufacturers, everything is reversed. Typically they must draw on many and varied supplies and skills outside themselves, they must serve a narrow market at the point where a market exists, and they must be sensitive to quick changes in this market. Without cities, they would simply not exist. Dependent on a huge diversity of other city enterprises, they can add further to that diversity. This last is a most important point to remember. City diversity itself permits and stimulates more diversity.

For many activities other than manufacturing, the situation is analogous. For example, when Connecticut General Life Insurance Company built a new headquarters in the countryside beyond Hartford, it could do so only by dint of providing—in addition to the usual working spaces and rest rooms, medical suite and the like—a large general store, a beauty parlor, a bowling alley, a cafeteria, a theater and a great variety of games space. These facilities are inherently inefficient, idle most of the time. They require subsidy, not because they are kinds of enterprises which are necessarily money losers, but because here their use is so limited. They were presumed necessary, however, to compete for a working force, and to hold it. A large company can absorb the luxury of such inherent inefficiencies and balance them against other advantages it seeks. But small offices can do nothing of the kind. If they want to compete for a work force on even terms or better, they must be in a lively city setting where their employees find the range of subsidiary conveniences and choices that they want and need. Indeed, one reason, among many others, why the much-heralded postwar exodus of big offices from cities turned out to be mostly talk is that the differentials in cost of suburban land and space are typically canceled by the greater amount of space per worker required for facilities that in cities no single employer need provide, nor any one corps of workers or customers support. Another reason why such enterprises have stayed in cities, along with small firms, is that many of their employees, especially executives, need to be in close, face-to-face touch and communication with people outside the firm—including people from small firms.

The benefits that cities offer to smallness are just as marked in retail trade, cultural facilities and entertainment. This is because city populations are large enough to support wide ranges of variety and choice in these things. And again we find that bigness has all the advantages in smaller settlements. Towns and suburbs, for instance, are natural homes for huge supermarkets and for little else in the way of groceries, for standard movie houses or drive-ins and for little else in

the way of theater. There are simply not enough people to support further variety, although there may be people (too few of them) who
would draw upon it were it there. Cities, however, are the natural
homes of supermarkets and standard movie houses *plus* delicatessens,
Viennese bakeries, foreign groceries, art movies, and so on, all of which
can be found co-existing, the standard with the strange, the large with
the small. Wherever lively and popular parts of cities are found, the
small much outnumber the large.[1] Like the small manufacturers, these
small enterprises would not exist somewhere else, in the absence of
cities. Without cities, they would not exist.

The diversity, of whatever kind, that is generated by cities rests on
the fact that in cities so many people are so close together, and among
them contain so many different tastes, skills, needs, supplies, and bees
in their bonnets.

Even quite standard, but small operations like proprietor-and-one-
clerk hardware stores, drug stores, candy stores and bars can and do
flourish in extraordinary numbers and incidence in lively districts of
cities because there are enough people to support their presence at
short, convenient intervals, and in turn this convenience and neighborhood personal quality are big parts of such enterprises' stock in
trade. Once they are unable to be supported at close, convenient intervals, they lose this advantage. In a given geographical territory, half as
many people will not support half as many such enterprises spaced at
twice the distance. When distance inconvenience sets in, the small, the
various and the personal wither away.

As we have transformed from a rural and small-town country into
an urban country, business enterprises have thus become more numerous, not only in absolute terms, but also in proportionate terms. In
1900 there were 21 independent nonfarm businesses for each 1,000 persons in the total U.S. population. In 1959, in spite of the immense
growth of giant enterprises during the interval, there were 26½ in-

---

[1] In retail trade, this tendency has been growing stronger, if anything. Richard
Nelson, the Chicago real estate analyst, examining the postwar trend of retail
sales in some twenty city downtowns, has discovered that the large department
stores have typically lost trade; the chain variety stores have stayed about even;
and the small and special stores have increased their business and usually have
also increased in number. There is no real competition outside the cities for these
small and various city enterprises; but it is relatively easy for the big and standardized, in their natural homes outside the city, to compete with what is big and
standardized within. This happens, incidentally, to be exactly what has occurred
in the neighborhood where I live. Wanamaker's, the big department store formerly
located in Greenwich Village, has gone out of business here and established itself
in a suburb instead, at the same time that small and special stores in its immediate former vicinity have increased by the score and flourished mightily.

dependent nonfarm businesses for each 1,000 persons in the population. With urbanization, the big get bigger, but the small also get more numerous.

Smallness and diversity, to be sure, are not synonyms. The diversity of city enterprises includes all degrees of size, but great variety does mean a high proportion of small elements. A lively city scene is lively largely by virtue of its enormous collection of small elements.

Nor is the diversity that is important for city districts by any means confined to profit-making enterprises and to retail commerce, and for this reason it may seem that I put an undue emphasis on retail trade. I think not, however. Commercial diversity is, in itself, immensely important for cities, socially as well as economically. Many of the uses of diversity . . . depend directly or indirectly upon the presence of plentiful, convenient, diverse city commerce. But more than this, wherever we find a city district with an exuberant variety and plenty in its commerce, we are apt to find that it contains a good many other kinds of diversity also, including variety of cultural opportunities, variety of scenes, and a great variety in its population and other users. This is more than coincidence. The same physical and economic conditions that generate diverse commerce are intimately related to the production, or the presence, of other kinds of city variety.

But although cities may fairly be called natural economic generators of diversity and natural economic incubators of new enterprises, this does not mean that cities *automatically* generate diversity just by existing. They generate it because of the various efficient economic pools of use that they form. Wherever they fail to form such pools of use, they are little better, if any, at generating diversity than small settlements. And the fact that they need diversity socially, unlike small settlements, makes no difference. For our purposes here, the most striking fact to note is the extraordinary unevenness with which cities generate diversity.

On the one hand, for example, people who live and work in Boston's North End, or New York's Upper East Side or San Francisco's North Beach-Telegraph Hill, are able to use and enjoy very considerable amounts of diversity and vitality. Their visitors help immensely. But the visitors did not create the foundations of diversity in areas like these, nor in the many pockets of diversity and economic efficiency scattered here and there, sometimes most unexpectedly, in big cities. The visitors sniff out where something vigorous exists already, and come to share it, thereby further supporting it.

At the other extreme, huge city settlements of people exist without their presence generating anything much except stagnation and, ultimately, a fatal discontent with the place. It is not that they are a different kind of people, somehow duller or unappreciative of vigor and diversity. Often they include hordes of searchers, trying to sniff out these attributes somewhere, anywhere. Rather, something is wrong with their districts; something is lacking to catalyze a district population's ability to interact economically and help form effective pools of use.

Apparently there is no limit to the numbers of people in a city whose potentiality as city populations can thus be wasted. Consider, for instance, the Bronx, a borough of New York containing some one and a half million people. The Bronx is woefully short of urban vitality, diversity and magnetism. It has its loyal residents, to be sure, mostly attached to little bloomings of street life here and there in "the old neighborhood," but not nearly enough of them.

In so simple a matter of city amenity and diversity as interesting restaurants, the 1,500,000 people in the Bronx cannot produce. Kate Simon, the author of a guidebook, *New York Places and Pleasures*, describes hundreds of restaurants and other commercial establishments, particularly in unexpected and out-of-the-way parts of the city. She is not snobbish, and dearly likes to present her readers with inexpensive discoveries. But although Miss Simon tries hard, she has to give up the great settlement of the Bronx as thin pickings at any price. After paying homage to the two solid metropolitan attractions in the borough, the zoo and the Botanical Gardens, she is hard put to recommend a single place to eat outside the zoo grounds. The one possibility she is able to offer, she accompanies with this apology: "The neighborhood trails off sadly into a no man's land, and the restaurant can stand a little refurbishing, but there's the comfort of knowing that . . . the best of Bronx medical skill is likely to be sitting all around you."

Well, that is the Bronx, and it is too bad it is so; too bad for the people who live there now, too bad for the people who are going to inherit it in future out of their lack of economic choice, and too bad for the city as a whole.

And if the Bronx is a sorry waste of city potentialities, as it is, consider the even more deplorable fact that it is possible for whole cities to exist, whole metropolitan areas, with pitifully little city diversity and choice. Virtually all of urban Detroit is as weak on vitality and diversity as the Bronx. It is ring superimposed upon ring of failed gray belts. Even Detroit's downtown itself cannot produce a respectable amount of diversity. It is dispirited and dull, and almost deserted by seven o'clock of an evening.

So long as we are content to believe that city diversity represents accident and chaos, of course its erratic generation appears to represent a mystery.

However, the conditions that generate city diversity are quite easy to discover by observing places in which diversity flourishes and studying the economic reasons why it can flourish in these places. Although the results are intricate, and the ingredients producing them may vary enormously, this complexity is based on tangible economic relationships which, in principle, are much simpler than the intricate urban mixtures they make possible.

To generate exuberant diversity in a city's streets and districts, four conditions are indispensable:

1. The district, and indeed as many of its internal parts as possible, must serve more than one primary function; preferably more than two. These must insure the presence of people who go outdoors on different schedules and are in the place for different purposes, but who are able to use many facilities in common.

2. Most blocks must be short; that is, streets and opportunities to turn corners must be frequent.

3. The district must mingle buildings that vary in age and condition, including a good proportion of old ones so that they vary in the economic yield they must produce. This mingling must be fairly close-grained.

4. There must be a sufficiently dense concentration of people, for whatever purposes they may be there. This includes dense concentration in the case of people who are there because of residence.

The necessity for these four conditions is the most important point I have to make. In combination, these conditions create effective economic pools of use. Given these four conditions, not all city districts will produce a diversity equivalent to one another. The potentials of different districts differ for many reasons; but, given the development of these four conditions (or the best approximation to their full development that can be managed in real life), a city district should be able to realize its best potential, wherever that may lie. Obstacles to doing so will have been removed. The range may not stretch to African sculpture or schools of drama or Rumanian tea houses, but such as the possibilities are, whether for grocery stores, pottery schools, movies, candy stores, florists, art shows, immigrants' clubs, hardware stores, eating places, or whatever, they will get their best chance. And along with them, city life will get its best chances. . . .

The Unheavenly City

EDWARD C. BANFIELD

Edward C. Banfield, professor of urban government at Harvard, has argued that our cities are more livable and equitable than we give them credit for. His book, The Unheavenly City, *in which he details his skepticism of altruistic attempts to renovate metropolitan America, won immediate public attention.*

. . . the clock is ticking, time is moving . . . , we must ask ourselves every night when we go home, are we doing all that we should do in our nation's capital, in all the other big cities of the country.

—President Johnson, after the Watts Riot, August 1965

That we face an urban crisis of utmost seriousness has in recent years come to be part of the conventional wisdom. We are told on all sides that the cities are uninhabitable, that they must be torn down and rebuilt or new ones must be built from the ground up, that something drastic must be done—and soon—or else.

On the face of it this "crisis" view has a certain plausibility. One need not walk more than a few blocks in any city to see much that is wrong and in crying need of improvement. It is anomalous that in a society as technologically advanced and as affluent as ours there should be many square miles of slums and even more miles of dreary blight and chaotic sprawl. And when one considers that as many as 60 million more people may live in metropolitan areas in 1980 than lived there in 1960, it seems clear that unless something drastic is done things are bound to get worse.

There is, however, another side to the matter. The plain fact is that the overwhelming majority of city dwellers live more comfortably and conveniently than ever before. They have more and better housing, more and better schools, more and better transportation, and so on. By any conceivable measure of material welfare the present generation of urban Americans is, on the whole, better off than any other large group of people has ever been anywhere. What is more, there is every reason to expect that the general level of comfort and convenience will continue to rise at an even more rapid rate through the foreseeable future.

It is true that many people do not share, or do not share fully, this general prosperity, some because they are the victims of racial prejudice and others for other reasons that are equally beyond their control. If the chorus of complaint about the city arose mainly from these disadvantaged people or on behalf of them, it would be entirely understandable, especially if their numbers were increasing and their plight were getting worse. But the fact is that until very recently most of the talk about the urban crisis has had to do with the comfort, convenience, and business advantage of the well-off white majority and not with the more serious problems of the poor, the Negro, and others who stand outside the charmed circle. And the fact also is that the number of those standing outside the circle is decreasing, as is the relative disadvantage that they suffer. There is still much poverty and much racial discrimination. But there is less of both than ever before.

The question arises, therefore, not of whether we are faced with an urban crisis, but rather, *in what sense* we are faced with one. Whose interest and what interests are involved? How deeply? What should be done? Given the political and other realities of the situation, what *can* be done?

The first need is to clear away some semantic confusions. Consider the statement, so frequently used to alarm luncheon groups, that 70 percent of the population now lives in urban places and that this number may increase to 80 percent in the next two decades if present trends continue. Such figures give the impression of standing room only in the city, but what exactly do they mean?

When we are told that the population of the United States is rapidly becoming overwhelmingly urban, we probably suppose this to mean that most people are coming to live in the big cities. This is true in one sense but false in another. It is true that most people live closer physically and psychologically to a big city than ever before; rural occupations and a rural style of life are no longer widespread. On the other hand, the percentage of the population living in cities of 250,000 or more (there are fifty-six of them in the 1970 census) is about the same now as it was in 1920. In census terminology an "urban place" is any settlement having a population of 2,500 or more; obviously places of 2,500 are not what we have in mind when we use words like "urban" and "city." It is somewhat misleading to say that the country is becoming more urban, when what is meant is that more people are living in places like White River Junction, Vermont . . . , and fewer in places like Boston, Massachusetts. . . . But it is not altogether misleading, for most of the small urban places are now close to large cities and part of a metropolitan complex. White River Junction, for example, is now close enough to Boston to be very much influenced by it.

A great many so-called urban problems are really conditions that we either cannot change or do not want to incur the disadvantages of changing. Consider the "problem of congestion." The presence of a great many people in one place is a cause of inconvenience, to say the least. But the advantages of having so many people in one place far outweigh these inconveniences, and we cannot possibly have the advantages without the disadvantages. To "eliminate congestion" in the city must mean eliminating the city's reason for being. Congestion in the city is a "problem" only in the sense that congestion in Times Square on New Year's Eve is one; in fact, of course, people come to the city, just as they do to Times Square, precisely *because* it is congested. If it were not congested, it would not be worth coming to.

Strictly speaking, a problem exists only as we should want something different from what we do want or as by better management we could get a larger total of what we want. If we think it a good thing that many people have the satisfaction of driving their cars in and out of the city, and if we see no way of arranging the situation to get them in and out more conveniently that does not entail more than offsetting disadvantages for them or others, then we ought not to speak of a "traffic congestion problem." By the same token, urban sprawl is a "problem," as opposed to an "unpleasant condition," only if (1) fewer people should have the satisfaction of living in the low-density fringe of the city, or (2) we might, by better planning, build homes in the fringe without destroying so much landscape and without incurring costs (for example, higher per-unit construction costs) or foregoing benefits (for example, a larger number of low-income families who can have the satisfaction of living in the low-density area) of greater value than the saving in landscape.

Few problems, in this strict sense, are anywhere near as big as they seem. The amount of urban sprawl that could be eliminated simply by better planning—that is, without the sacrifice of other ends that are also wanted, such as giving the satisfaction of owning a house and yard to many low-income people—is probably trivial as compared to the total urban sprawl (that is, to the "problem" defined simplemindedly as "a condition that is unpleasant").

Most so-called urban problems are more characteristic of rural and small-town places than of cities. We have been conditioned to associate "slums" with "cities," but in 1960 74 percent of all deteriorating and 81 percent of all dilapidated housing was *outside* cities of 100,000 or more population, and about 60 percent of all families in substandard housing lived outside metropolitan areas. The situation is similar in other matters. "Low verbal ability," Sloan R. Wayland of Columbia Teachers College has written, "is described as though it could only happen in an urban slum." Actually, he points out, all but a very small fraction of mankind has always been "culturally deprived," and the task of formal education has always been to attack such conditions.

Most of the "problems" that are generally supposed to constitute "the urban crisis" could not conceivably lead to disaster. They are— some of them—important in the sense that a bad cold is important, but they are not serious in the sense that a cancer is serious. They have to do with comfort, convenience, amenity, and business advantage, all of which are important, but they do not affect either the essential welfare of individuals or what may be called the good health of the society.

Consider, for example, an item that often appears near the top of the list of complaints about the city—the journey to work. It takes the average worker in a metropolitan area about half an hour to get to work, and only about 15 percent of workers spend more than three-quarters of an hour getting there. It would, of course, be very nice if the journey to work were much shorter. No one can suppose, however, that the essential welfare of many people would be much affected even if it were fifteen minutes longer. Certainly its being longer or shorter would not make the difference between a good society and a bad.

Another matter causing widespread alarm is the decline of the central business district, by which is meant the loss of patronage to downtown department stores, theaters, restaurants, museums, and so on, which has resulted from the movement of many well-off people to suburbs. Clearly, the movement of good customers from one place to another involves inconvenience and business loss to many people, especially to the owners of real estate that is no longer in so great demand. These losses, however, are essentially no different from those that occur from other causes—say, a shift of consumers' tastes that suddenly renders a once-valuable patent valueless. Moreover, though some lose by the change, others gain by it: the overall gain of wealth by building in the suburbs may more than offset the loss of it caused by letting the downtown deteriorate.

There are those who claim that cultural and intellectual activity flourishes only in big cities and that therefore the decline of the downtown business districts and the replacement of cities by suburbs threatens the very survival of civilization. This claim is farfetched, to say the very least, if it means that we cannot have good music and good theater (not to mention philosophy, literature, and science) unless customers do their shopping in the downtown districts of Oakland, St. Louis, Nashville, Boston, and so on, rather than in the suburbs around them. Public efforts to preserve the downtown districts of these and other cities may perhaps be worth what they cost; the return, however, will be in terms of comfort, convenience, and business advantage of the relatively well-off—and not in terms of anyone's essential welfare.

The same can be said about efforts to "beautify" the cities. That for the most part the cities are dreary and depressing if not offensively ugly may be granted: the desirability of improving their appearance, even if only a little, cannot be questioned. It is very doubtful, however, that people are dehumanized (to use a favorite word of those who complain about the cities) by the ugliness of the city or that they would be in any sense humanized by its being made beautiful. (If they were humanized, they would doubtless build beautiful cities, but that is an entirely different matter. One has only to read Machiavelli's history of Florence to see that living in a beautiful city is not in itself enough to bring out the best in one. So far as their humanity is concerned, the people of, say, Jersey City compare very favorably to the Florentines of the era of that city's greatest glory.) At worst, the American city's ugliness—or, more, its lack of splendor or charm—occasions loss of visual pleasure. This loss is an important one (it is surely much larger than most people realize), but it cannot lead to any kind of disaster either for the individual or for the society.

Air pollution comes closer than any of these problems to threatening essential welfare, as opposed to comfort, convenience, amenity, and business advantage. Some people die early because of it and many more suffer various degrees of bad health; there is also some possibility (no one knows how much) that a meteorological coincidence (an "air inversion") over a large city might suddenly kill thousands or even tens of thousands. Important as it is, however, the air pollution problem is rather minor as compared to other threats to health and welfare not generally regarded as "crises." According to the U.S. Public Health Service, the most polluted air is nowhere near as dangerous as cigarette smoke.

Many of the "problems" that are supposed to constitute the "crisis" could be quickly and easily solved, or much alleviated, by the application of well-known measures that lie right at hand. In some instances, the money cost of these measures would be very small. For example, the rush-hour traffic problem in the central cities (which, incidentally, is almost the whole of the traffic problem in these cities) could be much reduced and in some cases eliminated entirely just by staggering working hours in the largest offices and factories. Manhattan presents the hardest case of all, but even there, an elaborate study showed, rush-hour crowding could be reduced by 25 percent, enough to make the strap-hanger reasonably comfortable. Another quick and easy way of improving urban transportation in most cities would be to eliminate a mass of archaic regulations on the granting of public transit and taxi franchises. At present, the cities are in effect going out of their way to place obstacles in the paths of those who might offer the public better transportation.

The "price" of solving, or alleviating, some much-talked-about urban problems is largely political. The proposal to reduce transit jams in Manhattan by staggering work hours was quickly and quietly killed by the city administration because the business community preferred the traditional nine-to-five pattern.

If the rush-hour traffic problem is basically political, so is the revenue problem. A great part of the wealth of our country is in the cities. When a mayor says that his city is on the verge of bankruptcy, he really means that when the time comes to run for reelection he wants to be able to claim credit for straightening out a mess that was left him by his predecessor. What a mayor means when he says that his city *must* have state or federal aid to finance some improvements is (1) the taxpayers of the city (or some important group of them) would rather go without the improvement than pay for it themselves; or (2) although they would pay for it themselves if they had to, they would much prefer to have some other taxpayers pay for it. Rarely if ever does a mayor who makes such a statement mean (1) that for the city to pay for the improvement would necessarily force some taxpayers into poverty; or (2) that the city could not raise the money even if it were willing to force some of its taxpayers into poverty. In short, the "revenue crisis" mainly reflects the fact that people hate to pay taxes and that they think that by crying poverty they can shift some of the bill to someone else.

To some extent, also, the revenue problem of the cities arises from the way jurisdictional boundaries are drawn or, more precisely, from what are considered to be inequities resulting from the movement of taxable wealth from one side of a boundary line to another. When many large taxpayers move to the suburbs, the central city must tax those who remain at a higher rate if it is to maintain the same level of services. The "problem" in this case is not that the taxpayers who remain are absolutely unable to pay the increased taxes; rather, it is that they do not want to pay them and that they consider it unfair that they should have to pay more simply because other people have moved away. The simple and costless solution (in all but a political sense) would be to charge nonresidents for services that they receive from the city or, failing that, to redraw the boundary lines so that everyone in the metropolitan area would be taxed on the same basis.

That we have not yet been willing to pay the price of solving, or alleviating, such "problems" even when the price is a very small one suggests that they are not really as serious as they have been made out to be. Indeed, one might say that, by definition, a serious problem is one that people are willing to pay a considerable price to have solved.

With regard to these problems for which solutions are at hand, we will know that a real crisis impends when we see the solutions actually being applied. The solution, that is, will be applied when—and only when—the inconvenience or other disadvantage of allowing the problem to continue unabated is judged to have become greater than that of taking the necessary measures to abate it. In other words, a bad-but-not-quite-critical problem is one that it would almost-but-not-quite pay us to do something about.

If some real disaster impends in the city, it is not because parking spaces are hard to find, because architecture is bad, because department store sales are declining, or even because taxes are rising. If there is a genuine crisis, it has to do with the essential welfare of individuals or with the good health of the society, not merely with comfort, convenience, amenity, and business advantage, important as these are. It is not necessary here to try to define "essential welfare" rigorously: it is enough to say that whatever may cause people to die before their time, to suffer serious impairment of their health or of their powers, to waste their lives, to be deeply unhappy or happy in a way that is less than human affects their essential welfare. It is harder to indicate in a sentence or two what is meant by the "good health" of the society. The ability of the society to maintain itself as a going concern is certainly a primary consideration; so is its free and democratic character. In the last analysis, however, the quality of a society must be judged by its tendency to produce desirable human types; the healthy society, then, is one that not only stays alive but also moves in the direction of giving greater scope and expression to what is distinctively human. In general, of course, what serves the essential welfare of individuals also promotes the good health of the society; there are occasions, however, when the two goals conflict. In such cases, the essential welfare of individuals must be sacrificed for the good health of the society. This happens on a very large scale when there is a war, but it may happen at other times as well. The conditions about which we should be most concerned, therefore, are those that affect, or may affect, the good health of the society. If there is an urban crisis in any ultimate sense, it must be constituted of these conditions.

It is a good deal easier to say what matters are not serious (that is, do not affect either the essential welfare of individuals or the good health of the society) than it is to say what ones are. It is clear, however, that poverty, ignorance, and racial (and other) injustices are among the most important of the general conditions affecting the essential welfare of individuals. It is plausible, too, to suppose that these conditions have a very direct bearing upon the good health of the society, although in this connection other factors that are much harder to guess about—for example, the nature and strength of the consensual bonds that hold the society together—may be much more important. To begin with, anyway, it seems reasonable to look in these general directions for what may be called the serious problems of the cities.

It is clear at the outset that serious problems directly affect only a rather small minority of the whole urban population. In the relatively new residential suburbs and in the better residential neighborhoods in the outlying parts of the central cities and in the older, larger, suburbs, the overwhelming majority of people are safely above the poverty line, have at least a high school education, and do not suffer from racial discrimination. For something like two-thirds of all city dwellers, the urban problems that touch them directly have to do with comfort, convenience, amenity, and business advantage. In the terminology used here, these are "important" problems but not "serious" ones. In a great many cases, these problems cannot even fairly be called important; a considerable part of the urban population—those who reside in the "nicer" suburbs—lives under material conditions that will be hard to improve upon.

The serious problems are to be found in all large cities and in most small ones. But they affect only parts of these cities (and only a minority of the city populations). In the central cities and the larger, older suburbs the affected parts are usually adjacent to the central business district and spreading out from it. If these inner districts, which probably comprise somewhere between 10 and 20 percent of the total area classified as urban by the census, were suddenly to disappear, along with the people who live in them, there would be no serious urban problems worth talking about. If what really matters is the essential welfare of individuals and the good health of the society as opposed to comfort, convenience, amenity, and business advantage, then what we have is not an "urban problem" but an "inner-central-city-and-larger-older-suburb" one.

The serious problems of these places, it should be stressed, are in most instances not caused by the conditions of urban life as such and are less characteristic of the city than of small-town and farm areas. Poverty, ignorance, and racial injustice are more widespread outside the cities than inside them.

One problem that is both serious and unique to the large cities is the existence of huge enclaves of people (many, but not all of them, Negro) of low skill, low income, and low status. In his book *Dark Ghetto*, Kenneth B. Clark presents census data showing that eight cities—New York, Los Angeles, Baltimore, Washington, Cleveland, St. Louis, New Orleans, and Chicago—contain a total of sixteen areas, all of at

least 15,000 population and five of more than 100,000, that are exclusively (more than 94 percent) Negro. There are smaller Negro enclaves
in many other cities, and there are large Puerto Rican and large Mexican ones in a few cities. Whether these places can properly be called
ghettoes is open to some doubt. . . . However, there is no question but
that they are largely cut off both physically and psychologically from
the rest of the city. Whatever may be the effect of this separation on
the essential welfare of the individual (and it is arguable that it is trivial), it is clear that the existence of huge enclaves of people who are in
some degree alienated from it constitutes a kind of hazard not only to
the present peace and safety but also to the long-run health of the society. The problems of individual welfare that these people present are
no greater by virtue of the fact that they live together in huge enclaves
rather than in isolation on farms, or in small neighborhoods in towns
and cities (the problem of individual welfare *appears* greater when they
live in huge enclaves, but that is because in this form it is too conspic-
uous to be ignored). The problem that they present to the good health
of the society, on the other hand, is very different and vastly greater
solely by virtue of the fact that they live in huge enclaves. Unlike those
who live on farms and in small towns, disaffected people who live in
huge enclaves may develop a collective consciousness and sense of
identity. From many standpoints it is highly desirable that they do so.
In the short run, however, they represent a threat to peace and order,
and it must be admitted that even in the long run the accommodation
that takes place may produce a politics that is less democratic, less
mindful of individual rights, and less able to act effectively in the common interest than that which we have now.

This political danger in the presence of great concentrations of
people who feel little attachment to the society has long been regarded
by some as *the* serious problem of the cities—the one problem that
might conceivably produce a disaster that would destroy the quality of
the society. "The dark ghettoes," Dr. Clark has written, "now represent a nuclear stockpile which can annihilate the very foundations of
America." These words bring up-to-date apprehensions that were expressed by some of the Founding Fathers and that Tocqueville set forth
in a famous passage of *Democracy in America:*

> The United States has no metropolis, but it already contains sev-
> eral very large cities. Philadelphia reckoned 161,000 inhabitants,
> and New York 202,000, in the year 1830. The lower ranks which
> inhabit these cities constitute a rabble even more formidable than
> the populace of European towns. They consist of freed blacks, in
> the first place, who are condemned by the laws and by public
> opinion to a hereditary state of misery and degradation. They also

contain a multitude of Europeans who have been driven to the shores of the New World by their misfortunes or their misconduct; and they bring to the United States all our greatest vices, without any of those interests which counteract their baneful influence. As inhabitants of a country where they have no civil rights, they are ready to turn all the passions which agitate the community to their own advantage; thus, within the last few months, serious riots have broken out in Philadelphia and New York. Disturbances of this kind are unknown in the rest of the country, which is not alarmed by them, because the population of the cities has hitherto exercised neither power nor influence over the rural districts.

Nevertheless, I look upon the size of certain American cities, and especially on the nature of their population, as a rea danger which threatens the future security of the democratic republics of the New World; and I venture to predict that they will perish from this circumstance, unless the government succeeds in creating an armed force which, while it remains under the control of the majority of the nation, will be independent of the town population and able to repress its excesses.

Strange as it may seem, the mammoth government programs to aid the cities are directed mainly toward the problems of comfort, convenience, amenity, and business advantage. Insofar as they have any effect on the serious problems, it is, on the whole, to aggravate them.

Two programs account for approximately 90 percent of federal government expenditure for the improvement of the cities (as opposed to the maintenance of more or less routine functions). Neither is intended to deal with the serious problems. Both make them worse.

The improvement of transportation is one program. The urban portions of the national expressway system are expected to cost about $18 billion. Their main effect will be to enable suburbanites to move about the metropolitan area more conveniently, to open up some areas for business and residential expansion, and to bring a few more customers from the suburbs downtown to shop. These are all worthy objects when considered by themselves; in context, however, their justification is doubtful, for their principal effect will be to encourage—in effect to subsidize—further movement of industry, commerce, and relatively well-off residents (mostly white) from the inner city. This, of course, will make matters worse for the poor by reducing the number of jobs for them and by making neighborhoods, schools, and other community facilities still more segregated. These injuries will be only partially offset by allowing a certain number of the inner-city poor to commute to jobs in the suburbs.

The huge expenditure being made for improvement of mass transit facilities (it may amount to $10 billion over a decade) may be justifiable for the contribution that it will make to comfort, convenience, and business advantage. It will not, however, make any contribution to the solution of the serious problems of the city. Even if every city had a subway as fancy as Moscow's, all these problems would remain.

The second great federal urban program concerns housing and renewal. Since the creation in 1934 of the Federal Housing Authority (FHA), the government has subsidized home building on a vast scale by insuring mortgages that are written on easy terms and, in the case of the Veterans Administration (VA), by guaranteeing mortgages. Most of the mortgages have been for the purchase of *new* homes. (This was partly because FHA wanted gilt-edged collateral behind the mortgages that it insured, but it was also because it shared the American predilection for newness.) It was cheaper to build on vacant land, but there was little such land left in the central cities and in their larger, older suburbs; therefore, most of the new homes were built in new suburbs. These were almost always zoned so as to exclude the relatively few Negroes and other "undesirables" who could afford to build new houses. In effect, then, the FHA and VA programs have subsidized the movement of the white middle class out of the central cities and older suburbs while at the same time penalizing investment in the rehabilitation of the run-down neighborhoods of these older cities. The poor— especially the Negro poor—have not received any direct benefit from these programs. (They have, however, received a very substantial unintended and indirect benefit . . . because the departure of the white middle class has made more housing available to them.) After the appointment of Robert C. Weaver as head of the Housing and Home Finance Agency, FHA changed its regulations to encourage the rehabilitation of existing houses and neighborhoods. Very few such loans have been made, however.

Urban renewal has also turned out to be mainly for the advantage of the well-off—indeed, of the rich—and to do the poor more harm than good. The purpose of the federal housing program was declared by Congress to be "the realization as soon as feasible of the goal of a decent home and a suitable living environment for every American family." In practice, however, the principal objectives of the renewal program have been to attract the middle class back into the central city (as well as to slow its exodus out of the city) and to stabilize and restore the central business districts. Unfortunately, these objectives can be served only at the expense of the poor. Hundreds of thousands of low-income people have been forced out of low-cost housing, by no means all of it substandard, in order to make way for luxury apartments, office buildings, hotels, civic centers, industrial parks, and the like. Insofar as renewal has involved the "conservation" or "rehabilitation" of residential areas, its effect has been to keep the poorest of the poor out of these neighborhoods—that is, to keep them in the highest-density slums. "At a cost of more than three billion dollars," sociologist Scott Greer wrote in 1965, "the Urban Renewal Agency (URA) has succeeded in materially reducing the supply of low-cost housing in American cities."

The injury to the poor inflicted by renewal has not been offset by benefits to them in the form of public housing (that is, housing owned by public bodies and rented by them to families deemed eligible on income and other grounds). With the important exception of New York and the less important ones of some Southern cities, such housing is not a significant part of the total supply. Moreover, the poorest of the poor are usually, for one reason or another, ineligible for public housing.

Obviously, these government programs work at cross-purposes, one undoing (or trying to undo) what the other does (or tries to do). The expressway program and the FHA and VA mortgage insurance and guarantee programs in effect pay the middle-class white to leave the central city for the suburbs. At the same time, the urban renewal and mass transit programs pay him to stay in the central city or to move back to it.

In at least one respect, however, these government programs are consistent: they aim at problems of comfort, convenience, amenity, and business advantage, not at ones involving the essential welfare of individuals or the good health of the society. Indeed, on the contrary, they all sacrifice these latter, more important interests for the sake of the former, less important ones. In this the urban programs are no different from a great many other government programs. Price production programs in agriculture, Theodore Schultz has remarked, take up almost all the time of the Department of Agriculture, the agricultural committees of Congress, and the farm organizations, and exhaust the influence of farm people. But these programs, he says, "do not improve the schooling of farm children, they do not reduce the inequalities in personal distribution of wealth and income, they do not remove the causes of poverty in agriculture, nor do they alleviate it. On the contrary, they worsen the personal distribution of income within agriculture."

It is widely supposed that the serious problems of the cities are unprecedented both in kind and in magnitude. Between 1950 and 1960 there occurred the greatest population increase in the nation's history. At the same time, a considerable part of the white middle class moved to the newer suburbs, and its place in the central cities and older suburbs was taken by Negroes (and in New York by Puerto Ricans as

well). These and other events—especially the civil rights revolution—
are widely supposed to have changed completely the character of "the
urban problem."

If the present situation is indeed radically different from previous
ones, then we have nothing to go on in judging what is likely to happen
next. At the very least, we face a crisis of uncertainty.

In a real sense, of course, *every* situation is unique. Even in making statistical probability judgments, one must decide on more or less
subjective grounds whether it is reasonable to treat certain events as if
they were the "same." The National Safety Council, for example, must
decide whether cars, highways, and drivers this year are enough like
those of past years to justify predicting future experience from past.
From a logical standpoint, it is no more possible to decide this question
in a purely objective way than it is to decide, for example, whether the
composition of the urban population is now so different from what it
was that nothing can be inferred from the past about the future. Karl
and Alma Taeuber are both right and wrong when they write that we
do not know enough about immigrant and Negro assimilation patterns
to be able to compare the two and that "such evidence as we could
compile indicates that it is more likely to be misleading than instructive to make such comparisons." They are certainly right in saying
that one can only guess whether the pattern of Negro assimilation will
resemble that of the immigrant. But they are wrong to imply that we
can avoid making guesses and still compare things that are not known
to be alike in all respects except one. (What, after all, would be the
point of comparing immigrant and Negro assimilation patterns if we
knew that the only difference between the two was, say, skin color?)
They are also wrong in suggesting that the evidence indicates anything
about what is likely to be instructive. If there were enough evidence to
indicate that, there would be enough to indicate what is likely to happen; indeed, a judgment as to what is likely to be instructive is insepa-
rable from one as to what is likely to happen. Strictly speaking, the
Taeubers' statement expresses *their* guess as to what the evidence indicates.

The facts by no means compel one to take the view that the
serious problems of the cities are unprecedented either in kind or in
magnitude. That population growth in absolute numbers was greater
in the decade 1950 to 1960 than ever before need not hold much significance from the present standpoint: American cities have frequently
grown at fantastic rates (consider the growth of Chicago from a prairie
village of 4,470 in 1840 to a metropolis of more than a million in fifty
years). In any case, the population growth of the 1950's was not in the
largest cities; most of them actually lost population in that decade. So
far as numbers go, the migration of rural and small-town Negroes and

Puerto Ricans to the large Northern cities in the 1950's was about equal to immigration from Italy in its peak decade. (In New York, Chicago, and many other cities in 1910, two out of every three school-children were the sons and daughters of immigrants.) When one takes into account the vastly greater size and wealth of the cities now as compared to half a century or more ago, it is obvious that by the only relevant measure—namely, the number of immigrants relative to the capacity of the cities to provide for them and to absorb them—the movement in the 1950's from the South and from Puerto Rico was not large but small.

In many important respects, conditions in the large cities have been getting better. There is less poverty in the cities now than there has ever been. Housing, including that of the poor, is improving rapidly: one study predicts that substandard housing will have been eliminated by 1980. In the last decade alone the improvement in housing has been marked. At the turn of the century only one child in fifteen went beyond elementary school; now most children finish high school. The treatment of racial and other minority groups is conspicuously better than it was. When, in 1964, a carefully drawn sample of Negroes was asked whether, in general, things were getting better or worse for Negroes in this country, approximately eight out of ten respondents said "better."

If the situation is improving, why, it may be asked, is there so much talk of an urban crisis? The answer is that the improvements in performance, great as they have been, have not kept pace with rising expectations. In other words, although things have been getting better absolutely, they have been getting worse *relative to what we think they should be.* And this is because, as a people, we seem to act on the advice of the old jingle:

> *Good, better, best,*
> *Never let it rest*
> *Until your good is better*
> *And your better best.*

Consider the poverty problem, for example. Irving Kristol has pointed out that for nearly a century all studies, in all countries, have concluded that a third, a fourth, or a fifth of the nation in question is below the poverty line. "Obviously," he remarks, "if one defines the poverty line as that which places one-fifth of the nation below it, then one-fifth of the nation will always be below the poverty line." The point is that even if everyone is better off there will be as much poverty as ever, provided that the line is redefined upward. Kristol notes that whereas in the depths of the Depression, F.D.R. found only one-third of the nation "ill-housed, ill-clad, ill-nourished," Leon Keyserling, a former head of the Council of Economic Advisers, in 1962 published a book called *Poverty and Deprivation in the U.S.—the Plight of Two-Fifths of a Nation.*

Much the same thing has happened with respect to most urban problems. Police brutality, for example, would be a rather minor problem if we judged it by a fixed standard; it is a growing problem because we judge it by an ever more exacting standard. A generation ago the term meant hitting someone on the head with a nightstick. Now it often means something quite different:

> What the Negro community is presently complaining about when it cries "police brutality" is the more subtle attack on personal dignity that manifests itself in unexplainable questionings and searches, in hostile and insolent attitudes toward groups of young Negroes on the street, or in cars, and in the use of disrespectful and sometimes racist language. . . .

Following Kristol, one can say that if the "police brutality line" is defined as that which places one-fifth of all police behavior below it, then one-fifth of all police behavior will always be brutal.

The school dropout problem is an even more striking example. At the turn of the century, when almost everyone was a "dropout," the term and the "problem" did not exist. It was not until the 1960's, when for the first time a majority of boys and girls were graduating from high school and practically all had at least some high school training, that the "dropout problem" became acute. Then, although the dropout rate was still declining, various cities developed at least fifty-five separate programs to deal with the problem. Hundreds of articles on it were published in professional journals, the National Education Association established a special action project to deal with it, and the Commissioner of Education, the Secretary of Labor, and the President all made public statements on it. Obviously, if one defines the "inadequate amount of schooling line" as that which places one-fifth of all boys and girls below it, then one-fifth of all boys and girls will always be receiving an inadequate amount of schooling.

Whatever our educational standards are today, Wayland writes, they will be higher tomorrow. He summarizes the received doctrine in these words:

> Start the child in school earlier; keep him in school more and more months of the year; retain all who start to school for twelve to fourteen years; expect him to learn more and more during this period, in wider and wider areas of human experience, under the guidance of a teacher, who has had more and more training, and

who is assisted by more and more specialists, who provide an ever-expanding range of services, with access to more and more detailed personal records, based on more and more carefully validated tests.

To a large extent, then, our urban problems are like the mechanical rabbit at the racetrack, which is set to keep just ahead of the dogs no matter how fast they may run. Our performance is better and better, but because we set our standards and expectations to keep ahead of performance, the problems are never any nearer to solution. Indeed, if standards and expectations rise *faster* than performance, the problems may get (relatively) worse as they get (absolutely) better.

Some may say that since almost everything about the city can stand improvement (to put it mildly), this mechanical rabbit effect is a good thing in that it spurs us on to make constant progress. No doubt this is true to some extent. On the other hand, there is danger that we may mistake failure to progress as fast as we would like for failure to progress at all and, in panic, rush into ill-considered measures that will only make matters worse. After all, an "urban crisis" that results largely from rising standards and expectations is not the sort of crisis that, unless something drastic is done, is bound to lead to disaster. To treat it as if it were might be a very serious mistake.

This danger is greatest in matters where our standards are unreasonably high. The effect of too-high standards cannot be to spur us on to reach the prescribed level of performance sooner than we otherwise would, for that level is by definition impossible of attainment. At the same time, these standards may cause us to adopt measures that are wasteful and injurious and, in the long run, to conclude from the inevitable failure of these measures that there is something fundamentally wrong with our society. Consider the school dropout problem, for example. The dropout rate can never be cut to zero: there will always be some boys and girls who simply do not have whatever it takes to finish high school. If we continue to make a great hue and cry about the dropout problem after we have reached the point where all those who can reasonably be expected to finish high school are doing so, we shall accomplish nothing constructive. Instead, we shall, at considerable cost to ourselves, injure the boys and girls who cannot finish (the propaganda against being a dropout both hurts the morale of such a youngster and reduces his or her job opportunities) while creating in ourselves and in others the impression that our society is morally or otherwise incapable of meeting its obligations.

In a certain sense, then, the urban crisis may be real. By treating a spurious crisis as if it were real, we may unwittingly make it so.

The Law

ROBERT M. COATES

After living among the famous colony of "lost generation"
expatriates in Paris, Robert M. Coates (1898-1973) began
writing for The New Yorker *in 1927. He wrote more than a*
hundred short stories for the magazine, which said of him in
an obituary: "In his writings about the city, he conveyed the
impression that an immitigable evil brooded in the sunniest
of our streets."

The first intimation that things were getting out of hand came one
early-fall evening in the late nineteen-forties. What happened, simply,
was that between seven and nine o'clock on that evening the Triborough Bridge[1] had the heaviest concentration of outbound traffic in
its entire history.

This was odd, for it was a weekday evening (to be precise, a
Wednesday), and though the weather was agreeably mild and clear,
with a moon that was close enough to being full to lure a certain
number of motorists out of the city, these facts alone were not enough
to explain the phenomenon. No other bridge or main highway was affected, and though the two preceding nights had been equally balmy
and moonlit, on both of these the bridge traffic had run close to normal.

The bridge personnel, at any rate, was caught entirely unprepared.
A main artery of traffic, like the Triborough, operates under fairly predictable conditions. Motor travel, like most other large-scale human
activities, obeys the Law of Averages—that great, ancient rule that
states that the actions of people in the mass will always follow consistent patterns—and on the basis of past experience it had always been
possible to foretell, almost to the last digit, the number of cars that
would cross the bridge at any given hour of the day or night. In this
case, though, all rules were broken.

The hours from seven till nearly midnight are normally quiet ones
on the bridge. But on that night it was as if all the motorists in the
city, or at any rate a staggering proportion of them, had conspired

---

Reprinted by permission; copyright © 1947 The New Yorker Magazine, Inc.

[1] Triborough Bridge: a main traffic artery across New York's East River.

together to upset tradition. Beginning almost exactly at seven o'clock, cars poured onto the bridge in such numbers and with such rapidity that the staff at the toll booths was overwhelmed almost from the start. It was soon apparent that this was no momentary congestion, and as it became more and more obvious that the traffic jam promised to be one of truly monumental proportions, added details of police were rushed to the scene to help handle it.

Cars streamed in from all directions—from the Bronx approach and the Manhattan one, from 125th Street and the East River Drive. (At the peak of the crush, about eight-fifteen, observers on the bridge reported that the drive was a solid line of car headlights as far south as the bend at Eighty-ninth Street, while the congestion crosstown in Manhattan disrupted traffic as far west as Amsterdam Avenue.) And perhaps the most confusing thing about the whole manifestation was that there seemed to be no reason for it.

Now and then, as the harried tollbooth attendants made change for the seemingly endless stream of cars, they would question the occupants, and it soon became clear that the very participants in the monstrous tieup were as ignorant of its cause as anyone else was. A report made by Sergeant Alfonse O'Toole, who commanded the detail in charge of the Bronx approach, is typical. "I kept askin' them," he said, " 'Is there night football somewhere that we don't know about? Is it the races you're goin' to?' But the funny thing was half the time they'd be askin' *me*. 'What's the crowd for, Mac?' they would say. And I'd just look at them. There was one guy I mind, in a Ford convertible with a girl in the seat beside him, and when he asked me, I said to him, 'Hell, you're *in* the crowd, ain't you?' I said. 'What brings *you* here?' And the dummy just looked at me. 'Me?' he says. 'I just come out for a drive in the moonlight. But if I'd known there'd be a crowd like this . . .' he says. And then he asks me, 'Is there any place I can turn around and get out of this?' " As the *Herald Tribune* summed things up in its story next morning, it "just looked as if everybody in Manhattan who owned a motorcar had decided to drive out on Long Island that evening."

The incident was unusual enough to make all the front pages next morning, and because of this, many similar events, which might otherwise have gone unnoticed, received attention. The proprietor of the Aramis Theatre, on Eighth Avenue, reported that on several nights in the recent past his auditorium had been practically empty, while on others it had been jammed to suffocation. Lunchroom owners noted that increasingly their patrons were developing a habit of making runs on specific items; one day it would be the roast shoulder of veal with pan gravy that was ordered almost exclusively, while the next everyone would be taking the Vienna loaf, and the roast veal went begging. A man who ran a small notions store in Bayside revealed that over a period of four days two hundred and seventy-four successive customers had entered his shop and asked for a spool of pink thread.

These were news items that would ordinarily have gone into the papers as fillers or in the sections reserved for oddities. Now, however, they seemed to have a more serious significance. It was apparent at last that something decidedly strange was happening to people's habits, and it was as unsettling as those occasional moments on excursion boats when the passengers are moved, all at once, to rush to one side or the other of the vessel. It was not till one day in December when, almost incredibly, the Twentieth Century Limited[2] left New York for Chicago with just three passengers aboard that business leaders discovered how disastrous the new trend could be, too.

Until then, the New York Central, for instance, could operate confidently on the assumption that although there might be several thousand men in New York who had business relations in Chicago, on any single day no more—and no less—than some hundreds of them would have occasion to go there. The play producer could be sure that his patronage would sort itself out and that roughly as many persons would want to see the performance on Thursday as there had been on Tuesday or Wednesday. Now they couldn't be sure of anything. The Law of Averages had gone by the board, and if the effect on business promised to be catastrophic, it was also singularly unnerving for the general customer.

The lady starting downtown for a day of shopping, for example, could never be sure whether she would find Macy's department store a seething mob of other shoppers or a wilderness of empty, echoing aisles and unoccupied salesgirls. And the uncertainty produced a strange sort of jitteriness in the individual when faced with any impulse to action. "Shall we do it or shan't we?" people kept asking themselves, knowing that if they did do it, it might turn out that thousands of other individuals had decided similarly; knowing, too, that if they *didn't*, they might miss the one glorious chance of all chances to have Jones Beach,[3] say, practically to themselves. Business languished, and a sort of desperate uncertainty rode everyone.

At this juncture, it was inevitable that Congress should be called on for action. In fact, Congress called on itself, and it must be said that it rose nobly to the occasion. A committee was appointed, drawn from both Houses and headed by Senator J. Wing Slooper (R.), of Indiana,

---

[2]Twentieth Century Limited: famous fast passenger train on the New York-Chicago route.

[3]Jones Beach: a popular state park near Long Island.

and though after considerable investigation the committee was forced reluctantly to conclude that there was no evidence of Communist instigation, the unconscious subversiveness of the people's present conduct was obvious at a glance. The problem was what to do about it. You can't indict a whole nation, particularly on such vague grounds as these were. But, as Senator Slooper boldly pointed out, "You can control it," and in the end a system of reeducation and reform was decided upon, designed to lead people back to—again we quote Senator Slooper —"the basic regularities, the homely averageness of the American way of life."

In the course of the committee's investigations, it had been discovered, to everyone's dismay, that the Law of Averages had never been incorporated into the body of federal jurisprudence, and though the upholders of States' Rights rebelled violently, the oversight was at once corrected, both by Constitutional amendment and by a law—the Hills-Slooper Act—implementing it. According to the Act, people were *required* to be average, and, as the simplest way of assuring it, they were divided alphabetically and their permissible activities catalogued accordingly. Thus, by the plan, a person whose name began with "G," "N," or "U," for example, could attend the theatre only on Tuesdays, and he could go to baseball games only on Thursdays, whereas his visits to a haberdashery were confined to the hours between ten o'clock and noon on Mondays.

The law, of course, had its disadvantages. It had a crippling effect on theatre parties, among other social functions, and the cost of enforcing it was unbelievably heavy. In the end, too, so many amendments had to be added to it—such as the one permitting gentlemen to take their fiancées (if accredited) along with them to various events and functions no matter what letter the said fiancées' names began with— that the courts were frequently at a loss to interpret it when confronted with violations.

In its way, though, the law did serve its purpose, for it did induce —rather mechanically, it is true, but still adequately—a return to that average existence that Senator Slooper desired. All, indeed, would have been well if a year or so later disquieting reports had not begun to seep in from the backwoods. It seemed that there, in what had hitherto been considered to be marginal areas, a strange wave of prosperity was making itself felt. Tennessee mountaineers were buying Packard convertibles, and Sears, Roebuck reported that in the Ozarks their sales of luxury items had gone up nine hundred per cent. In the scrub sections of Vermont, men who formerly had barely been able to scratch a living from their rock-strewn acres were now sending their daughters to Europe and ordering expensive cigars from New York. It appeared that the Law of Diminishing Returns was going haywire, too.

QUESTIONS

1a. What do you think "future shock" is? What evidence of it do you see in your own life or the lives of those around you? If you don't see any evidence, why do you suppose you don't?

 b. In presenting his views, author Toffler has marshalled evidence carefully and written in very persuasive prose. Examine his evidence critically, and see if you can interpret differently some of the situations which he cites.

2a. What is the life of the individual city-dweller like in each of Lewis Mumford's urban cycles? Describe what a journey through each of his six types of cities would be like.

 b. Are New York or Los Angeles in the megalopolitan stage now? What evidence (perhaps from Toffler or readings earlier in this book) do you see that they are or are not? Is it possible to determine from inside a city-culture whether it is in growth or decay? Why or why not?

3a. Harvey Cox uses the switchboard and the cloverleaf as symbols to discuss modern urban man. How does he develop these symbols specifically? What other symbols might be used to illustrate aspects of city life?

 b. How do Cox's defenses of "anonymity" and "mobility" compare with your own feelings about these two aspects of urban living? Did his defense surprise you? Why or why not? How would you answer the criticism that Cox is inviting people to keep aloof from others, to forsake their families, to be loners?

 c. When you finish school, do you expect to live in the same neighborhood or the same town or the same state you now live in? Does it make any difference to you if you do or not? If so, why? If not, why not?

4a. Whether you live in an urban area or not, compare the diverse and non-diverse parts of your community according to Jane Jacobs's standards.

 b. What more do you think is needed in the diverse parts to meet her criteria of a district realizing its "best potential"?

5a. What is Edward Banfield's view of the "urban crisis"? Are you persuaded by his argument? Why or why not?

 b. Banfield's article includes his analyses of "action" already taken against urban problems and of priorities for the future. He also has observations on the political realities of urban culture and on the influence of rising expectations. Make as broad a survey as possible in your own community, testing people's reactions to Banfield's conclusions about each of these points.

6a. What portions of your daily life depend upon the law of averages in the way Robert M. Coates writes about it?

b. Following his example, write a fantasy about the consequences of the law of averages—or some other "law" of daily life, such as the 24-hour day or our routines of eating, sleeping, and working—being suspended in a particular instance.

FURTHER SOURCES

A trio of writers concerned about the future of urban man provide a sample of the plentiful sources looking to the future. See Constantinos A. Doxiadis, *Ekistics: An Introduction to the Science of Human Settlements* (Hutchinson, 1968); R. Buckminster Fuller, *Operating Manual for Spaceship Earth* (Southern Illinois University Press, 1969) and *Earth, Inc.* (Anchor Press, 1973); and Paolo Soleri, *Arcology: The City in the Image of Man* (MIT Press, 1969). For imaginative speculation about what cities could become, see the science fiction of Ray Bradbury, particularly his collected stories *The Martian Chronicles* (Bantam, 1970) and his short story "The Lost City of Mars" in *I Sing the Body Electric* (Bantam, 1971).

For films, see *Futurists* and *Games Futurists Play* (both from Contemporary/McGraw-Hill Films, 1221 Avenue of the Americas, New York, N.Y. 10020).

New York Faces Future Shock *Alvin Toffler* The author's book *Future Shock* (Random House, 1970) has been an important bestseller. For critical reviews of it, see *Book World*, September 6, 1970, p. 4, and the *New York Times Book Review*, July 26, 1970, p. 3. Also available is the McGraw-Hill film titled *Future Shock*.

Cycle of Growth and Decay *Lewis Mumford* The author has written several dozen books in his long career. Three highly regarded ones which bear on urban problems are *The Culture of Cities* (Harcourt, 1938); *The City in History* (Harcourt, 1961); and *The Pentagon of Power* (Harcourt Brace Jovanovich, 1971).

The Shape of the Secular City *Harvey Cox* Frequent articles by this theologian can be found in national magazines since the mid-1960s. Another writer intent on seeking contemporary urban relevance in religion is Malcolm Boyd, author of *Are You Running With Me, Jesus?* (Avon Books, 1965).

The Generators of Diversity *Jane Jacobs* This urban critic has written a pair of highly regarded books: *The Death and Life of Great American Cities* (Random House, 1961) and *The Economy of Cities* (Random House, 1969). A profile of the author and her community work is Clark Whelton's article, "Won't you come home, Jane Jacobs?" in *The Village Voice*, July 6, 1972, p. 1.

The Unheavenly City *Edward C. Banfield* For articles about Banfield and his controversial views, see "A Theory of the Lower Class: Edward Banfield—The Maverick of Urbanology," by Richard Todd, *Atlantic*, Sept., 1970, pp. 51-55; and "Rethinking Cities," *Time*, June 1, 1970, pp. 64-65.

The Law *Robert M. Coates* The short stories of this writer can be found in issues of *The New Yorker* from 1927 to 1967.